RECONSIDERATIONS ON THE REVOLUTIONARY WAR

Contributions in Military History
Series Editors: *Thomas E. Griess* and *Jay Luvaas*

Schoolbooks and Krags: The United States Army in the Philippines, 1898-1902
John M. Gates

American Gunboat Diplomacy and the Old Navy, 1877-1889
Kenneth J. Hagan

The Image of the Army Officer in America: Background for Current Views
Robert C. Kemble

The Memoirs of Henry Heth
Henry Heth, edited by James Morrison

Against the Specter of a Dragon: The Campaign for American Military Preparedness, 1914-1917
John P. Finnegan

The Way of the Fox: American Strategy in the War for America, 1775-1783
Dave R. Palmer

History of the Art of War Within the Framework of Political History
Hans Delbruck, translated by Walter J. Renfroe, Jr.

The General: Robert L. Bullard and Officership in the United States Army, 1881-1925
Allan R. Millet

The Twenty-First Missouri from Home Guard to Union Regiment
Leslie Anders

The Politics of the Second Front: American Military Planning and Diplomacy in Coalition Warfare, 1941-1943
Mark A. Stoler

The Anatomy of a Small War: The Soviet-Japanese Struggle for Changkufeng/Khasan, 1938
Alvin D. Coox

RECONSIDERATIONS ON THE REVOLUTIONARY WAR

═══════SELECTED ESSAYS

Edited by Don Higginbotham

Contributions in Military History, Number 14

GREENWOOD PRESS
WESTPORT, CONNECTICUT • LONDON, ENGLAND

Library of Congress Cataloging in Publication Data

Main entry under title:

Reconsiderations on the Revolutionary War.

  (Contributions in military history; no. 14
ISSN 0084-9251)
  "Papers presented at a symposium . . . held at the United States Military Academy, West Point, New York, on April 22-23, 1976."
  Includes bibliographical references and index.
  1. United States—History—Revolution, 1775-1783
—Congresses. 2. Strategy—Congresses. I. Higgin-
botham, Don. II. Series: Contributions in military
history; no. 14.
E204.R4   973.3   77-84757
ISBN 0-8371-9846-1

Library of Congress Catalog Card Number: 77-84757
ISBN: 0-8371-9846-1
ISSN: 0084-9251

First published in 1978

Greenwood Press, Inc.
51 Riverside Avenue, Westport, Connecticut 06880

Printed in the United States of America
10 9 8 7 6 5 4 3 2 1

To Colonel Thomas E. Griess
and Colonel Roy K. Flint
Scholar-Soldiers of the Republic

CONTENTS

PREFACE   ix

1 The American War of Independence in World Perspective   3
   William H. McNeill

2 British Strategy: The Theory and Practice of
   Eighteenth-Century Warfare   14
   Ira D. Gruber

3 American Strategy: A Call for a Critical Strategic History   32
   Russell F. Weigley

4 Logistics and Operations in the American Revolution   54
   R. Arthur Bowler

5 American Society and Its War for Independence   72
   John Shy

6 The American Militia: A Traditional Institution with
   Revolutionary Responsibilities   83
   Don Higginbotham

7 American Generals of the Revolution: Subordination and
   Restraint   104
   Richard H. Kohn

8 Time: Friend or Foe of the Revolution?   124
   Richard Buel, Jr.

9 The Relationship Between the Revolutionary War and
   European Military Thought and Practice in the Second
   Half of the Eighteenth Century   144
   Peter Paret

   AFTERWORD   158
   Don Higginbotham

   NOTES   166

   INDEX   211

PREFACE

This book consists of a series of papers presented at a symposium on the American Revolutionary War held at the United States Military Academy, West Point, New York, on April 22-23, 1976. Except for the first paper by William H. McNeill of the University of Chicago—an after-dinner address that examined the Revolution in world focus—these essays deal with broad themes of the American War of Independence: strategy, logistics, militia forces, civil-military relations, social and economic aspects of the home front, and our Revolution's place in the thought and practice of European eighteenth-century warfare. In an "afterword," I endeavor to sketch some of the overall implications of the war and its outcome that these collective efforts call to my mind. My perceptions as well as those of the other contributors were sharpened by the numerous insightful observations from the large and responsive audience that attended the two days of sessions. We especially appreciate the thoughtful remarks of those scholars who presided and served as official commentators on the various panels: John R. Alden of Duke University, William B. Willcox of Yale University, Jay Luvaas of Allegheny College, Piers Mackesy of Oxford University, Theodore Ropp of Duke University, and Edward M. Coffman of the University of Wisconsin at Madison.

The symposium was made possible by a generous grant to the military academy from the National Endowment for the Humanities; the findings and conclusions of the symposium, of course, do not necessarily represent the views of the endowment. We authors are deeply indebted to the military academy—to the superintendent, Lieutenant General Sidney B.

Berry; to the dean, Brigadier General Frederick A. Smith; and to the
Department of History and its efficient secretarial staff presided over by
Mrs. Sally French. Most of all, however, we owe our thanks to Colonel
Thomas E. Griess, the head of the department, and to Colonel Roy K.
Flint, his deputy; they initiated, planned, and executed the symposium in
a manner that made it a most pleasant occasion for all of us. As visiting
professor of military history at the academy that year I had the good
fortune to play some small part in the different aspects of the symposium,
for which I extend to the academy's fine historians my personal
appreciation.

Don Higginbotham
Chapel Hill, N. C.

RECONSIDERATIONS ON THE REVOLUTIONARY WAR

1
THE AMERICAN WAR OF INDEPENDENCE IN WORLD PERSPECTIVE

William H. McNeill

I bring peculiar credentials to this undertaking. Canadian-born, I was brought up to believe that it was honorable to be able to write "UEL," United Empire Loyalist, after one's name. As a schoolboy, I also learned that the softness of life in the republic to the south of us set the virtues of Canada—the true north, strong and free—into a suitably high relief. Yet my childhood indoctrination into these matters also carried a strain of sympathy for the revolutionary movement that gave birth to the United States. Indeed, family tradition declares that one of my ancestors conducted a mini-revolution of his own in Prince Edward Island two years before the Yankees got around to following his lead. He had built his cabin on the site now occupied by the House of Confederation in Charlottetown, and when the governor sent out a dragoon to dispossess him, John McNeill responded by flattening the redcoat with his fist. Having thus expressed his opinion of constituted authority, my ancestor found it expedient to take off into the woods and set up housekeeping on the north shore of the island, some fifteen miles beyond the reach of the governor's wrath. For this, and perhaps for some other reasons, two of the fifteen English-speaking colonies of North America did not revolt against His Majesty King George III in 1776; and in time an English-Canadian consciousness came into existence in competition with and contrast to both French Canada and the national traditions of the United States.

Early inoculation with un-American ideas, counterbalanced by a middle western upbringing and education, invites a displacement from familiar points of view. That, at any rate, is what I conceive my task to be, so let us get down to the War of Independence in world perspective.

It is traditional in this country to give the War of Independence a central role in modern world history. Don Higginbotham has written:

The American Revolution was an upheaval of profound significance. It was a people's war for political independence, the first successful struggle to sever an imperial relationship in modern times. In one way or another it helped to shake human society to its very foundations—first in Europe, then in Latin America, and eventually in Africa and Asia, where the impact continues even today.[1]

Quite so: and even if the American War of Independence was not unique nor quite so novel as these sentences imply, still Higginbotham's careful wording stands. The war we celebrate was successful; it did command wide attention at the time and afterward; and it did help to trigger what a school of U.S. historians has dubbed the "democratic revolution," whose echoes still resound throughout the world a full two centuries later.

Yet there remains a nagging inadequacy in this flattering and familiar recital of the world significance of the War of Independence. Our horse-and-buggy revolution of 1776 has recently had to compete with newer models, most notably the Russian "Marx-mobile" of 1917 and the Chinese "Mao-Marx-II" of 1949. In that competition, more often than not, it is the shiny new models that attract the most attention. Hence the world, instead of moving toward a closer approximation to the United States' liberties and ideals, seems to be running in a different—if not an opposite—direction.

Something seems off the track. Is it us, as Marxist revolutionaries loudly proclaim? Or is it them, as American patriots assert, perhaps with diminishing assurance? Or is it rather the very notion of a single track along which human societies are all destined to go that is at fault?

Surely it is this third alternative that points to the fundamental error of our familiar thought patterns. Indeed, if we want to understand adequately what is happening in the world around us, we must give up the whole notion of revolution for export—whether our own or somebody else's. Early in the nineteenth century, when our revolution was still the latest thing, efforts to transfer its principles to European and Latin American soil turned out to be notoriously unsuccessful. Similar slogans and parallel aspirations produced sharply different results when injected into different historical, geographical, and human contexts. The same is just as true of the Russians' efforts to export their revolution, whether to eastern Europe or to China—or further afield. Frankly, it is naive to expect that old practices and patterns of behavior can somehow miracu- lously be swept away in the heat of revolutionary excitement. If there is any lesson to be learned from a study of history, it is the compelling force of continuity. ''Plus ça change, plus c'est la même chose'' is truer than we sometimes realize. Surely everyone now can see in Communist Russia massive carry-overs from czarism, and Mao Tse-tung's historic role begins to parallel that of the founders of new Chinese dynasties of the past.

What we need, then, is a juster perspective on our own and other revolutionary episodes in order to achieve a closer match-up between expectation and experience. It is sad to observe how stubbornly our own foreign policy has been governed since 1917 by the faulty assumption that all the world was waiting and eager to accept our ideals and borrow our institutions, so as to become as much like us as possible. We need a new foreign-policy idea badly. Ruthless power politics, assuming spheres of interest and radical amoralism—the most obvious alternative to the naive missionary impulse—is not in the least adequate as a substitute, if only because such a program cannot possibly command general support from the American public. But without solid public support, our government is hamstrung, as recent history surely demonstrates.

How then ought we to think of the American War of Independence? It seems fruitful to suggest that it was an episode in the expansion of European-style society and civilization: one of a class of similar conflicts that arose in the eighteenth century along the periphery of European settlement and imperial governance. Let us look briefly at three parallel revolutionary episodes—in addition to that family affair in Prince Ed- ward Island—and then offer a generalization about the significance and success these episodes attained.

The earliest came in 1710 in Recife, Brazil. A local quarrel there pitted planters against a modernizing governor sent out from Portugal. The rebels toyed halfheartedly with the idea of republican independence. But Bernardo Vieira de Mella, the only individual who is known to have advocated severance of all ties with Portugal, soon found himself in jail; and within a year, organized fighting ended in compromise and the planters' submission to another, more politic, governor. Not much of a revolution to be sure, but still an upheaval in which the elements later to boil over in the thirteen English colonies of North America are clearly recognizable. And just as we in this country have relied on the slogans of the War of Independence to support the United States' national identity, so also the affair at Recife has served, at least in a small way, to sustain modern Brazilian national consciousness.

The second instance of revolution on the periphery of an expanding Europe comes from Corsica. That Mediterranean island may seem too close to Europe's heartland to be really peripheral; yet in the eighteenth century the Corsicans were a wild, clannish people perpetually divided by blood feuds and subject to the imperial rule of Genoa. Discontent against the expanding reach of Genoese administration, based in a few coastal towns, led to chronic guerrilla warfare. Resistance took on a new character and scale after 1755, when Pasquale Paoli returned to his native land after years in exile and quickly assumed leadership of the clans fighting against the Genoese. Paoli was a man of the Enlightenment: a Freemason, like George Washington, and a deist. He welded the separate clans of the island together by exhortation and stern prohibition of blood feud. But his success rested mainly on his appeal to democratic principles of self-government—embodied, incidentally, in a written constitution— which assured that all-important decisions were made in the presence of freely elected representatives of the men of each clan who would have to do the fighting and abide by the results of any action agreed upon.

Paoli excited much admiration in England, and he received a trickle of military supplies from British sympathizers. His fame echoed even across the ocean, as the name of a suburb of Philadelphia attests to this day. But when the French came to the rescue of the defeated Genoese with a powerful expeditionary force and took over title to the island in 1769, English sympathy did *not* extend to sending ships and soldiers to the scene. Consequently, the cause of Corsican independence met defeat. Paoli fled to England, and the first written constitution of European history ceased to function. Twenty years later, when the French Revolution came along, Paoli returned in triumph to his native land, only to fall out with the authorities in Paris and once again meet defeat, this time despite naval help from Britain. Yet memories of Paoli's career and the aspirations it embodied are still alive in Corsica. As a result, agitation for Corsican independence constitutes a minor, but persistent, theme in contemporary French public life.

Still a third example of eighteenth-century peripheral revolution comes from Russia, where in 1773 an illiterate cossack named Emilian

Pugachev led a revolt against the advancing power of the imperial government. Pugachev's revolt started in the region where the Ural River flows southward across the steppe into the Caspian Sea. Human tinder for his revolt was provided by cossacks of that region whose traditional liberties and rude egalitarian, strikingly democratic way of life were endangered by the actions of governors and other officials sent out from distant St. Petersburg. The defense of traditional liberties and the right to local self-government were familiar rallying cries in our own American Revolution; and it is not a mere trick of words to suggest that the ideals that initially brought support for Pugachev's rising were similar to those that had stirred Brazilians and Corsicans and were soon to stir Americans into revolt against constituted, bureaucratic, and imperial authority.

But the cossacks and Bashkirs of the Ural region were more old-fashioned in their political ideas than their fellow revolutionaries of other segments of Europe's eighteenth-century frontier. Republicanism was inconceivable to them, so the rebels instead claimed that their leader was the rightful czar, Peter III. Czar Peter had in fact been murdered some eleven years previously after a reign of only six months, and the conspirators who killed him had put his young German wife, Catherine, on the throne. The fact that she was a woman and a foreigner, with no hereditary claim to rule Russia, obviously made Pugachev's challenge to her legitimacy all the more dangerous to the authorities in St. Petersburg.

Yet Pugachev also failed. He himself and those who followed him knew what they were against—injustice and inequality, supported by the alien rule of a distant imperial capital and the bureaucratic machine that served it. But Pugachev did not have any viable substitute to offer: Cossack and peasant freedom meant anarchy and automatic execution of landlords and nobles who fell into their hands—nothing more. Hence the fabric of Catherine's imperial command structure held in face of Pugachev's challenge: army disicipline was not affected, and as soon as the war with Turkey that had absorbed the resources of the imperial government for six long years took a favorable turn, Catherine was able to send sufficient troops down the Volga to capture Pugachev and disperse his followers.

The imperial government subsequently tried to erase all trace of Pugachev's name and movement. Yet Russian peasants remembered the hope of freedom he had embodied, even if only in a confused and partial way; and these memories surfaced again during the revolutions of 1905-06 and 1917. Official historians since 1917 have made much of Pugachev as a revolutionary forerunner of Lenin and the Bolsheviks. He too has thus become a national hero alongside Washington, Paoli, and the Brazilian, de Mella.

In bracketing these diverse expressions of local revolt against distant, oppressive regimes together with the American War of Independence, I do not mean to imply that there were not important differences that distinguished each episode of revolutionary violence from the others. Such differences were real and important. Besides, the North American revolution was the only revolt against imperial authority that succeeded. This elemental fact assured it of a constitutive role in shaping the national tradition of the United States and therefore sustained its prominence in world history, as Higginbotham pointed out. Unsuccessful risings, obviously, could not command any comparably continuous and reverent attention. Moreover, the ideas that justified the American Revolution, the men who led it, the ironical way in which French intervention in the New World soon precipitated revolution in Paris—all these familiar facts gave to our War of Independence far greater importance in world history than anything generated by its sister movements of the eighteenth century.

Yet despite these differences, all four of the revolutionary outbreaks shared one elementary characteristic: each of them began as an effort to resist a tightening up of imperial administration and control. Officials appointed from the capital sought to make distant subjects conform to rules and regulations like those already accepted by populations living nearer to the seat of power. This meant paying more taxes, contributing more services, surrendering special liberties and peculiar local practices that had previously exempted peripheral communities from a full share in the burdens—and advantages—of civilized existence.

These rebellions, therefore, may be seen as episodes in the expansion of European patterns of society and government. Like the shock waves that arise when an airplane breaks the sound barrier, these upheavals registered local instabilities generated by sporadic but persistent advances in the art of governance at a distance. If this is the right perspective, clearly it is a mistake to think of the success that crowned the efforts of George Washington and his fellow patriots as a mainstream of modern history. On the contrary: men have continued to devise more and more effective means of exercising power at a distance throughout modern times. Local immunities and liberties have correspondingly diminished in scope within every sovereign state on earth. In the eighteenth century, the human reality of imperial government was exceedingly weak by comparison with modern bureaucratic administration. Communications took weeks or even months to pass between ministers of state in London or St. Petersburg and their local agents in North America or Siberia. Armed action at a distance presented even more formidable difficulties, as British administrators discovered by 1778 at the latest.

Yet despite these, to us, all but unimaginable handicaps, even in the eighteenth century the balance of forces favored the advance of centralized, bureaucratic administration. The defeats that three of the four rebellions against central authority met is evidence of this; and as we all know, even the American patriots could not have prevailed without massive assistance from the French. It is always chastening to recollect that French sailors and soldiers present at Cornwallis's surrender far outnumbered Americans under arms at Yorktown; and even before the open and massive armed French intervention, Washington's forces had derived essential munitions and other supplies from France. Hence it was by tapping resources available to the French administrative machine that successful American revolt against the British imperial system became possible.

What would the world have been like if de Mella had secured French support, if Pugachev had been able to get aid from the Turks, or if Paoli had received British munitions in his time of need? Different, no doubt; but not so very different. Even if foreign help had permitted de Mella, Pugachev, and Paoli to succeed as Washington succeeded—that is, if each of these men had been able to set up a new state independent of older imperial structures—the larger processes of acculturation and transfer of civilized skills to new ground would not have been much affected. And these are the processes that seem to have mattered most. Whether peripheral revolts succeeded or failed, the process of consolidation of governmental power along with other aspects of civilization continued.

Assuredly, establishment of a new American government between 1776 and 1789 did not slow the process whereby the western shores of the Atlantic were assimilated to the patterns of life long established in western Europe. If anything, development went faster than it would have if the imperial tie with Great Britain had somehow survived 1776. As a result, during the nineteenth century, what was once on the periphery rapidly came abreast of the center of European civilization. Consequently, by 1917, if not before, the government of the United States emerged as an equal to, and, in some important respects, the superior of any European state.

The rise of marcher states from backwardness and relative weakness to a level of parity with and superiority to states nearer the center of an expanding civilization is an old, old story. It is manifest in the history of ancient China, of ancient India, and of the ancient Middle East—as well as in the classical Mediterranean age when first Macedon and then Rome played the role of marcher state with respect to the Greek city-states of antiquity. And in recent times the rise of the United States on Europe's western horizon paralleled the rise of another superpower on Europe's eastern flank, first Czarist and then Soviet Russia.

In a sense, putting our national history into such a perspective may seem to devalue it, denying uniqueness to what happened on these shores, and making our achievement less clearly the result of human will and action and more likely the consequence of massive, largely unconscious processes that operated at a level below deliberate political-military planning and action. Yet a Calvinist world view—perhaps perversely—can be mildly reassuring. For one thing, if history really does move in this way, accidents of leadership matter less. As circumstances take on a larger role, errors of judgment and defects of individual performance tend to be canceled out by someone else's unusually successful conduct. In other words, impersonal process creates a more reliable order in the world than we could otherwise enjoy. Order means limits, and such a vision of historical process ought also to remind us that we are never wholly sovereign, whether as individuals or as citizens of even the greatest of states. This is true today; it was just as true in 1776—and on both sides of the Atlantic.

If one is willing to concede the force of circumstances and the reality of massive processes of civilizational expansion across space and through time, it is perhaps a useful exercise to compare the circumstances of Great Britain in 1776 with those of the United States of America in 1976. In many senses, we play today the world role Great Britain played in 1776. Comparisons run remarkably close: British supremacy on the high seas in 1776 was still a relatively new thing, the result of victory in two world wars. France and Britain fought the first eighteenth-century-style world war between 1740 and 1748 on the European continent, in the Americas, and in India. It is known in United States history as King George's War and in European history as the War of the Austrian Succession. East Asia and the Pacific remained outside the theater of action, and in this sense perhaps this war and its successors should be called semi-world wars or perhaps hemispheric wars. Whatever name we give it, the struggle of 1740-48 was inconclusive. Accordingly, the contest was soon resumed, from 1754 to 1763. This time Britain won decisively in both America and India and humbled the French on the continent of Europe as well. French revenge, of course, came later, through their successful intervention in the American War of Independence.

The two world wars of the twentieth century involved the United States in a similarly rapid rise to dominion over wide reaches of land and sea; and the responsibility we felt after 1945 for defending clients and assisting friends in Latin America, Europe, Asia, and Africa is, of course, what got us into the dilemmas and painful frustration of the Vietnam War.[2] Overconfidence, based on the belief that all the world ought to be ready to conform to our example and accept our goodwill in trying to help them to help themselves to become more like us, lay behind our policy. Very similar thoughts dominated the councils of the British government from 1763 to 1776 in its dealings with the American colonies. A wish to see the colonies conform more exactly to English ways of life and forms of government and to forward the interests of those sober and responsible elements in the American population that were ready and willing to support British initiatives was characteristic of that policy. When armed opposition manifested itself, British pride and defective information about the strength and determination of the patriot party led the British ministers from one blunder to another. The eventual success that came to the Continental army resulted from this long string of miscalculations and misunderstandings.

Parallels with our recent experience in Vietnam leap to mind. We find ourselves now in the world role Britain formerly enjoyed—or suffered from—and we have made very similar mistakes. The bitter divisions of opinion in Great Britain about the war of 1776-83 were remarkably similar to those we have recently experienced in our own country. Our official reliance on logistical superiority and professionalism and our unwillingness to take seriously the power of popular feeling mobilized against foreign invaders in 1965-74 closely resembled the miscalculations of British policy in 1776-83. Moreover, the dismay that descended upon King George and his advisers as the error of their ways was slowly brought home to them may resemble the current or very recent state of American official opinion. The fact that Britain rallied from the defeat of 1783 and played a leading and honorable role in world affairs for more than another century may also reassure those who felt or feel that our Vietnam experience was an irretrievable disaster.

In short, at a given time in human affairs there is an appropriate role for particular states and peoples to play; and force of circumstances seems such as to assure that they *will* play those roles, well or badly, with conviction and skill or bumblingly and ineffectually. It was natural and to be expected in the days of the Founding Fathers that men in North America should resist tightened control from London. It is no less natural that we in 1976 should wish to assure a rule of law throughout the world and should dislike, even fear, local outbreaks of violence that reject legal processes. Of late, our heritage of revolutionary rhetoric interfered with a clear vision of what our changed circumstances have begun to require us to do in the world. Yet when those circumstances nonetheless prevailed, we often acted covertly, as though ashamed. On several occasions, unprincipled and short-sighted support of reactionary elements in other societies—being unconnected with any ideal or world view the American public as a whole could support or sympathize with—led our government into ineffective, as well as demoralizing, alliances and encounters.

It is time to think better, to view the world more clearly, and to recognize the force of circumstance as it limits and channels our national conduct and as it affects the behavior of other peoples and social groupings in other parts of the world. If we can attain such a vision, both the revolutionary strivings of peripheral and weak peoples and the Big Powers' efforts to channel such movements into predictable and relatively moderate paths—a policy pursued as much by the U.S.S.R. and China as by our own government in recent years—will become understandable. Improved understanding will in turn allow us to play our allotted role in world affairs with a clear conscience and, one may hope, with somewhat better effect, because we will know what we are doing and feel no shame in trying to do it well and wisely—favoring evolution as against revolution, and moderation as against fanaticism. Above all, we will be prepared to recognize the limits of our power far more sensitively than has recently been the case.

Let us hope that the Bicentennial stimulus to reassessment and reaffirmation of national purposes will conduce to such a result all across the nation. Adolescent rebellion gives way in most of us to adult responsibility. It is in such a light that we should view the shift in roles that two centuries have brought to this nation; and if studying the past allows us to avoid some of the errors of that past—both our own and others'—so much the better.

2 BRITISH STRATEGY: THE THEORY AND PRACTICE OF EIGHTEENTH-CENTURY WARFARE

Ira D. Gruber

In the past forty years historians have become increasingly interested in the relationship between eighteenth-century military doctrine and British defeat in the War for American Independence. Some have gone so far as to argue that the British failed to achieve decisive results in the opening campaigns because they applied conventional European strategies to the unconventional circumstances of a revolutionary war. According to this interpretation, the British tried before 1778 to end the rebellion by waging a conventional war of posts—by avoiding the hazards of a general engagement and by concentrating on depriving the rebels of their cities, magazines, and lines of supply and communication. These measures were not sufficient to destroy the Continental army or to break the spirit of determined revolutionaries, but orthodox practice simply did not encourage a more aggressive use of regular forces or a heavier reliance on irregular, loyalist units.[1] In pursuing this line of argument, historians have never really looked closely at what they call conventional strategy. They have assumed that military doctrine was essentially the same throughout western Europe, that British and French and German officers planned their campaigns according to the same general principles.[2] No one has attempted to isolate and analyze British military thought in the eighteenth century, to see whether there was a separate strategic tradition in the British army or how such a tradition might have affected the War for American Independence. This essay attempts to do just that, by asking what strategic theories held sway in Britain at the time of the American War and how far those theories influenced the performance of ministers and commanders-in-chief.

To pursue these questions requires a circuitous route. There is simply not enough evidence to establish precisely what individual British leaders knew of strategic theory or how they applied what they knew. Although each of those leaders has been studied intensively and many of their papers have been preserved, little specific information remains about the early training that any of them received. Moreover, there is little in their later correspondence or memoirs that provides direct connections between the strategic theories they held and the plans they made. Most were much too preoccupied with the particular circumstances of the American War to provide theoretical justifications for what they were doing. It is, however, possible to show that nearly all of those who shaped British strategy were familiar with current military practices—familiar enough to have absorbed those theories of strategy held most widely in the British army. It is also possible to suggest what those theories were and how they, in turn, influenced British strategy in the American War.

Consider first the training and experience of the king and those ministers who had the most to do with managing the American War. With the exceptions of Lord North, principal minister throughout the war, and the earl of Dartmouth, secretary of state for America until November 1775—men whose experience had been almost exclusively in politics and public administration—the king and his closest advisers had more than a passing acquaintance with military affairs. George III regularly supervised the assignment and promotion of officers, collected books on the art of war, and attended summer encampments.[3] The earl of Sandwich, first lord of the admiralty from 1772 to 1782, was both the senior official in the navy and a general in the army. If he had not seen active duty since the Jacobite Rebellion in 1745, he continued to subscribe to military literature.[4] Lord George Germain, who succeeded Dartmouth as colonial secretary in November 1775, was until the age of forty-three as much a soldier as a politician. Germain had served brilliantly as a junior officer during the War of the Austrian Succession and the Jacobite Rebellion; he had been a protégé of Marshal Ligonier and a friend of James Wolfe, two of the most distinguished professional officers of his day, and he had risen to second in command of allied forces in Germany before being banished from the service for disobedience at the Battle of Minden in 1759.[5] The only career officer in the goverment was Lord Amherst, the commander in chief. Amherst began his service with Ligonier during the War of the Austrian Succession, won a reputation as a devoted student of strategy, and, during the Seven Years' War, became commander in chief of British forces in America.[6] He helped plan, and he presided over, the conquest of Canada. It should, of course, be emphasized that the king and all of his closest advisers, save Amherst, were more experienced in politics and government than in warfare and that political, economic, and diplomatic considerations probably weighed more heavily with them in planning a war than did any strategic theory.

By contrast, the men who would command British armies in America during the Revolutionary War were all professional soldiers. With two exceptions they had distinguished themselves not merely by their energy and bravery in the wars of mid-century but also by their unusual interest in the art of war. They were men who by instinct and attainment would be more inclined than their ministerial superiors to emphasize current military practice, to pursue current strategic theory in planning a campaign. Thomas Gage, commander in chief at Boston when the war began, and Guy Carleton, commanding in Canada until 1778, were the exceptions: they were better known as administrators than as battlefield commanders or students of warfare.[7] Quite the contrary was true of Gage's successors, William Howe and Henry Clinton, who commanded in the middle colonies, 1775-78 and 1778-82, respectively. Howe, a protégé of Ligonier and Wolfe, had made a name for himself on both sides of the Atlantic as an aggressive regimental commander and an authority on light infantry tactics. Clinton, too, served with Ligonier, earned a reputation for gallantry in Germany between 1760 and 1762, and returned to the Continent just before the American War to examine battlefields and observe the Russian and Austrian armies.[8] Like Clinton, John Burgoyne, who commanded the Canadian army in 1777, had studied and fought on the Continent. After spending more than seven years in France evading his creditors and reading books on the art of war, Burgoyne went home to England, began a second career in the army, and served with distinction in Portugal at the close of the Seven Years' War. Thereafter he resumed his studies on the Continent and wrote an essay comparing the Prussian, Austrian, and French armies. Earl Cornwallis, who commanded in the southern colonies in 1780 and 1781, was one of the few British officers of his time to have studied at a military academy. He had also served most effectively in Germany as aide-de-camp to the commander of British troops and as a lieutenant colonel of a regiment in the last stages of the Seven Years' War.[9] Although none of these officers had had the experience of an independent command in wartime or the opportunity to plan a campaign, all except Gage and Carleton were proven regimental commanders and unusually devoted students of warfare.

Considering, then, that the king and most of his ministers and commanders were familiar with current military practice, it does seem likely that they would have been aware of those strategies that were most widely held in the British army on the eve of the American War. Considering as well that they were conventional men, it also seems that they would have been influenced by the most popular strategies. But what were those strategies? If there is not evidence enough to establish what strategies the king and his closest advisers preferred, if the correspondence and memoirs of the most prominent men of that time do not supply the answer, how will it be possible to analyze the preferences of British officers in general?

Such an analysis may at least be attempted by examining books on the art of war. At a time when there was no military academy in England (except for engineers and artillerymen), no uniform system of training within the army, and little opportunity in peacetime for any service, books were an important means of conveying thought and experience from one generation of officers to another. But as a great variety of books on war was available during the eighteenth century, there would be little advantage in using them indiscriminately. It is essential, therefore, to determine which books were most influential among British officers and what those particular books had to say about strategy. Such an approach does have its limitations. There is no way to be sure that strategies described in the most influential books dominated the thinking of officers in general, or, by extension, shaped the plans of those particular men who managed the American War. But in the absence of other evidence, this approach does seem preferable to any that has been tried.

To determine which books were most influential it is necessary to establish what books were read and regarded as authorities. Although there are few inventories or catalogues of complete eighteenth-century officers' libraries, it has been possible to examine fourteen: eight of libraries gathered by officers who served during the first four decades of the century, and six by officers whose careers flourished between 1740 and 1770.[10] These lists reflect the taste of men of varied rank, wealth, experience, and professional interests, including Howe, Clinton, and Lord Ligonier, the patron of Amherst, among those who served after

1740. Taken together the lists provide evidence of changes that were taking place in officers' attitudes during the first three-quarters of the century—specifically, a growing interest in professional literature and in books on tactics and strategy. The post-1740 lists also provide evidence of the preferences of officers who served during the wars of mid-century when men like Germain, Howe, Clinton, Burgoyne, and Cornwallis were being trained. These later lists strongly suggest the importance of particular books and particular kinds of books. But these suggestions must be tested against other evidence—against the publishing history of individual titles, the records of book auctions, and the writings of British officers.

Applying these tests to titles found in inventories and catalogues of libraries assembled after 1740 makes it clear that British officers did not rely heavily on books written by their countrymen. Of the fifty-eight books in these libraries that deal in any way with strategy, only twelve, or slightly more than 20 percent, were written by Englishmen. And only one of these seems to have been considered a standard work: the earl of Orrery's *Treatise of the Art of War* (1677), which was frequently cited or quoted by British authors but belonged to only one of six post-1740 libraries and was not in demand when offered for sale in 1773.[11] The most popular British books of the 1760s—Samuel Bever, *The Cadet* (1756 and 1762), and Campbell Dalrymple, *Military Essay* (1761)—had scarcely more appeal than Orrery: they were included in two of the six libraries surveyed, warranted between them one reprinting, and sold no better than Orrery. No wonder that Bever and Dalrymple lamented the shortage of English authorities on war; that Bever urged his fellow officers to study history, the classics, and French theorists; and that Dalrymple, despising the French, proposed that British generals be required to keep strategic notebooks for the benefit of their successors.[12] John Burgoyne, who believed in devoting a portion of each day to professional reading, went so far as to encourage his subordinates to learn French: "The best modern books upon our profession are written in that language."[13]

Many officers seem to have shared Burgoyne's opinion. More than 50 percent of the books on strategy in the six officers' libraries assembled after 1740 were French; nearly 20 percent, classical; and 10 percent, Italian, Prussian, or Austrian. Although these rough proportions tend to overemphasize the importance of French books and undervalue the classics, they do convey accurately the predominance of foreign over domestic books. There were perhaps half a dozen contemporary French books that were more influential among British officers than any English work. The most important of these were the marquis of Feuquières's *Memoirs* and Marshal Saxe's *Reveries*. Feuquières's *Memoirs*, first published in 1711 but reprinted repeatedly thereafter in French and English, appeared in three of six libraries after 1740 in seven editions, was frequently cited by English authors, and remained in demand in 1773.[14] Saxe's *Reveries*, which was not published until 1753, enjoyed sudden and widespread popularity. It was reprinted in French and English within four years, included by two of six officers in their collections, and considered by both Bever and Dalrymple to be the foremost continental work on war.[15] But even more influential than Feuquières or Saxe—than any contemporary study of war—were two classical works, Vegetius's *Military Institutions* and Caesar's *Commentaries*. Vegetius belonged to two of six professional collections, was cited or quoted in nearly every English book on war, merited a new translation in 1767, and was still in demand when British troops marched to Lexington in April 1775.[16] Even so, Vegetius was not so popular as Caesar, whose book was included in three of six libraries in seven editions, was available in three English translations, and was clearly regarded as required reading for any officer who aspired to high command. According to Orrery, the most famous generals took "the Ancients, but especially *Julius Caesar* for their Example." Caesar was, said William Duncan in 1753, the one "Leader, whom all succeeding Ages have agreed to regard as the most finished Pattern of Military Merit."[17]

Few officers shaped their careers or planned their campaigns to suit any single "Pattern of Military Merit." Many eighteenth-century British officers took little interest in improving themselves professionally, were quite indifferent to patterns of military merit, and felt quite content with whatever rudimentary training they received when on active duty.[18] But the officers who were interested in their professional education clearly preferred some patterns to others. Those who took the trouble to assemble professional libraries and to write books on the art of war were discriminating in their choice of authorities: they owned, bought, read, and cited some books far more frequently than others. It is also clear that those officers who would serve in the ministry or in high command during the American War were deeply interested in their professional development. They had taken considerable trouble to serve under particular commanders, to observe military practices in other countries, and to improve themselves by studying between the wars. Such men would have been familiar with the arguments expressed in those books that were widely regarded as authoritative, such as Caesar's *Commentaries,* Feuquières's *Memoirs,* and Saxe's *Reveries.* What, then, would they have learned—either directly or indirectly—from those books?

No one can be sure. But it is possible to describe the nature and limits of strategic theory available in the most popular books on war. Caesar's *Commentaries* demonstrated the advantages both of an aggressive, mobile strategy—of seeking, engaging, and destroying the opposing army whenever feasible—and of a thorough exploitation of victory. It is true that Caesar occasionally declined to fight (particularly against fierce and numerous Germanic tribes), that he tried at the outset of the civil war to negotiate with Pompey's followers, and that when outnumbered he sometimes preferred to besiege rather than assault an opposing army. Yet in most of his campaigns in Gaul and during the later stages of the civil war, he waited only for the most favorable moment to attack and destroy his enemy; and once he had gained a victory, he did not fail to take advantage of it, whether by the most ruthless or the most generous measures. He was able to employ such a bold and flexible strategy because he could depend on having an almost inexhaustible supply of reliable, skilled, and self-sufficient troops and because he usually had as much political as military authority when in command. Nevertheless, his *Commentaries* argued forcefully that destroying the opposing army in battle was the best way to decide a campaign or a war.[19]

Vegetius, Feuquières, and Saxe, by contrast, argued explicitly for more prudent strategies. Assuming that no commander would have unlimited men and supplies and knowing that general engagements were usually costly to both sides, all advocated strategies that promised victory without the risks of a decisive battle. Vegetius preferred to starve the enemy: "The main and principal point in war is to secure plenty of provisions and to weaken or destroy the enemy by famine." He would attack only when sure of success or when given an opportunity to slaughter a disorganized or retreating army.[20] Feuquières believed in being a bit more aggressive. He would invade enemy territory to demoralize the population, disrupt the flow of supplies, and look for a chance to disable the opposing army by capturing its artillery and baggage. But he would be reluctant to offer or accept a general engagement: "General actions of one army against another, often deciding the success of the whole war and almost always that of the campaign . . . ought to be given only under necessity and for important reasons."[21] Although Saxe was probably more aggressive than either Vegetius or Feuquières, he too advocated a war of attrition. Rather than hazard a single climactic battle, he would exhaust the enemy with frequent, limited attacks on its men and supplies. "I do not mean to say by this that when an opportunity occurs to crush the enemy that he should not be attacked. . . . But I do mean that war can be made without leaving anything to chance. And this is the highest point of perfection and skill in a general." It should be added that, in spite of his reservations about battle, Saxe was one of the few generals of the mid-eighteenth century to advocate relentless pursuit of a defeated army and that both he and Feuquières were remarkably offensive-minded for their day.[22]

There were, of course, fundamental differences between the strategies recommended by Vegetius, Feuquières, and Saxe and those employed by Caesar. British authors did little to reconcile those differences. The earl of Orrery, like Vegetius, Feuquières, and Saxe, expressed an aversion to battle. Believing that battles were too often decided by chance, Orrery preferred to "weary" out the enemy with skirmishes, sieges, and maneuvers. When on the defensive, he would gather his troops in fortified camps, strip the countryside of provisions, and try to avoid a general engagement until shortages forced the enemy to retire. On the offensive and with superior forces, he might attack the enemy to maintain his reputation. Even then, said Orrery, "whoever has his Enemy at such an advantage, as he must submit in a short time without hazarding a Field, ought on no terms to expose his Army to Battle." Although Orrery emphasized the risks inherent in battle, he also admired a commander, like Caesar, who knew how to engage, defeat, and destroy an enemy.[23] Similarly, Samuel Bever believed not merely that wars should be waged with moderation—with as little killing and rancor as possible—but also that Caesar was the greatest of all generals: *"Hannibal, Marius, Pompey,* and *Marc Anthony,* gained Victories, but their later Actions did not correspond with their beginnings; they have left us to doubt whether they owed their Victories to Fortune or to Conduct. Caesar *only* was a Conqueror."[24]

The strategies of Vegetius, Feuquières, and Saxe were scarcely compatible with those of Caesar. But in the century before the American Revolution, many British officers could not resist embracing both styles of making war. Orrery knew that the cautious strategies of Vegetius were better suited to the small national armies of the late seventeenth century than were the bold measures of Caesar, that it was better for a general with a limited number of troops to starve or maneuver the enemy into submission than to resort to a pitched battle. But Orrery was not entirely satisfied with cautious strategies, and he suspected that many of his countrymen would not be—that many were so accustomed to seeing campaigns decided in a single battle that they would not have the patience for a war of attrition.[25] In fact, during the first three-quarters of the eighteenth century many British officers retained their enthusiasm for an aggressive style of warfare. They bought, read, and quoted Caesar's *Commentaries* more frequently than any contemporary book on war; they admired officers like Marlborough and Wolfe who sought victory in battle; and they never completely adopted the prudent continental strategies of a Feuquières or a Saxe. So it was that British officers were, at the beginning of the American Revolution, heirs to an ambiguous strategic tradition, one that was shaped as much by Caesar as by Saxe.

This tradition was also quite narrow—primarily because it was created by professional officers, by men who did not as yet presume to consider more than the military dimensions of a campaign or war. Kings and ministers did make strategy in the broadest sense. They did take politics, economics, diplomacy, and ideology into account when deciding how best to use force, and they sometimes explained what they had done in Parliament or in their memoirs. But they rarely contributed to theoretical discussions of war or strategy. Those discussions were carried on mainly in books on the art of war. Such books, written by officers for other officers, dealt almost exclusively with tactics, administration, and siegecraft—with the skills needed to manage soldiers in camp, on the march, in battle, and during a siege. When these books did touch on strategy, on the planning of a campaign or war, they usually considered only the military aspects of strategy: When should a commander begin a campaign? Under what circumstances should he offer or accept battle? And, what were the best ways of attacking and defending a country? Most authors assumed that political, economic, diplomatic, and ideological considerations would be left to the king and his ministers.

How then did this ambiguous and narrow strategic heritage affect

British efforts to put down the American rebellion of 1775? Initially—
that is, between January 1775, when the ministry first decided to use
force to sustain its authority in the colonies, and July 1775, when it
learned of the Battle of Bunker Hill—strategic theory had little influence
on the British. During these months, the king and his advisers made their
plans to suit their understanding of the political climate in the mother
country and the colonies. They were anxious to end what they regarded as
a rebellion in Massachusetts and to force other mainland colonies to obey
acts of Parliament, but they wished to do so in a way that would create as
little resentment as possible, particularly in England. Thus they decided
to use a limited amount of force at Boston, to add a modest number of
troops to those under General Thomas Gage and have him "take a more
active & determined Part" in support of royal government. He was to
arrest leaders of the provincial congress, prevent the colonists from
assembling under arms, dismantle or occupy forts, and seize rebel
magazines. The king and the ministry hoped that these firm measures,
together with restrictions on colonial trade and vague offers of concilia-
tion, would soon overturn the rebels in Massachusetts and encourage the
rest of the colonies to return to their allegiance. They anticipated that the
people of Massachusetts might resist, meeting force with force, but they
assumed that Gage with only such troops as could be spared from the
peacetime establishment (no more than 6,000 men) would be equal to any
emergency. They refused as yet to prepare for war, to raise a vast
expeditionary force or pursue a regular plan of campaign.[26] After learning that Gage's troops had met resistance at Lexington and Concord, that
they had subsequently been besieged at Boston, and that colonists everywhere were in arms, the ministry did order a more aggressive use of the
fleet and sent arms to the loyalists of North Carolina. Still, it persisted in
thinking that with a few additional men Gage would be able to disperse
the rebels gathered about Boston or to capture New York.[27]

The Battle of Bunker Hill persuaded ministers and commanders alike
that they were at war, that they would have to raise an army and conduct a
regular campaign to retain their American colonies. Nearly all agreed that
they should begin by conquering New England. Their strategy reflected
both the realities of the American rebellion and the ambiguous, narrow
strategic heritage of the British army. As the terrain in New England was
too difficult and the population too hostile for a regular offensive from
Boston, Gage and his successor, William Howe, recommended that the

conquest of New England be undertaken from New York and Quebec. With reinforcements they would leave Boston, capture New York, and send detachments of ships and men to take Rhode Island and impose a tight blockade on the coasts from New York to Maine. They would also send an army north along the Hudson River to cut off New England from the middle colonies and to join with another army from Canada in attacking the frontiers of Massachusetts and Connecticut.[28] These plans, which promised to strangle New England without taking the British far from waterborne supplies and without requiring a direct assault on the rebels near Boston, would have pleased a Feuquières or a Saxe. But Géneral Howe, who became commander in chief in October 1775 and whose plans were warmly supported by the ministry, believed that a war of attrition alone would not end the rebellion, that the British would also have to defeat the Continental army in "a decisive Action, than which nothing is more to be desired or sought for by us as the most effectual Means to terminate this expensive War."[29] Howe was expressing a sensible appreciation of the strength of the rebellion as well as a typically British desire to do more than "weary" out the enemy.

Soon after reaching New York to open the campaign of 1776, Howe began to modify his plans, to put a greater emphasis on "wearying" out the rebels. It is not clear why, temporarily, he lost his enthusiasm for destroying the Continental army in battle. Perhaps he was inhibited by warnings from the ministry not to engage prematurely, perhaps by a desire to preserve his army, "the stock upon which the national force in America must in the future be grafted." He may even have been influenced by his brother, who as peace commissioner, as well as commander of the American squadron, was anxious to minimize the fighting until negotiations had been tried.[30] Whatever his reasons, from early August until the end of October, General Howe pursued a strategy of maneuver, limited engagements, and carefully consolidated gains that won Long Island and New York City but lost opportunities to trap and perhaps to destroy the Continental army.

At the end of October and against the advice of his generals, he tried briefly at White Plains to precipitate a general action. Forestalled by rain, he reverted quickly to a war of attrition: securing the remainder of Manhattan, forcing the Continental army to withdraw into Pennsylvania, sending Clinton to capture Rhode Island, and establishing a line of armed camps across New Jersey to provide security for loyalists and British foraging parties. Such a prudent, deliberate strategy seemed to be threatening the rebellion until Washington scored his brilliant victories at Trenton and Princeton, victories that forced Howe to concede he saw no "prospect of terminating the war but by a general action."[31] In 1776 Howe had emphasized flanking maneuvers, limited encounters, and territorial acquisitions. Yet he had not been able to put a decisive battle completely out of his mind.

For the ensuing campaign, the British managed to develop or, at least, to pursue two separate and incompatible plans. Both of these plans embodied the ambiguity, if not the narrowness, of Britain's strategic heritage. One, very much like the basic plan for 1776, grew out of suggestions made by General John Burgoyne, who was second in command in Canada and who had taken leave in the autumn of 1776 to return home, discuss strategy, and promote his own career. Stimulated by his "Thoughts for Conducting the War from the Side of Canada," and assuming that the campaign of 1776 could have been decisive if the Canadian army had not stopped short at Lake Champlain, the ministry decided to try once again not merely to isolate and conquer New England but also to create an opportunity for a climactic battle with the Continental army. To these ends, Burgoyne and Sir William Howe both would lead armies toward Albany—Burgoyne proceeding south from Quebec across Lake Champlain and Lake George, and Howe north from New York along the Hudson. The convergence of these powerful armies would, presumably, force Washington to make a stand in order to keep the British from completely isolating New England. As in 1776, detachments of ships and men would complement operations in the interior by attacking the coasts of Connecticut, Massachusetts, and New Hampshire.

When these plans were made, Lord George Germain, the secretary of state for America, knew that Howe was planning to begin the campaign by capturing Philadelphia and that he intended to leave only a small, defensive corps on the lower Hudson. Nevertheless, Germain failed to make sure that Howe would cooperate with Burgoyne. Preoccupied with the costs of the war and the task of encouraging his commanders to act decisively, Germain merely assumed that Howe would do his part and only belatedly and equivocally told him to. Germain and the ministry also assumed that their strategy would destroy the Continental army, subdue New England, and end the war in 1777—all without a substantial increase in British forces.[32]

Having no explicit instructions from Germain and knowing only that there would be few reinforcements to work with, Howe made separate plans for 1777. He decided that he had not the mobility to bring Washington to a decisive action, that he should concentrate instead on capturing Philadelphia and enlisting the support of the loyalists said to be living in the Delaware Valley. He would leave garrisons at New York and Newport, warn the commander of the Canadian army to expect little help from him, and take the remainder of his army by sea to Pennsylvania. If successful in raising loyalist forces to release regulars from garrison duty, he hoped to recover substantial portions of Pennsylvania, New Jersey, and New York by the end of the year. This plan, which may have been inspired by Howe's desire to show that there were loyalists in the Delaware Valley—that he had not been rash in extending his posts to Trenton and Princeton during the previous winter—owed little to contemporary strategic theory. But Howe followed this plan only fitfully during the remainder of the campaign. More often, between the end of May and the beginning of December, he oscillated between the poles of British strategic theory, between seeking a decisive battle and relying on maneuvers to take important posts and distress the enemy. In late May, while preparing to leave New York, he learned that Washington had advanced from Morristown to Boundbrook. On the chance that he might be able to precipitate a general engagement, he spent nearly a month in futile maneuvers along the Raritan. Then, after refusing to acknowledge any obligation to cooperate with Burgoyne, after rejecting instructions brought by a special emissary as well as the arguments of Sir Henry Clinton (his second in command, who had just returned from England and knew Germain's plans well), Sir William embarked for Philadelphia. En route he decided to go by way of the Chesapeake both to avoid an opposed landing in the Delaware and to cut off Washington from his principal magazines at York and Carlisle, Pennsylvania. At the Head of Elk he changed strategies once again. Finding the population hostile and Washington prepared to fight for Philadelphia, Howe decided to attack in force. On September 11 he won the Battle of Brandywine, but, as on Long Island in 1776, he failed to exploit the victory. He spent the next two months consolidating his hold on Philadelphia and denying responsibility for Burgoyne's surrender at Saratoga. Briefly in early December, Sir William made one last, vain effort to engage Washington and destroy his army at Whitemarsh.[33]

Burgoyne's surrender created problems that went beyond the competence of any commander in chief, problems that only the ministry could attempt to solve. It left Canada vulnerable to attack, reduced the forces available for carrying on the war against the rebels, diminished parliamentary support for coercive policies, and encouraged France to take a more overt role in behalf of the rebels. The ministry had no intention of abandoning the war or of conceding American independence, but it could not ask Parliament for all of the forces it needed to defend Canada, garrison posts in the middle colonies, and proceed with a conquest of New England. Necessity as well as the optimistic reports of the former royal governors of Georgia and the Carolinas led the ministry to adopt alternative ways of continuing the war—to experiment with strategies for which there were few theoretical precedents. On March 8, 1778, the ministry ordered Sir Henry Clinton, who had been appointed to succeed Howe as commander in chief, to rely mainly upon the British navy and loyal colonists in combatting the rebellion. If unable to bring Washington to action at the beginning of the campaign, Clinton was to send detachments to raid and blockade rebel ports from New York to Nova Scotia. He was then to embark 7,000 regular troops to join with loyalists in recovering Georgia, the Carolinas, and Virginia. Once royal government had been reestablished in the South, the remainder of the colonies could be left to wither under a blockade.[34] In ordering Clinton to seek a general action and to attack the coasts of New England, the ministry was close to conventional practice, close to traditional British reliance on a combination of decisive battles and "wearying" measures. But in telling him to enlist the population, the ministry was, it seems, responding far more to the circumstances of a revolutionary war than to any strategic theory. The ministry relied on the loyalists both to furnish badly needed troops and to persuade Parliament that the war should be continued—that it should be continued for the sake of the majority of the colonists who remained loyal and who fought against the tyranny of a few ambitious rebels.

Although forced to delay the execution of its new strategy for some months, the ministry would remain strongly committed to that strategy—or, at least, to its principal features—for the remainder of the war. On March 13 the French government announced that it had concluded a

Treaty of Amity and Commerce with the United States. This announce-
ment so provoked the king and his advisers that they decided at once to
divert 8,000 men from North America to attack the French island of St.
Lucia and to bolster the defenses of Florida. In so doing, they agreed to
withdraw from Philadelphia and temporarily suspend offensive operations against the rebels. Not until August 5 would the ministry tell Clinton
to revert to his instructions of March 8—specifically, to consider attacking colonial ports and sending a winter expedition to Georgia and South
Carolina.[35] The ministry's instructions for the following year were much
the same. Anticipating that Clinton would have significantly larger
forces—6,600 recruits, all the regulars that could be spared from St.
Lucia and Nova Scotia, and additional loyalist troops—the ministry did
provide for more extensive operations in the middle colonies. Clinton
would begin the campaign by trying to lure Washington into a decisive
battle or, that failing, by driving him into the Highlands of the Hudson so
that royal government might be reestablished in portions of New York
and New Jersey. But he would also send detachments of 4,000 men to
destroy rebel shipping in the Chesapeake and on the coasts of New
England, and he would take care not to neglect the South. He was to
maintain the forces already in Georgia and to remember that the ministry
regarded "the Recovery of South Carolina . . . an object of . . . great
Importance."[36] Thenceforth the ministry would provide little further
encouragement for operations in the middle colonies; it would stress with
increasing force and frequency the importance of relying on the fleet and
on loyalists in the South. Germain lost no opportunity to express his
enthusiasm whenever Clinton sent, or proposed to send, expeditions to
the Chesapeake and the Carolinas. In 1781 the king and the entire cabinet
joined Germain in telling Clinton that "the Recovery of the Southern
Provinces, & the Prosecution of the War by pushing Our Conquests from
South to North is to be considered as the chief and principal Object for the
Employment of all the forces under [your] Command"[37]

How did Sir Henry Clinton respond to these directions? During his first
two years as commander in chief, he followed in general the strategies
required or recommended by the ministry, strategies that encouraged him
to divide his efforts between the middle colonies and the deep South—
between conventional and unconventional warfare. Those strategies
made it all too easy for him to indulge his inherent lack of persistence. On
assuming command in May 1778 he had few choices to make. He was

required by the ministry and by circumstances to leave Philadelphia, defend New York, and prepare expeditions for St. Lucia and the Floridas. But beginning in the autumn of 1778, when the ministry told him to consider a winter expedition to Georgia and South Carolina, he was continually tempted to pursue now one strategy and now another. Although he was unwilling at first to invest more than 1,000 men in Georgia, he was so impressed with their success that he thought briefly of going to South Carolina in force.[38] He decided instead to carry out the ministry's proposal for a summer campaign in the middle colonies, a proposal that reflected conventionally ambiguous strategic thinking. After sending troops to raid the Chesapeake, he began the campaign by taking Stony and Verplanks points. As these posts controlled an important crossing of the Hudson, Clinton hoped not merely to disrupt American communications but also to tempt Washington to fight, to risk a general action. Finding that Washington refused and not having troops enough to secure New York and New Jersey while the Continental army remained intact, Clinton spent much of the summer waiting for reinforcements and conducting raids on the coast of Connecticut.[39] By late August he was eager to turn his back on New York and make a full-scale effort to restore loyalists to power in South Carolina. He was so much delayed by reports that a French fleet was returning to North America that he did not sail from New York until December nor reach South Carolina until February. On May 12, 1780, he captured Charleston.[40]

Thus far Clinton had kept reasonably close to strategies suggested by the ministry. During the next year he would frequently act to suit himself. His success in South Carolina—the taking of Charleston and more than 5,000 rebels, the rapid progress of British forces pushing into the interior, and the initially favorable response of the population—led him to think of restoring royal government throughout the South. It did not lead him to give priority to such an undertaking, even though he knew that the ministry was most enthusiastic over his going to Charleston and willing to forgo a summer campaign in the middle colonies. He told Earl Cornwallis, who would command in the South for the remainder of the war, not merely to defend South Carolina and Georgia but also to consider, in the proper season, "a *solid* move into North Carolina." But he left him with only 28 percent of the regular forces in the rebellious colonies.[41] Clinton then returned to New York, to secure that place against the French and to pursue a conventionally ambiguous strategy. He tried and failed once again to precipitate a decisive battle with Washington; he decided against attacking the French after they had taken possession of Rhode Island; and he exhausted the remainder of the summer considering a variety of "wearying" measures: expeditions to the Chesapeake, a raid on magazines at Philadelphia, and an excursion up the Hudson to take advantage of Benedict Arnold's offer to betray the American fortress at West Point. Not until mid-October did he send Major General Alexander Leslie with 2,500 men to the Chesapeake to assist Cornwallis.[42] During the ensuing winter, at the insistence of the ministry and in response to the recommendations of his generals, he gradually committed larger forces to the Chesapeake: 1,900 in December, 2,400 in March, and an additional 1,900 in May. He still had no intention of making Virginia the seat of the war or of giving priority to the ministry's strategy of employing loyalists to recover the South.[43] But by the time Cornwallis reached Petersburg in May 1781, nearly two-thirds of all British troops were in the South, and Clinton found it impossible, subsequently, to recover those troops before a French fleet arrived to trap many of them at Yorktown.[44]

It is not possible to demonstrate conclusively how theory affected practice in British strategy during the War for American Independence. This essay has tried merely to expand the discussion of that subject. It has suggested that British strategic thinking in the years before the American War was more complicated than historians usually have assumed, that the British were heirs to an ambiguous, if somewhat limited, strategic tradition. To judge by the books that they owned, read, wrote, and admired, British officers never completely accepted the prudent war of posts that was fashionable on the Continent in the eighteenth century and they never completely abandoned the aggressive war of movement and battles that owed as much to their own military tradition as to the classical past. This essay has also suggested that British strategy in the American War frequently reflected the ambiguities peculiar to contemporary British strategic theory. The ministry did make plans—at the beginning of the war and after Burgoyne surrenderd—that owed little to any theory. These plans were designed primarily to suit the circumstances of a revolutionary war, to recover the colonies piecemeal by enlisting the support of the population. But the ministry relied as well on strategies that were consistent with conventional theory or, at least, on strategies that embodied both conventional and unconventional ways of waging war. In 1776 and

1777 it encouraged Howe both to pursue a war of attrition and to seek a decisive battle; in 1779 it ordered Clinton not merely to enlist loyalist support in recovering the middle colonies and the South but also to try to destroy the Continental army in battle and to exhaust the rebels with raids in the Chesapeake and on the coasts of New England. The ministry was not, of course, so familiar with or restricted by military theory as were the commanders in chief. Howe and Clinton occasionally made plans to take advantage of loyalist support. More often they sought to end the rebellion with a strategy that depended on both a climactic battle and such "wearying" measures as destroying the rebels' magazines, cutting their lines of supply and communication, capturing their cities, attacking their ports and shipping, and driving their armies into barren and inhospitable country. Indeed, it seems that prevailing doctrine encouraged Howe and Clinton to dissipate their energies swinging between prudent and aggressive measures and to divert their forces from any systematic effort to enlist loyalists. If they had pursued exclusively a strategy of destroying the Continental army, they might well have broken American resistance at the beginning of the war when Washington was all too willing to fight. If they had pursued a prudent war of posts, they might eventually have exhausted the rebels. Or, if they had concentrated on restoring loyalists to power in one region after another, they might gradually have pushed the rebels into oblivion. As it was, they proceeded with an ambiguous strategy that contributed at last to defeat and to the loss of America.

3

AMERICAN STRATEGY: A CALL FOR A CRITICAL STRATEGIC HISTORY

Russell F. Weigley

George Washington may never have used the word *strategy*. In the eighteenth century, the word was just beginning to come into military discourse as a derivation from the Greek *strategos*, or leader, to signify the art practiced by the military leader. To the limited extent that the term was employed at all in Washington's day, *strategy* had a much closer relationship than it now retains to *stratagem*, a ruse or trick. Partly that was true because eighteenth-century European war had grown so mechanical and ritualistic that a mere unexpected trick could sometimes prove of decisive advantage in war. More important, when Washington lived, the study of strategy as a major branch of the military art still lay in the future; for strategic studies were to be born in the nineteenth century when Jomini and Clausewitz attempted to explain the revolution in warfare symbolized by Napoleon.[1]

Thus Washington missed the opportunity to prepare himself for his responsibilities as principal American strategist of the Revolution in the way that later American strategists of the Civil War were to be prepared, by studying the erudite reflections of Jomini and his disciples upon the virtues of interior versus exterior lines and by learning from Jomini that the exploitation of the interior lines was the secret of Napoleon's success. In this, Washington may well have been fortunate. The whole body of Jominian strategic study came to revolve around his invention of the concept of the interior and exterior lines. In presenting this concept and pointing out the advantages of the interior position, Jomini was essentially codifying an insight as old as maneuver by organized bodies of armed men; but he and his followers also complicated the insight by burying it within multiple layers of complex deductions from it about reentering angles and eccentric retreats and what not. These strategists tended to blur the vision of generalship by making commonsense principles seem so esoteric that one must study and restudy how they apply to any given situation. By the time such studying is completed in real war, a resourceful, commonsensical opponent is likely to have left the calculations of the Jominian scholar-general trailing well behind his own maneuvers. Thus resulted the unhappy experiences of such Jominian Civil War strategists as George B. McClellan and Henry Wager Halleck against less studious soldiers of the stamp of Stonewall Jackson and Nathan Bedford Forrest.

If Washington benefited from antedating the birth of the modern study of strategy he also suffered a penalty, since he was unlucky in the effect that the timing of his career was to have upon his stature in military history. So were all the strategists of the American Revolution. Their misfortune was that they so immediately preceded the revolution in war identified with the French Revolution and Napoleon. With vast military changes occurring promptly after their own campaigns, they came to seem military antiques before their bodies were cold in their graves, or indeed before they entered their graves. The modern study of strategy at its birth concentrated upon Napoleon and his marshals and rivals. Such pre-Napoleonic European strategists as Marshal Saxe and Frederick the Great retained a foothold in strategic study because they had preceded Napoleon by just long enough to have entrenched themselves in the company of great commanders and, moreover, because their campaigns and writings could be searched for sources of Napoleonic warfare. But the Americans seemed outside the mainstream of evolutionary development, as well as obsolete overnight. When the systematic study of strategy began early in the nineteenth century, even among Americans the object lessons were almost entirely Napoleonic and almost never Washingtonian. Early West Point strategists had their Napoleon Club, not their Washington Club. The first American books about strategy, Dennis Hart Mahan's and H. W. Halleck's, contained much about Napoleon and little about Washington, in particular virtually nothing about his strategy.[2]

The first American textbook on military strategy designed to break free from exclusively European models, Captain John Bigelow's *Principles of Strategy: Illustrated Mainly from American Campaigns,* did not appear until the closing years of the nineteenth century. By then, predict-

ably, it chose its American campaigns overwhelmingly from the Civil
War. Washington's Trenton-Princeton campaign receives an unimagina-
tive three-page synopsis as an example of a counteroffensive operation.
Somewhat longer sections on the Saratoga campaign and the southern
campaigns focus on British rather than American strategy.[3] Matthew
Forney Steele's *American Campaigns,* long the standard introduction to
American military history especially among American soldiers, is much
more a tactical than a strategic study.[4] On the naval side, Alfred Thayer
Mahan preferred the British and French navies of the American Revolution as objects of strategic study, for the American navy was too small to
essay any strategy except that of the *guerre de course,* which in Mahan's
scheme of things was futile by definition.[5]

Since the time of Bigelow and Steele, European as well as American
writers on strategy have come to incorporate American historical examples into their teachings. But the examples remain those of the Civil War
and later wars. George Washington and his comrades still make no
appearance in B. H. Liddell Hart's influential *Strategy;* and J. F. C.
Fuller's *Military History of the Western World,* while giving two
"chronicles" and two chapters to the American Revolution, follows the
pattern of concentrating its strategic discussion on the British. The
British, of course, bore the more complex strategic problems of offensive
war and attempted conquest, but Fuller hints that not everything of
strategic interest was on their side when he lauds Nathanael Greene as
"one of the greatest of small war leaders." Having said that much,
however, he does not bother either to spell Greene's Christian name
correctly ("Nathaniel") or to offer any clear evidence in support of his
praise.[6]

Similarly, the two most frequently used surveys of world military
history, Theodore Ropp's *War in the Modern World* and Richard A.
Preston's and Sydney F. Wise's *Men in Arms,* reserve their considerations of the strategy of the American Revolution almost entirely to the
British. Ropp is unusually generous in the space he allots to the Revolution, but his section on the Continental army deals mainly with organizational problems.[7] Field Marshal Viscount Montgomery's massive *History of Warfare* dismisses the American Revolution with one short
paragraph in well over 500 pages; from Montgomery we learn merely
that while Washington was never more than a mediocre leader, he
benefited from British blunders, such as fighting in red uniforms while

"the Americans camouflaged themselves in green and fought largely as irregulars."[8]

Professor Ropp, in several very sound paragraphs, and Field Marshal Montgomery, in an absurdly inaccurate one, touch what has been the main theme of the American Revolution, even for those writers who as specialists in American military history have been obliged to deal more fully with the Revolution than have students either of the art of strategy or of Europe's or the whole world's military history. The importance of the Revolution in the history of war has tended to be seen by such historians as residing in the way the American rebels formed their army: in their breaking away from the European conventions of the professional army of long-service enlisted men for the army of the citizen-soldier, in their corollary departure from the conventional rigid tactics possible only to long-service soldiers, and in their consequent foreshadowing of the "nation in arms" and a revolution in warfare, both tactical and organizational. To American military historians of the Emory Upton school, themselves largely professional soldiers, these changes have generally appeared deplorable. The changes allegedly prolonged the War of the Revolution itself, because citizen-soldiers could not fight as effectively as a properly trained army could have done. And the Revolution gave the United States an unfortunate military tradition of excessive reliance on the citizen-soldier and denigration of the military professional, prolonging all subsequent American wars as well.[9] Many civilian historians have made a nearly opposite evaluation, that the civilianization and democratization of war occurring in the American Revolution, while they may have had the unfortunate ultimate consequence of making war more terrible, were of immediate advantage in the winning of American independence. Walter Millis's *Arms and Men,* generally the most satisfying of all surveys of American military history, takes the latter view when it lists the armed citizenry as a principal source of American victory: "The combination of an armed populace, a loose-knit and democratically organized administration offering few points of attack and a huge terrain was too much for British arms.[10]

Whatever value judgments are made about the American rebels' employment of an armed citizenry, however, treating the citizen-soldier as the central contribution of the American Revolution to the evolution of warfare rescued the Revolution from the neglect of the strategic historians at the expense of creating new difficulties of historical interpretation. For one thing, even so accurate and sophisticated a historian as Walter Millis runs the risk of creating an exaggerated impression of revolutionary America as a nation in arms when he lists "an armed populace" as first among the factors that undid the British. For another, though the American Revolution did to a limited degree foreshadow the French recourse to the nation in arms a decade and a half later, it did so only on an exceedingly limited scale. The French would surely have called on the *levée en masse* to preserve their own revolution against the united monarchies of Europe no matter what precedents the distant Americans had or had not set for them: the French armed citizenry does not stand in a direct line of succession from the American. Finally, emphasis on the armed citizenry tends to lead into a further emphasis on the Americans' employment of unconventional tactics appropriate to an unconventional soldiery, and this emphasis in turn to the belief that a tactical revolution commenced in America, the beginning of the end for the close-order linear tactics of the eighteenth-century European battlefield. But Peter Paret has shown that the movement toward looser, open-order skirmishing tactics had its roots less in the western than in the eastern marches of European civilization, reaching the major powers through the *Jäger* and *Schützen* of the German states, and that the British army despite its direct American experience was slow to adopt tactics of skirmishing and marksmanship for the main body of its infantry.[11]

The neglect of the American strategy of the Revolution by both historical and strategic scholars and writers is of course consistent with the prolonged colonial status of America in things military. Except for the brief interlude of the Civil War, the United States Army until the twentieth century was a tiny force compared with the armies of the European powers and, in many ways, less an army than a frontier constabulary. Consequently, the United States remained largely in tutelage to Europe for military ideas. Only well along into the twentieth century did the United States effectively assert its declaration of independence from European military thought and examples. Yet the entrance of the armed forces of the United States into the world military arena much earlier in this century—and especially the American insistence during World War I that an American army must fight as independently as possible of its European associates—created a motive for Americans to search their history in hopes of discovering their own tradition of successful military strategy and command. If they had to work implicitly within the framework of American military tutelage to Europe, nevertheless Americans might find that within those boundaries American strategists had demonstrated enough originality and ability to merit a more prominent place than was customarily given them in the history of military strategy. Finding historical examples of American strategists and commanders of high stature might lend added sanction to General John J. Pershing's latter-day claims for an autonomous American army, with autonomous strategy and command.

Against the background of World War I, two military officers who were also amateur historians sought with particular conspicuousness to complete such a search, by applying modern strategic interpretations to the career of General George Washington, in a manner that would enhance his reputation by adding to the familiar portrait of the patriotic hero the lineaments of an accomplished strategist. These two officers were Captain Thomas G. Frothingham, United States Reserves, with *Washington: Commander in Chief,* and Captain Dudley W. Knox, United States Navy, with *The Naval Genius of George Washington.* [12] In focusing upon Washington, both writers—as Knox's title especially suggests—betrayed a certain persistence of the filiopietistic strain in Revolutionary War history that had so long been among the principal causes of neglect of critical strategic study. But both also made it clear that Washington was the dominant figure in American Revolutionary strategy. Congress through various military committees and the Board of War attempted to supervise strategy, initiating the 1775 invasion of Canada, pressing Washington to attempt a military defense of New York City in 1776, and later pushing for another effort toward Canada. Congress also enjoined Washington to heed the advice of his generals in councils of war, a duty that Washington faithfully performed. But the interest of Congress was always, and necessarily, more in military administration than in military strategy. Also, despite occasional congressional carping and the flirtation of some congressmen with intrigues against the commander in chief (such as the so-called Conway Cabal), the legislature was remarkably consistent in its endeavors to be helpful to Washington in his strategic role. Washington never had to face congressional criticism at all resembling that which plagued so many Union generals of the Civil War. Especially after his stimulation of the sagging American cause at Trenton and Princeton, Congress deferred to

Washington as *the* American strategist of the Revolution. The ascendancy of Washington over most of his generals assured him that position despite the required councils of war. If Major General Nathanael Greene was also to win deserved laurels as a strategist, it was as a regional leader that he did so, not as a rival to Washington in shaping the whole direction of the war.[13]

Clausewitz defined strategy as *"the theory of the use of combats for the object of the War."* Tactics, in contrast, he defined as *"the theory of the use of military forces in combat."*[14] The distinction of Frothingham's and Knox's books was that, while earlier military studies of the Revolution had examined in detail the use of military forces in combat on the battlefield, the tactics of the war, they were the first to attempt to review the battles and campaigns as links in a chain that properly put together would draw the colonies on to independence. Frothingham and Knox provided the first systematic studies of how the American leadership, and particularly Washington, used combats for the object of the war.

In this effort to see the war as a strategic whole, Frothingham became one of the first military historians to recognize clearly that with the expulsion of the British army from Boston on March 17, 1776, the Americans had thus early in the war taken a giant step toward achieving the objects they sought: the rebels were already in practical control of the thirteen colonies stretching from New England to Georgia. From then on, the Americans needed only to hold what they had gained; the British had to reconquer. To be sure, the American strategists' effort to add Canada to the rebellion had failed with Richard Montgomery's and Benedict Arnold's campaigns in the fall and winter of 1775-76. But Frothingham regarded the Canadian effort as a mistake on the part of Congress and Washington anyway, misguided because the Canadians did not want to join the Revolution, the venture was supported by insufficient resources, and success would have chained the Americans to a strategic albatross.[15]

Henceforth the Revolution was to be a defensive war for the Americans. In this defensive war, Frothingham perceived two fundamental strategic factors: first, the ability of the British armies to go anywhere and capture any place—but only as long as they were operating near enough to the coast that the Royal Navy could assure their supply by sea;[16] and second, the ability of the Americans to turn back or at least hold off the British whenever the redcoat armies attempted to penetrate into the countryside beyond ready access to the sea—because there the British could not sustain themselves, and also because in wooded country not suitable to formalized European warfare the Americans could resort to irregular tactics.[17] Though the Americans could never offer the British equal battle in European terms, the balancing off of the two strategic factors placed the war nevertheless in a strategic impasse. The American defensive war could not defend the coast; but it could always defend the interior.[18]

A still more modern note than one might expect of a post-World War I study was Frothingham's realization that in such circumstances a trump card of American strategy was partisan warfare. Washington "could always count his enemy as being at a marked disadvantage in irregular warfare."[19] To be sure, Frothingham did not mean all that "irregular warfare" may connote in the age of Vo Nguyen Giap and Mao Tse-tung. He included within the term the colonials' conduct of the Lexington-Concord affair, which—though fought by irregular troops according to methods not contemplated by contemporary European soldiers—would not strike the late-twentieth-century observer as quite amounting to irregular or partisan war. Yet Frothingham did emphasize partisan war as a fundamental asset of American strategy, the factor that ensured the inability of the British armies to sustain themselves at any appreciable distances from the sea.[20]

Frothingham's appreciation of the utility of partisan war for the defensive strategy of the Americans led him to a shrewd and, again to the student in the late twentieth century, a seemingly very modern appraisal of how Nathanael Greene's use of combats contributed to the object of the war. Of Greene's campaign in the South in 1781-1782 he said:

> Greene's conception of his task was nothing less than inspired. Instead of ignoring the partisan bands, as [Horatio] Gates had done, he made them important in his strategy. . . . He constituted his army the nucleus for rallying all these American forces, for the irregular harassing warfare, which was always most effective against the British of that formal school. He made the country what Cornwallis called a "hornets' nest." At times Greene's army was united. At other times it was divided into partisan bands. But it was always attacking and harassing the Regulars. Yet Greene's most daring moves were always controlled by the resolve never to put his army in a position where it might be sacrificed in a set battle.[21]

In part, Frothingham on Greene anticipated Mao Tse-tung on the cooperation of the main organized army with the guerrillas: "This army is powerful because of its division into two parts, the main forces and the regional forces, with the former available for operations in any region whenever necessary and the latter concentrating on defending their own localities and attacking the enemy there in co-operation with the local militia and the self-defense corps.''[22] But more to the point, Frothingham's comments on Greene reflect his larger judgment that it was necessary, despite their trump card of partisan war, for the Americans to build as strong as possible a conventional army, capable of the best showing possible against the British in European-style warfare, if they were to be able to exploit their advantages in irregular war and in British logistical difficulties.

For Frothingham believed that irregular, partisan warfare alone could not have won the Revolution for two basic reasons. First, though a conventional American army must always fight at a disadvantage, nevertheless it could neutralize the British main forces, preventing them from dispersing enough to track down the partisans. If they had not had to concentrate their main forces to check an American conventional army, the British might well have found means to deal with the partisans after all. Secondly, a conventional American army was necessary for symbolic purposes: to represent the continuity, stability, and indeed dignity of the Revolutionary cause and to provide a permanent nucleus around which transient militia and irregulars might rally.[23]

Washington's principal claim to distinction as a commander was his creation, in the midst of revolutionary change and flux, of this permanent, stable nucleus of military resistance: the Continental army. His similar claim to distinction as a strategist was a clear and consistent recognition that preserving the army he had created was the first strategic essential for the American cause. Washington intensified this recognition after his own mistakes and those urged on him by Congress almost lost the army in the futile battles for New York in the summer of 1776. Coming to perceive the importance of preserving the Continental army over all other means to the end of independence, Washington henceforth rightly eschewed both further defensive stands in perilous locations and hazardous offensive operations, especially any new incursion into Canada after 1775-76.[24]

With the limited resources in military education that were at the disposal of the commander in chief and his officers, and with the newly independent country's other limitations in manpower and materiel,

Washington's "nondescript and ill-equipped troops" were "never strong enough to hope to destroy their enemy."[25] Nevertheless, Washington could "use the Continentals he had created as a nucleus for stiffening the raw levies into troops able to take the field against the British. It was his application of this principle, in 1777, that had transformed the gathering of militia into the formidable American army that had overwhelmed Burgoyne."[26] The Continentals became effective enough soldiers that Washington could use them for counterstrokes against enemy detachments (as at Trenton and Princeton) and even against large enemy forces (as at Germantown). "Washington's logical strategic aim was, to keep before the eyes of the people the existence of an opposing American army, which would curb the British army and defend the surrounding country."[27]

So well did Washington exploit the existence of his army and the memory of the stings that it inflicted at Trenton and Princeton and, in time, Germantown and Stony Point that the fear of encountering the Continental army in combination with swarming unconventional troops in an inhospitable country left the British forces virtual prisoners in the seacoast enclaves that the power of the Royal Navy permitted them to conquer. The psychological balance of the war was turned against them; even on the coast, they felt trapped rather than victorious. Once Washington's organizational and strategic talents had created such a situation, not only was the already accomplished liberation of the bulk of the United States assured, but the stage was set for complete British disaster when the French alliance should deprive Great Britain of control of the sea.

With weaker forces, in the face of difficulties and discouragements that seemed insurmountable, Washington . . . had baffled and beaten off the superior British main army, until it lay huddled on the coast, after giving up all efforts to overrun the country. . . . This went far beyond any mere matter of the events of battles. It marked an actual decision won by Washington over the British main army—for it meant the defeat of the whole object of the main British army in the Revolution.[28]

The most dramatic consequence of Washington's success in confining British operations to the seacoast—the Yorktown campaign—formed the climax of Captain Knox's study of Washington as a naval strategist. Knox traced Washington's course from a strategist helplessly "baffled"[29] by sea power that he could not hope to counter to a master strategist of sea power himself when the French alliance placed a strong navy at his disposal. It was "in the vital relation of naval supremacy to vigorous and decisive military operations," said the naval Captain Knox, "that Washington's genius chiefly lay."[30]

The filiopietistic strain certainly remains present in Knox's book. It required no genius to recognize what it was that was baffling American strategy in the early part of the war, when sea power enabled the British to descend wherever they pleased on the rebel coast. Major General Charles Lee in fact described the source of frustration more pungently than Washington ever did, in a letter from Williamsburg during his tenure of command in the Southern Department:

I am like a Dog in a dancing school. I know not where to turn myself, where to fix myself, the circumstances of the Country intersected by navigable rivers, the uncertainty of the Enemy's designs and motions, who can fly in an instant to any spot They choose with their canvass wings, throw me, or would throw Julius Caesar, into this inevitable dilemma. I may possibly be in the North, when, as Richard says, I should serve my Sovereign in the West. I can only act from surmise, and have a very good chance of surmising wrong.[31]

Yet Knox was correct in treating Washington not only as the central American strategist of the Revolution but also as the strategist who most consistently recognized how sea power might serve the American cause once it was available. "Next to the loan of money," Knox quoted Washington regarding the French alliance, "a constant naval superiority on these coasts is the object most interesting. . . . This superiority, with an aid of money, would enable us to convert the war into a vigorous offensive."[32] Sea power alone could turn American strategy from the defensive to a decisive offensive that could complete the job of driving the British army from the American coasts by driving them from the interior as well.

From the close of 1778, when d'Estaing had left Boston for the West Indies, Washington had done practically nothing with his army except to hold it in readiness for coöperation with a naval superiority. At every subsequent occasion when the hope of such superiority presented itself, he made extensive preparations and showed the strongest determination to undertake a vigorous and decisive offensive on land.[33]

Washington, said Knox, was a better admiral than the French admirals on whose naval force he had to depend. If Washington could have communicated rapidly enough with Admiral Chevalier Destouches in February, 1781, and if Destouches had acted upon his advice, instead of dividing his squadron the French admiral would have confronted the British with a decisive naval superiority in the Chesapeake at the very outset of that critical year.[34] And more successfully, "the General's influence dissuaded de Barras from his proposed eccentric Newfoundland expedition, and brought him instead to a junction with de Grasse in the Chesapeake, thus cleverly applying the fundamental principle of the maximum concentration of forces at the vital point at the critical time."[35] And in the decisive campaign, said Knox, "Washington's profound and brilliant naval strategy of the Yorktown campaign is too obvious to be dwelt upon. In this it is sufficient proof of his naval genius to recognize the unquestionable fact that his was the master mind," that is, the mind that planned, held to the plan, and executed the campaign.[36]

World War II, much more than World War I, stimulated an interest in military history among civilian American historians. Like World War I, it offered appallingly dramatic evidence of the importance that arms could have in human affairs. Unlike World War I, it continued in retrospect to seem to the overwhelming majority of Americans, including most historians, to demonstrate that arms could contribute to the preservation and advancement of their country's traditional values. Taking up arms to defend traditional American values stimulated a new nationalism among American historians. Together, the neo-nationalist mood and the demonstration of the possible utility of war prompted in particular a reexamination of the military aspects of the country's origins. The military history of the American Revolution emerged from the keeping of military men such as Frothingham and Knox and entered the domain of civilian professional historians to a degree unprecedented since the appearance of history as a professional academic discipline in America in the late nineteenth century. When Willard M. Wallace's *Appeal to Arms: A Military History of the American Revolution* was published in 1951, it was, as Don Higginbotham described it, "the first comprehensive treatment of revolutionary warfare since 1911,"[37] and the 1911 survey of the military history of the war had been written by a military writer, Colonel Francis Vinton Greene.[38] Now Wallace's book proved to be merely the first of four surveys of the military history of the Revolution to appear in as many years, only one of them by a writer who might at all be considered as much a military man as a historian.[39]

By 1964, Higginbotham could add two further overall surveys of Revolutionary military history to the post-World War II accounting of "American Historians and the Military History of the American Revolution," along with nineteen recent biographies of American soldiers and sailors of the Revolution.[40] The approach of the Bicentennial of the Revolution has assured that this tide should continue to rise. And Higginbotham, who surveyed the tide in 1964, presently contributed to it his own one-volume military history of the Revolution.[41] Nor could the American revulsion against warfare accompanying the Indochina War stem the rise of Revolutionary War history; the revulsion itself produced an introspective search for the deepest roots of American military involvement in Southeast Asia, a search that reached to the roots of American methods of warfare and of American values and thus back again to the American Revolution.

The most imposing single landmark of the post-World War II surge of Revolutionary War history is Douglas Southall Freeman's seven-volume biography of George Washington, three volues of which encompass the history of Washington's command of the Continental army. This book is fully worthy of a place beside its author's monumental Civil War studies, *R. E. Lee* and *Lee's Lieutenants*—and higher praise than that can scarcely be accorded a work in American military history.[42] But it is also significant that like Freeman's Civil War books, his military biography of Washington is primarily a history of tactics, operations, and administration, not of strategy. In this, Freeman's *Washington* is a representative work among the new Revolutionary military histories. The post-World War II historians have brought the military history of the Revolution into the mainstream of American historical literature; they have not brought the Revolution, at least the American side of it, into the mainstream of strategic studies or the history of strategy.

In his twenty-four pages summarizing his conclusions about Washington's military leadership, Freeman characteristically devoted less than four full pages to Washington as a strategist. The rest is about Washington as administrator, disciplinarian, respecter of civilian supremacy as embodied in the Congress, and admirable character.[43] Of "Washington's strategy, his tactics, his leadership," all taken together, Freeman asked, "Did these distinguish him or merely show him fortunate?"[44]

Freeman's verdict was that in these aspects of his command, Washington was in large part fortunate—"in nothing so fortunate, strategically, as his adversary's lack of enterprise." Except for Cornwallis and Benedict Arnold, none of the British leaders "acted as if the United States were a foe to be destroyed."[45] Washington's strategic contribution to his own good fortune had to be mainly one of caution. "To have described his Army is to make plain the fundamental of all the cumbering factors: Washington's strategy had to be patiently defensive."[46] By temperament, Washington would have preferred to be aggressive, but until 1781 he could never secure the means for an offensive that might hope to drive the enemy from America. Through careful intelligence work to uncover the enemy's dispositions and careful secrecy on his own part, he sought to make his defensive an offensive-defensive wherever possible, by hurling swift strokes at exposed portions of the enemy. But his risks and commitments had to be severely limited: "In strategy, as in land speculation, Washington habitually was a bargain hunter. He always sought the largest gain for the least gore."[47]

The emphasis of the other post-World War II studies that focus on the American side of the Revolution also lies predominantly elsewhere than on the strategy of Washington or the other American leaders. The other recent multivolume biography of Washington, James Thomas Flexner's, is less a military biography than Freeman's, but rather a character study. In any event, its military history is mainly tactical.[48] Marcus Cunliffe's *George Washington: Man and Monument,* on the whole a stimulating interpretative book, devotes more of its military chapter on "General Washington" to British strategy than to Washington's.[49] Like Cunliffe's essay on the commander in chief in George Athan Billias's collection, *George Washington's Generals,* that chapter stresses instead Washington as a military organizer and administrator, especially his efforts and achievement toward creating not an army that would be revolutionary in its very approach to warfare, but as close as possible a replica of a European army for fighting conventional war. Though Cunliffe is concerned with analyzing how Washington the man came to be a monument, rather than with worshipping the monument, he also finds himself obliged to dwell on those admirable qualities of character that probably made Washington indispensable to holding the Revolution together.[50]

Theodore Thayer is something of an exception to these generalizations about the post-World War II military historians' lack of interest in

American strategy, especially in his writings on Major General
Nathanael Greene: a full-length biography, *Nathanael Greene: Strategist of the American Revolution,* and an essay in the Billias collection,
"Nathanael Greene: Revolutionary War Strategist."[51] Greene indeed
indicated an interest in strategy by having waged in the South a victorious
campaign to drive the British from the Carolinas and Georgia despite
such severe limitations as a tactician that he lost every sizable battle he
fought; his success was the triumph of a strategist so masterful that he
could make even tactical defeats contribute to his Clausewitzian pursuit
of the objects of the war. His success was also that of a strategist attractive
to the modern observer as the only general in American history to offer a
fair claim to mastery of the strategy of unconventional war, as the
quotations about Greene from Fuller and Frothingham have already
suggested. But the rub is that the phrase "Strategist of the American
Revolution" as the subtitle of a biography of Greene is misleading.
Greene was never the strategist at the center of the war. The difference
between a regional strategist and one who bears the responsibility of
winning a war altogether is considerable—even in its impact on a given
general's own strategy, as witness the difference between the subtle
strategy of maneuver of U. S. Grant in the Vicksburg campaign and his
bludgeoning strategy of annihilation once he became commander of all
the Union armies. The American strategist of the Revolution remained
George Washington.

In lingering over British strategy in a chapter about "General
Washington," Marcus Cunliffe explained his choice of emphasis by
stating that while Washington's "duty, though desperately demanding,
reduced itself to simple essentials . . . [to] endure, evade, exhort[,] Howe
in comparison had almost an excess of alternatives."[52] The British, cast
in the aggressive role of having to conquer thirteen provinces already in
the control of the Revolutionaries, faced a puzzling variety of possible
strategies from which they had to select the one most likely to succeed.
The consequent complexity of their strategic problems, multipled still
again when for them the War of the American Revolution became a world
war against multiple enemies, no doubt goes far to account for the fact
that British strategy, unlike American, has received notable attention in
the post-World War II resurgence of Revolutionary War military studies.
Beginning in 1945, William B. Willcox has contributed a succession of
articles on British strategy, an edition of General Sir Henry Clinton's

account of his American strategy and campaigns, and finally a biography of Clinton.[53] The British historian Eric Robson's *American Revolution in its Political and Military Aspects, 1763-1783*—although balancing two chapters called "Why British Defeat?" with one called "Why American Victory?"—approaches both questions from the British viewpoint.[54] Another British historian, Piers Mackesy, in *The War for America, 1775-1783,* has offered a study of overall British strategy and administration that has no counterpart in the literature of the American side of the war.[55] Ira D. Gruber, *The Howe Brothers and the American Revolution,* deals amply with battles and tactics but is largely concerned with the Howes' designs for conducting the whole war, that is, with their strategy.[56]

The studies of the American effort in the Revolution have remained, in contrast, histories principally of tactics and operations rather than of strategic conception, planning, and decision. Lieutenant Colonel Dave Richard Palmer is correct when he says: "Foremost among the considerations slighted by historians would have to be the strategic concepts under which the war was waged."[57]

In time for the observation of the Revolutionary War Bicentennial, Colonel Palmer himself has made a noteworthy contribution toward remedying this omission: *The Way of the Fox: American Strategy in the War for America, 1775-1783.* The fox, of course, is the major American strategist, Washington. The book is admirably ambitious in that it not only attempts to deal with Washington's strategy per se; it also presents two chapters reviewing the modern history of strategic thought, and it attempts to place the American strategy of the Revolution into the history of the evolution of strategy. Less admirably, the book is ambitious as well in its continual quarrelsome challenging of other historians, for Palmer argues that not only have other writers neglected strategy; when they have incidentally brushed against the topic, he contends, their judgments about it have almost invariably been wrong.[58]

Unfortunately, Palmer himself begins to go wrong here. In trying to convert the complex conclusions of other historians into plainly marked targets that he can aim at and shoot down, he distorts by oversimplification of what the other historians have said. In trying to show that practically everybody who preceded him in touching on Washington as a strategist misunderstood the Revolutionary commander in chief, Palmer has the other historians depicting Washington as a more simply Fabian strategist than they did. It is not true to say, as Palmer does, that "if strategy is mentioned at all [in military studies of the Revolution], it is likely to be couched in terms of the much ballyhooed—but possibly misconstrued—Fabian streak in George Washington and Nathanael Greene."[59] It is hard to find writers who call Greene a Fabian. Of Washington, Marcus Cunliffe wrote well before Palmer: "Others might talk of Fabian tactics, even approvingly; he himself seems never to have invoked the name of Fabius Cunctator, the Delayer."[60] To be sure, Palmer has to acknowledge that not every student has found Washington to be a Fabian strategist. But he professes to find it merely puzzling, or symptomatic of his predecessors' confusion, that Don Higginbotham should write: "It is surprising that older histories depict him [Washington] as a Fabius, a commander who preferred to retire instead of fight. . . . While Washington has been criticized for excessive caution, he was actually too impetuous";[61] or that Freeman should have said both that "Washington's strategy had to be patiently defensive"[62] and that "if a choice had to be made, he [Washington] preferred active risk to passive ruin. . . ."[63] That is, Palmer considers the proposition that Washington was bold by temperament but cautious by restrained judgment as too subtle to be tenable.

Palmer goes about his task of depicting Washington as a more aggressive strategist than previous writers have perceived by dividing Washington's strategy into four phases. The first, from April 1775 to July 1776, "was the 'revolutionary' period of the Revolutionary War,"[64] in which the insurgents expelled British civil and military power from the thirteen rebellious colonies and tried to expand their rebellion into Canada. The second, from July 1776 to December 1777, was admittedly a defensive phase, in which "Patriot generals" saw their task "as the defense of national shores against a foreign invader," and Washington's "foremost imperative was to prevent a decisive defeat of his own army."[65] In the third phase, January 1778 to December 1781, the French alliance deprived the British of uncontested command of the sea, and consequently "the entire thrust of Washington's strategy could be reversed. Whereas he had been limited to the strategic defensive while Great Britain remained superior at sea, the arrival of a French fleet would make it feasible for him once again to pass over to the offensive."[66] Finally, the fourth phase, January 1782 to December 1783, after Yorktown, was one in which "with independence virtually assured . . . preserving the Continental Army was now more important than defeating the enemy army. Washington informed his officers that offensive actions were to be undertaken only when the Patriots had a 'moral certainty of succeeding.' "[67] But "it would be wrong to portray his attitude during this period as defensive," because Washington now again turned his attention to territorial expansion, in the West and in Canada.[68]

Though Palmer's treatment of Washington is new in its consistent focus upon his strategy rather than his tactics and administration, the picture that emerges is not so new as Palmer implies—because earlier historians have never perceived only a defensive Washington as consistently as he suggests. No one would deny Washington's aggressiveness in the first phase of the war. When treating the months during which the commander in chief sponsored Arnold's invasion of Canada and sought persistently for a means to drive the British from Boston, no historian could gainsay Washington's offensive-mindedness. Frothingham described Washington in this period as always "anxious to fight" and thought that in pushing the attack on Canada he was aggressive to excess.[69] Freemen said that "impatiently, at last, Washington cast aside his earlier theory that his strategical task was simply to confine the British to Boston. He must do more—but what and where and how?"[70] If not the same large-offensive-mindedness, in a broader sense the aggressive phase of Washington's generalship extended beyond July 1776 into Palmer's second period, to encompass Washington's several bold—not to say reckless—invitations to the British to meet his army in head-on combat during the New York campaign of the summer and autumn.

For it was only in the battles around New York that Washington learned the full measure of the inferiority of his ill-trained army to British and German regulars on the battlefield. Though he was persuaded to attempt a defense of New York in part by political, rather than military, considerations and by the sentiments of Congress, before General William Howe began moving the king's forces from Staten Island to Long Island Washington was relatively sanguine: "tho' the appeal may not terminate so happily in our favor as I could wish . . . yet they [the British] will not succeed in their views without considerable loss. Any advantage they may get I trust will cost them dear."[71] Or as Washington himself described the transition in his attitudes from before to after the Battle of Long Island: "Till of late I had no doubt in my own mind of defending this place [New York], nor should I yet, if the men would do their duty, but this I despair of.''[72] It was from this time when he despaired of his men's doing their duty—that is, fighting as disciplined soldiers—that Washington went over consistently to the strategic defensive. It was thenceforth that he consistently described his strategy in terms such as these:

> In deliberating on this Question [of strategy] it was impossible to forget, that History, our own experience, the advice of our ablest Friends in Europe, the fears of the Enemy, and even the Declarations of Congress demonstrate, that on our Side the War should be defensive. It has even been called a War of Posts. That we should on all Occasions avoid a general Action, or put anything to the Risque, unless compelled by a necessity, into which we ought never to be drawn.[73]

Yet once obliged to form such conclusions, Washington held to them throughout almost the entire war. He maintained the strategic defensive from mid-1776 until mid-1781. In that long time span, Washington avoided not only the attack but even, after the New York campaign, major defensive battle against the main forces of his tactically superior enemy, except when he felt obliged in 1777 to face Howe's whole army in open combat rather than yielding the Continental capital, Philadelphia, without a fight. Of course, during that long time span Washington did stage hit-and-run attacks, such as at Trenton, Princeton, and Stony Point, but these raids were mere incidents of a strategic defensive. Even Palmer, who does not wish to concede that Washington was at all a Fabius, interprets the strategy of the second phase of the war as defensive, " 'The Old Fox' . . . playing his game to perfection.''[74] Of Washington's letter on avoiding a general action and not putting anything to risk, Palmer in fact writes:

> It was a masterpiece of strategic thought, a brilliant blueprint permitting a weak force to combat a powerful opponent. Indeed, there is a curiously modern ring to the ideas, even to the phraseology itself. Mao Tse-tung could have used Washington's letter in the twentieth century while preparing his thesis on the protracted war, the two concepts are so similar.[75]

But curiously, Palmer is unwilling to concede that Washington went on to wage protracted defensive war. He terminates the second phase of the Revolution with December 1777 and has Washington reversing ''the

entire thrust'' of his strategy,''to pass over to the offensive'' from January
1778 to December 1781.[76] Once again, no historian could deny that
Washington eventually went over to the offensive, to trap Cornwallis at
Yorktown with the aid of the Comte de Rochambeau's French army and
the indispensable aid of de Grasse's French fleet. Washington's ability
from the beginning of the French alliance to envision the offensive
possibilities opened up by French sea power is what Captain Knox's book
is all about. But it also strains interpretation to call the whole period of the
war from Janaury 1778 to December 1781 an offensive phase. From the
beginning of the French alliance Washington recognized the offensive
potential in the alliance, but to recognize it was not to be able to seize it.
Realizing the potential depended upon the French; and for three and a half
years they were too preoccupied with the West Indies to send a prepon-
derant fleet to North American waters, or the French admirals who came
to North America were too cautious, or both, to permit Washington to use
the French navy as he wanted to use it, as he continually tried to persuade
the French to allow him to use it, and as he ultimately did use it to trap
Cornwallis. Meanwhile, with French naval superiority on the North
American coast only a hope, Washington went on waging the same sort
of defensive war—avoiding major actions and seeking only opportunities
to raid the enemy's outposts—that he had felt obliged to resort to since the
battles for New York. On several occasions in this period, as when the
enemy twice thrusted toward Springfield, New Jersey, in 1780 and when
the Pennsylvania line mutinied at the beginning of 1781, even a defensive
war seemed almost beyond Washington's resources.

It also strains interpretation to give an offensive coloring to Washington's post-Yorktown strategy by emphasizing expansionist schemes directed toward Canada and the West. The main burden of Washington's
command after Yorktown was merely to hold the semblance of an army
together and to restrain its discontented remnants not only from desertion
but also from an enlisted men's mutiny or an officers' coup d'état.

It may be that the first book-length study of Washington as a strategist
thus informs us less about the strategy of the Continental commander in
chief than, by implication, about the reasons why the appearance of such
a book has been so long delayed. Colonel Palmer presses hard to make
Washington appear to have been primarily a strategist of the offensive. In
my judgment, Palmer strains evidence and interpretation to make

Washington something other than the primarily defensive strategist he was. It was noted that a major reason why Washington as a strategist has been so long neglected is that he preceded and too quickly was followed by Napoleon. More specifically, Napoleon brought into vogue an offensive style in strategy—the strategy of annihilation of the enemy army—that by promising quick and dramatic decision in war made Washington's patient, time-consuming defensive strategy seem obsolete. Colonel Palmer has attempted to rescue Washington as a strategist from the neglect he has suffered ever since he so quickly fell under the shadow of Napoleon—by the expedient of transforming Washington himself into a strategist of the offensive, not so unlike Napoleon after all.

In Washington's own army, even more than in most armies of the Western world since Napoleon, the favored strategy has come to be that of the offensive, with a Napoleonic annihilation of the opposing armed forces as its first objective. The wealth in military resources and manpower that the United States achieved in the nineteenth century in remarkably swift transformation from the poverty of the Revolution made Washington's patient defensive no longer imperative in America's subsequent great wars, the Civil War and the two world wars. In these conflicts, the United States could afford to expend resources with the lavishness required by a Napoleonic offensive strategy. As American national character and national attitudes concerning the nature of war evolved, they exerted pressures upon the American military to end wars swiftly and decisively, still further discouraging a strategy of the patient defensive such as Washington had had to employ. By the time in the twentieth century when strategic thought hardened into formal doctrine in the various Western armies, the military doctrine of the United States was preeminently that of the offensive, on every level from strategy to minor tactics. An American professional soldier seeking to write about Washington in a way that would secure the strategic reputation of the Revolutionary commander in chief would have been thoroughly prepared by his own professional education and conditioning to perceive Washington as an offensive-minded strategist.

But the *offensive à outrance* is no longer so evidently appropriate to America's objectives and interests, political or military, in the world position of the United States today or in the kinds of wars in which involvement has been most likely since 1945, as it was for Abraham Lincoln's government in the Civil War or for Franklin D. Roosevelt's in

World War II. Reflection on the ability of the first American strategists, particularly General George Washington, to employ with success a patiently defensive strategy, to be strategists not of annihilation but of erosion and attrition, may be peculiarly fitting in the Bicentennial era. But the utility of such reflection for the concern of the present, as well as the demands of historical truthfulness, would be better served by careful reexamination of American Revolutionary strategy as it was, not as post-Napoleonic strategic doctrine might suggest it should have been.[77]

4

LOGISTICS AND OPERATIONS IN THE AMERICAN REVOLUTION

R. Arthur Bowler

In the history of war, a tradition only now beginning to wither is that logistical problems are treated in the light of the old maxim "it is a poor workman who blames his tools." The traditional emphasis is on politics, strategy, and tactics; and even when the historian does consider logistical problems, they seldom enter into his final assessments in any serious way. There is, of course, often good reason for this—a lack of easily available information. Successful tacticians are great writers of memoirs and there seems to be a compulsion to reach for pen and paper that strikes eyewitnesses of battles. Commissaries and quartermasters, on the other hand, seldom write of their experiences, and the records of their work are often not considered worth keeping; their activities are prosaic and usually boring. Without records the full logistical story and the ways in which it is interwoven with the other aspects of a war are difficult to revive.

But if much of the history of logistics is irretrievable, the growth of bureaucratic government since the seventeenth century has meant that the records since that time at least are often remarkably complete. The price of overlooking the story they can tell is ignorance of factors just as significant as the tactical and strategic decisions of military commanders in deciding the course and final outcome of a war. For no war is this more true than the American Revolutionary War. When Sir Henry Clinton, commander of the British forces in America for most of the war, wrote to England that "I have no money, no provisions, nor indeed any account of the sailing of the Cork fleet, nor admiral that I can have the least dependence on, no army. In short I have nothing left but the hope for better times and a little more attention,"[1] and when Washington wrote to Congress that "with truth I can declare that no Man, in my opinion, ever had his measures more impeded than I have, by every department of the army,"[2] both were speaking to problems that took up a large part of their time and energy throughout the war. These problems could give reason to their actions with as much force as any other consideration.

That the American army faced enormous logistical problems is common knowledge to every school child who has read about Valley Forge. What is seldom realized, however, is that the difficulties experienced at Valley Forge were repeated at every winter encampment of the war except that of 1775-76 and were the result not of momentary failings but of fundamental problems arising, in part, from the immature structure of the American government, economy, and society.[3] One of the most basic of these problems was that the economies of the thirteen colonies were primarily agricultural. Americans produced very little not only of the wide variety of hardware demanded by an army but even of such fundamentals as cloth and canvas for uniforms and tents. The war enormously increased American capacity to supply these articles but never to the point that large and regular imports were not required. When they failed, the army suffered. And to pay for the imports there had to be exports. Although France was generous with loans and gifts, much that was imported could be paid for only by American exports. And in the reliance on imports and exports lay another problem. Throughout most of the war the British navy, abetted by loyalist privateers, controlled the seas, so imports were expensive and deliveries, in terms of both dates and place, uncertain.

British control of the sea had another serious effect. It threw the army, its logistical support, and, indeed, the whole economy of the colonies back on a totally inadequate land communications system. Before the Revolution, and for several generations after, communications between the colonies and even within individual colonies depended on water transport. Roads, where they existed, were often quagmires except in winter freezes and summer droughts. The best of them quickly broke down under the strain of an army on the march with all its equipment or even the regular passage of heavy supply wagons. The need to marshal and maintain the huge numbers of horses and wagons needed to move and supply the army, and to operate them over inadequate roads, was a persistent problem of nightmare proportions through much of the war.

The innumerable unbridged rivers running into the sea made north-south land transport over any distance slow and outrageously expensive.[4]

But without question, the most persistent and deadly problem of army logistical support was organization and administration. The process of building a logistical organization, like that of building the army and, indeed, the federal government itself, had to start from scratch in 1775. Inevitably, especially given the conditions of revolution and war under which the building was done, there were many mistakes, many poor decisions and false starts.

Throughout the war, Congress was a relatively small body of men, many of whom had experience in legislation but few in administration. Yet it was called on to be both a legislative and an administrative body and, to make matters worse, it had only slightly more real power than a debating society. It could recommend and even act, but its recommendations could be turned down or ignored and its actions repudiated by the states. If it had real power, it lay in the fact that it was the only body that could speak and act for the states as a whole; the state governments were usually well aware of the need for unity but often lacked the capacity to act decisively and effectively themselves.

Because of its unique position, Congress was flooded with work, of which establishing the army and its logistical support was only one part. In June 1775 it appointed George Washington as commander in chief and gave him a commissary general of stores and purchases and a quartermaster general, but nothing more.[5] Not until a year later, in June 1776, was the Board of War and Ordnance created, charged with overseeing all military stores, superintending the raising, equipping, and dispatching of the land forces, and supervising the army generally. Even then, however, the board had no executive function; it was merely a standing committee that reported and recommended to Congress. None of its members had experience in military administration, and not until a year after its establishment did it even have any members who were not also burdened with regular congressional duties.[6] Even at the best of times, however, the Board of War was seldom efficient, as Henry Laurens, president of Congress, had occasion to note: "I sent for Mr. Nourse Secretary pro tem. at the War Office," he wrote, "and between chiding for the repeated losses and miscarriages of public papers in that Office, and entreaties to search diligently. . . , I prevailed on him at an unseasonable hour, not any such in my four and twenty, to rummage, horrible idea to rummage, in an Office which ought to be accurate in all things.''[7] The ever changing makeup of the board over the years also meant that there was a dangerous lack of continuity in its policy and a continuous temptation to tinker with or even drastically alter basic administrative establishments. The latter was particularly evident in 1777, when an extensive reorganization was attempted in an effort to bring the army departments under closer congressional control.[8] The result was such enormous confusion that Washington was led to complain that virtually his every plan for that year "was either frustrated or greatly impeded by the want of a regular supply of provisions."[9] Not until late 1781 was a regular executive office, the War Office headed by the secretary at war, established.

The absence or slow growth of a stable, well-organized, experienced executive to look after army affairs had serious results. One was a lack of clear definitions of tasks. The original commissary general and quartermaster were given no instructions, no clear definitions of their functions, no limits to their authority. And despite their appointment, Congress went ahead and also commissioned independent purchasing agents for army stores.[10] Who had authority? Even after 1776, when Congress was able to turn its attention more fully to the army and undertake more systematic planning of the army services, areas of responsibility remained blurred. Throughout the war various agents of the army services regularly competed against each other, against agents of state governments, and against civilians for scarce supplies, bidding up prices, to the detriment of everyone but the purchasing agents, who received a commission on all money that passed through their hands.[11] The other end of the problem was those cases in which no one seemed to have authority. In 1779, for instance, when much of the army was in rags, 10,000 suits of clothing lay in storehouses in France and another large quantity in the West Indies because various agents of Congress could not decide whose business it was to ship them.[12] At the lowest level, the army had to invent regulations in1777 to stem the enormous losses by theft or carelessness of common tools. Not until 1779 were regulations introduced to make soldiers strictly accountable for their weapons. Up to that time carelessness and the tendency of soldiers on short-term enlistments to take their issue weapons home with them had resulted in a requirement for 5,000-6,000 new muskets at the beginning of each campaign.[13]

Such problems in organization meant that commissaries and quartermasters were frequently tempted to spend more time with Congress or the

Board of War lobbying for workable systems and divisions of responsibility than with the army, often with unhappy results. Appointed commissary general of forage in mid-1777, Clement Biddle received virtually
no direction from his superior, Quartermaster General Thomas Mifflin,
because Mifflin was seldom with the army in the months before his
resignation. Biddle's attempts to lay in stocks that fall and winter were
regularly frustrated because he had no authority over the many other
purchasers of forage.[14]

It was in large part inexperience and new and inadequate organization—although incompetence cannot be discounted entirely—that
produced the near-disastrous conditions under which the army had to
exist at Valley Forge. By early 1777 the army service departments were
just beginning to achieve a respectable degree of organization. Then
disaster began to build. In August the commissary general of purchases,
Joseph Trumbull, and a good part of his staff resigned as a result of
changes in departmental organization and rates of pay instituted by
Congress.[15] The new appointee, William Buchanan, was probably not as
incompetent as he has been pictured; but he was not particularly competent, and he was one of those who spent as much time attending Congress
as the army. Buchanan resigned the following March; in the meantime
departmental activity slackened and the vital process of laying in stores
for the following winter was not well attended to.[16]

Then in October 1777, Quartermaster General Mifflin, after largely
neglecting his duties for some months, resigned.[17] Because he was not
replaced by Nathanael Greene until February 1778, his department was
without adequate central direction for almost six months. Further, two
newly created and vital offices in the quartermaster department, the
Forage and Wagonmaster offices, were also weak. The Forage Office,
responsible for organizing the feeding of all the army's horses, was
established and put under the direction of Clement Biddle on July 1,
1777. Biddle was to prove to be a very competent administrator in time,
but at this period he was new to office and lacked guidance from above
and clear authority. The result was that the Forage Office was far less
efficient than it could and should have been that fall and winter; the
army's horses suffered accordingly.

More important than the forage problem, though, was the weakness in
the wagon department. Congress had appointed a wagonmaster that
spring and approved the purchases of several hundred wagons and teams

for the army's use. Joseph Thornsbury, the first appointee, however, resigned his office in October without accomplishing anything significant and was not replaced until December.[18] But more important than Thornsbury's inability to organize the army's own wagon train was the failure to deal with problems involving hired wagons. Throughout the war the army depended primarily on privately owned wagons. Whether the wagons were freely hired or impressed, this service had to be carefully organized if the army was to be adequately served. It was not.[19] The low rates of hire set by Congress made impressment necessary, and poor organization meant that the burden of such service tended to fall most heavily on farmers near the army's encampments. Further, neither horses nor wagons fared well in the army service due to inadequate forage, poor maintenance facilities, and inexperienced wagoneers. Farmers took to hiding horses and wagons when army press parties were out and those who were impressed not infrequently deserted at the first opportunity, leaving their cargoes at the roadside.[20]

The result of these many failures—this coordinated ill-fortune, if you wish—was privation in the midst of plenty. For there is no doubt that the fertile farms of the central states could easily have fed the small American army. Washington even had the power to confiscate supplies if necessary, although, wisely, he was extremely reluctant to use it. The problem was one of organizing the supply and getting it to the army. It was clear throughout the fall of 1777 that a crisis was approaching, but the army was powerless to prevent it. Only by the narrowest of margins did Washington's December prediction that the army would have to "dissolve or disperse in order to obtain subsistence" not come true.[21]

By the spring of 1778, however, new leadership, better organization, and a substantial increase in the prices Congress authorized commissaries and quartermasters to pay for provisions and equipment began to have their effect.[22] Supplies of all sorts, although never all that were desired, became better and more regular, and the development of a system of magazines along the main lines of communications from the Hudson to Virginia gave the army the mobility it needed to respond to British initiatives.[23] The success of the logistical services at this period may be judged in part from army vital statistics for the winter of 1778-79: Washington was able to maintain the largest force-in-being of any winter of the war that season, and the sickness rate dropped to less than half of its level over the previous two winters.[24]

But even while the logistical services were improving, a new disaster was building, largely the result of the precarious finances of the new nation. Congress, without taxing powers, financed the central administration of the war by issues of paper money—Continental bills. For the first two years of the war the Continentals maintained their value but that situation could have continued only if the state governments had retired the bills when they came in as payment for taxes. This was not done; indeed, most states even issued their own paper money. By late 1777 the inevitable depreciation had set in and ever larger issues of paper were required to purchase the same quantities of goods and services. In September of 1779, when Continental issues had reached the then frightening sum of $200 million, Congress called a halt.[25]

The end of Continental issues, however badly depreciated they were, was disastrous for the army. The service departments, already handicapped by shortages of funds and a reluctance on the part of suppliers to accept Continental bills, virtually collapsed just when they should have been at their busiest, and the army had to live from hand to mouth through the harshest winter of the war. Of this period Baron de Kalb wrote, "Those who have only been in Valley Forge and Middlebrooke during the last two winters, but have not tested the cruelties of this one, know not what it is to suffer."[26]

By early 1780 Congress devised and put into effect a new system for supplying the army, but it was a poor expedient. This was the system of specific supplies—requisitions upon each state for quantities of beef, pork, flour, and so on, with the promise that the value would be credited towards each state's part of Congress's debt. As a measure of economy, Congress also cut back and reorganized, somewhat, the army service departments.[27]

The new system never worked well. The states had not imposed taxes to support congressional expenditures and were not much more enthusiastic about expenditures in kind. Appeals to forward quotas frequently went unanswered or, alternatively, resulted in more than could possibly be used before rot set in.[28] But even when adequate supplies were forthcoming, the army still faced an overwhelming problem. The supplies were collected at central depots in each state, but it was then up to the army to move them to wherever they were needed. The problem was that transportation, which could not be by sea, was always difficult to obtain and often far more expensive than the supplies themselves. The result was severe and persistent shortages that virtually crippled the army.[29]

Lafayette's attempts to halt Benedict Arnold's ravages in Virginia in March 1780 were completely frustrated by logistical problems, and in May, when news came from France that an army and fleet were being prepared to aid the American cause, Washington reported that his army was "pinched for provisions" and "reduced to the very edge of famine."[30] Nathanael Greene, dispatched to take command of the southern army late in the year, took the precaution of asking the legislatures of several states for all the supplies he needed in the hope that they might, together, come up with his total requirement.[31] Nevertheless, when he actually took command, his first move had to be to split the army and dispatch the parts to areas where it was hoped that adequate supplies of food and forage could be obtained.

The main army under Washington was in bad shape throughout the year. There were desperate and persistent shortages of food, clothing, and money for pay, and by early fall it was reduced to living on what it could borrow, impress, and confiscate. The near mutiny of two Connecticut regiments in May 1780 was a result of the dreadful conditions these problems produced; the Pennsylvania line needed only the addition of enlistment grievances to bring it to mutiny in January 1781. And all of these problems occurred despite the fact that the army was at a generally lower strength than it had been at any time since the first eight months of 1777.[32] Indeed, Washington had to disband part of the army when he went into winter quarters in 1780 because "want of clothing rendered them unfit for duty, and want of flour would have disbanded the whole army if I had not adopted this expedient."[33]

The net result of the financial crisis and its logistical repercussions was that the Continental army was handicapped almost to the point of immobility for the best part of two years. Only heroic efforts, extensive reorganization, and French gold permitted the cooperation with Rochambeau and de Grasse that brought Cornwallis's surrender and effectively ended the war.[34]

What comes out of a survey—even one as brief as this—of the logistical position of the American army during the Revolutionary War is a clear appreciation of the enormous hardships that dogged the life of the Continental soldier. But it also reveals the fundamental limitations that logistics placed on the size and operational capacity of the Continental

army. America in the eighteenth century was a relatively rich and popu-
lous country. On the basis of a simplistic computation, it should have
been able to field a large army and, indeed, at one stage Congress
envisioned a force of 75,000 men.[35] In fact, Washington never commanded more than 19,000 regulars and on several occasions had less than
10,000.[36] The problem was that America in the mid-eighteenth century
was a country ill-suited to waging war, for reasons made clear by the two
crises that have been outlined here, those of 1777-78 and 1779-80. State
governments were generally weak, and Congress was even weaker;
administration was rudimentary and often had to be invented as the need
arose; financial organization, at least of the kind necessary for war
finance, was almost nonexistent; transportation and communications
were appalling; and, by no means of least importance, the people were
suspicious of governments and armies, even their own.

The American army of the Revolution was small, far smaller than the
military situation demanded. It was kept small and was hamstrung in its
operation in very considerable measure by inadequate logistics and
administration. For most of the war it remained, of necessity, on the
defensive. When it did undertake offensive operations, they were usually
on a relatively small scale and of short duration.

The obvious question arising from this analysis is why, if the Continental army was so weak, did not it and the Revolution fall easy victim to
the British army? The answer to that question, if it can ever be satisfactor-
ily answered, is at best highly complex. As others have pointed out, the
quality and sense of purpose of British generalship was a large factor,[37] as
was administrative and strategic confusion in Britain.[38] What is
suggested here, however, is that Britain's military failure must be seen in
part in terms of the logistical problems that her army encountered when it
attempted to function in Revolutionary America.

The British army had, of course, operated successfully in America
before, during the Seven Years' War, and it is tempting to assume that the
same logistical conditions existed during that war and the American
Revolution. Such was not the case; logistically there were fundamental
differences between the two situations. To understand the differences the
British system of logistical administration must first be examined.

In the eighteenth century, British army logistics were the responsibility
of a number of executive departments of the government. The Board of
Ordnance, the War Office, and the Navy Board all had a part in it. But the

largest responsibility rested with the Treasury. With it lay the burden of supplying all food, forage, wood, barrack supplies, cash, and land and coastal transport. For the most part, however, the Treasury carried out this responsibility by contracting. It either let contracts itself directly with London merchants or authorized its principal agent with the army, the commissary general, to let contracts himself or purchase directly through agents all that the army needed. This was the system by which the army in America during the Seven Years' War was supplied, and it was carried on for the forces that remained after that war. As it actually worked out, however, virtually all the supplies for which the Treasury was responsible came from America itself, for the London merchants who accepted the prime contracts turned to American subcontractors for the actual procurement and delivery.[39]

With the coming of the Revolution this system broke down almost completely. One of the first actions of patriot committees throughout the thirteen colonies after news of Lexington and Concord had arrived was to cut off supplies destined for the army at Boston. By May 10, Gage had to write to the Treasury that "all the ports from whence our supplies usually came have refused suffering any provisions or necessary whatsoever to be shipped for the King's use . . . and all avenues for procuring provisions in this country are shut up."[40]

Right from the beginning of the war, then, the army was forced back on Britain for supplies it had normally obtained in America. Nevertheless, this did not cause any great concern at first. On several occasions during the Seven Years' War it had also been necessary to procure some provisions in Britain. The contractors were notified, and before fall they had on its way a large flotilla filled with ample and, it has even been suggested, luxurious supplies for the troops. Even live sheep, pigs, and cattle were included in the cargo. But then disaster struck: the fleet, consisting of thirty-six ships, was caught in fierce autumnal storms that drove some back to England and others to the West Indies. A number of those that survived the storm fell easy prey to American privateers and the fledgling American navy. These same war vessels also picked up a number of other ships attempting to supply the army at Boston from Nova Scotia.[41]

The results of this first disastrous supply attempt—besides short rations for the army—was a steep rise in rates of shipping hire and insurance. The contractors informed the Treasury that they could no longer take the responsibility for delivering provisions. The Treasury, never an active department in this way, promptly asked the Navy Board, which already looked after the transport of ordnance stores, to take on the task. When it refused, the Treasury had no choice. It remained directly responsible for provisions shipping until 1779, when the Navy Board, under due persuasion, finally relented.[42]

But in early 1776 there was no thought that anything more than temporary supply from Britain would be necessary. Already in late 1775 it had been decided that the army would move its base from Boston to New York City. That would not only be a better base for operations, but, everyone expected, virtually all the supplies the army needed could be obtained locally.[43] For the fall of 1776, these expectations were fully realized. As Washington was forced successively out of Long Island, lower New York, and New Jersey, the commissaries were able to procure huge quantities of supplies. By November, Commissary General Daniel Chamier was able to report that he was already putting up meat and flour for the next year's campaign and expected that the supplies from England could be substantially reduced in the near future.[44]

As it turned out, he spoke too soon. On December 26, Washington proved that although he could not defeat the British army as a whole, he was quite capable of destroying it piecemeal. The annihilation of the Hessian brigade at Trenton and the mauling of Mawhood's brigade at Princeton that quickly followed sent the British army tumbling out of New Jersey. With them went the hope of supplying the army from America. Washington took up a position at Morristown and adopted a strategy that he was to follow throughout the war in the central colonies from such bases as Valley Forge, Middlebrook, and the Hudson highlands. Morristown was a strong natural position in which Washington's relatively weak force was reasonably secure and it was far enough from the British base to ensure against surprise attack. From that base he could launch offensives if the British were ever again so foolish as to divide their army up into isolated detachments in order to hold large areas. Although both the commissary general and Howe hoped that the move to Philadelphia might change the situation and Pennsylvania might become the breadbasket of the army, they were soon disappointed.[45] After an initial period of abundance, the army was again locked into a tight perimeter and Howe found that he had to provide covering forces of several thousand men in order to obtain even the most meagre supplies from the countryside.

Thus, from the very beginning of the war, most of the army's basic food had to come from Britain. And the supply depended, first of all, on a department, the Treasury, which was neither prepared for nor wanted the job. It was to be five years before a consistent and adequate flow of supplies was organized: by that time the war was lost.[46] This is not to say that the British army suffered horribly from want of provisions. Far from it. On only a few occasions did rations have to be cut, and the British soldier probably received his rations more fully and more regularly than did his American counterpart. The problem lay not with day-to-day supply but with reserves.

If the war was to be won, the army had to take the offensive, the rebel strongholds reduced, and Washington's army destroyed. But few eighteenth-century commanders, and Clinton least of all, would ever have even considered taking to the field without adequate supplies. The British supply route was 3,000 hazardous miles long, and both Howe and Clinton insisted on having provisions on hand before they began a campaign. An offensive that stalled for lack of supplies would be at best frustrating, at worst disastrous. Thus both generals in their turn recommended that shipments from Britain always be sufficient to keep a six-month reserve on hand in America. When France entered the war and her navy became a threat to the Atlantic supply line, Clinton sought a doubling of the reserve.[47]

Even when no operations were in the offing, a reserve sufficient for at least two months was necessary if the army's position and, indeed, the army itself were not to be jeopardized. For when reserves fell to that level, the commander in chief had to think in terms of evacuation. To move the army with all its equipment and support personnel and with all the loyalists who depended on it for protection required shipping resources larger than the army ever had on hand. Even when Boston was evacuated in 1776, a move planned months in advance, many ships had to make two trips to Halifax. Only about 15,000 people were evacuated from Boston: there were seldom less than 50,000 who would have had to leave New York. Thus the decision to evacuate, if it were possible at all, had to be made while there were still provisions to feed the army during the time the move was organized and effected.

Thus, the need for reserves of provisions was vital, and the Treasury was regularly informed of that fact. Most certainly Britain was capable of supplying them, yet the army was seldom adequately supplied. The war in America lasted, effectively, for seventy-nine months—from the battles at Lexington and Concord in April 1775 to Cornwallis's surrender in October 1781—but for no more than twenty-three of those months did the army have the minimum six-month reserve that the commanders considered necessary for offensive operations. During twenty-eight months supplies were at the three- to five-month level and for eight months they were sufficient for no more than two to three months. During an additional eleven months, reserves fell to a paralyzing thirty to sixty days; and at least once in each year except 1777, for a total of five months, the army had less than thirty days' provisions on hand. Put another way, during only two summers of the war did the army have an adequate and consistent reserve on hand.[48]

The reasons for these failures were many: bad provisions, inadequate accounting on both sides of the Atlantic, unexpected calls for rations, shipping shortages, and confused convoy schedules. But the basic problem lay in the Treasury itself. That department never seriously attempted to adapt to its new responsibility or even, it could be argued, clearly understood what it involved. Although it set standards of quality for provisions, it could never force contractors to live up to them; nor would it make allowances in the size of contracts for the fact that even under the best of conditions a proportion of the provisions shipped would be unusable on arrival in America. Year after year it received reports from the commissaries in America of the shortages caused by bad provisions. Yet when it was suggested that the problem could be eliminated by increasing the contracts by one-eighth, the Treasury responded that it could act only after a commissary had supplied evidence, attested to by a board of officers, that specific shipments were bad; then they would be replaced. Throughout the period of its responsibility, despite losses at sea and on land, despite reports of bad provisions, the Treasury never contracted for more than one ration per man per day on the basis of reported strengths and insisted on believing that every pound of food shipped became available to the army.[49]

The list of Treasury failings could go on, but they are summed up in the fact that despite the repeated pleas of Howe and Clinton and its own assertions that its was planning such a move, the Treasury never seriously committed itself to building up and maintaining army provision reserves. When provisioning was being turned over to the Navy Board in 1780, Secretary of the Treasury John Robinson admitted, "This Board do not contract for greater quantities of provisions than may be ample supply for the troops on the respective service, and if possible to keep such a supply a few months ahead."[50]

It would be difficult to attempt here to sort out from all the other problems that beset the British army, including Clinton's very complex character, the particular effects of inadequate provisions reserves. Nevertheless, there is an interesting correlation between those reserves and offensive operations. In 1776 and 1777 reserves were consistently adequate and the army moved. From 1778 through mid-1781, reserves were high on only three occasions; on the first of those Clinton moved against Charleston. However viewed, though, provisions reserves were a fundamental problem for the British army.

But there was another aspect of the British logistical situation that was equally significant. For whatever the state of supplies from Britain, there were still commodities that the army needed that could be obtained only locally. The most significant of these were forage for the army's horses, fresh food, and wood. Of these, forage, and particularly hay, was the most strategically important. Without hay the army could not feed the 3,000-4,000 horses it usually maintained; without horses it could not mount a sustained offensive. The problem was where to get hay. Early in the war the Treasury agreed, reluctantly, to supply from Britain the oats that the army required but absolutely refused, because of the cost of transportation and the scarcity of shipping, to provide hay. Instead, it sent several hay presses and told Howe to find his own supplies.[51] The army had no choice but to look to America, and Howe planned the capture of Rhode Island in 1776 in part because he wanted its hay resources.[52]

The requirements for livestock—horses, sheep, and cattle—fresh food of all kinds, and firewood were equally important. Horses were needed first to build up and then to replace the army's cavalry transport service. The wood, in quantities of up to 70,000 cords a year, was necessary to keep the army from freezing. The cattle and other items provided some variations from the monotonous and potentially deadly basic diet of salt meat and bread. On some occasions they were necessary simply to keep the army alive.

Because of these requirements no British army could remain completely within the tight cantonments that were established after 1776. Regular foraging expeditions had to be sent out into the countryside, and once out they became targets. Washington recognized immediately this weak spot in the British armor. A letter he wrote to General William Heath in February 1777 is well worth quoting at length since it lays out a policy he was to follow throughout the war:

The securing the Forage in West Chester county, for our own use, or depriving the enemy from carrying it off for theirs, is an object of so much moment, that I desire some measures may yet be fallen upon to effect one or the other. Suppose a light body of troops, under an active officer, sufficient to repel any foraging parties of the enemy, except they come out in very large bodies, should be left behind, and stationed as near Kingsbridge as possible. While they kept a good look out they never could be surprised, for not being encumbered with any baggage, they could always move at a moment's warning, if the enemy came out with a superior force, and move back when they returned. This would oblige them to forage, with such large covering parties, that it would in a manner harass their troops to death. We have found the advantage of such practices with us, for by keeping four or five hundred men far advanced, we not only oblige them to forage with parties of 1500 and 2000 but every now and then give them a smart brush.[53]

Those who picture the winters of the war as periods of idleness when the Americans sat around their campfires bewailing their lack of shoes and the British turned to dissipation, miss a neglected, but most fundamental, aspect of the war. The need for supplies drove the British with relentless regularity out into the countryside. There dispersed and encumbered by wagons, they were met and opposed by Washington's detachments, local militia, and the banditti who roamed the no-man's-land between the two armies.

In very short order, foraging parties became foraging expeditions involving as many as 5,000 troops. Howe had to employ that many to protect wagons bringing in 1,000 tons of hay from Darby to Philadelphia in December 1777, and an expedition to Salem, New Jersey, the following spring to bring in livestock and forage required the deployment of three regiments of regular troops, two provincial corps, and a navy frigate.[54] The story of the previous winter is well told in the diaries of two British officers, John Peebles and James Robertson.[55] Their regiments were engaged in as many as ten such expeditions a month. Sometimes the expeditions went without incident but more often they were a series of short, sharp clashes on the order of Lexington and Concord. And as in those battles, the British more often than not came out the losers. One officer felt that this sort of warfare was a positive advantage to the Americans: "The Rebel soldiers, from being accustomed to peril in the skirmishes, begin to have more confidence, and their officers seldom meet with foraging parties, but they try every ruse to entrap them, and tho' they do not always succeed, yet the following the people as they return, and the wounding and killing of our rearguards, gives them the notion of victory, and habituates them to the profession." The result of this kind of opposition to British foraging, he continued, was that it "kept the army the whole winter in a perpetual harassment, and upon a modest computation, lost us more men than the last campaign."[56]

But the need to forage did more than open the British army to the kind of warfare at which Americans could win—guerrilla war, *la petite guerre,* or "a dirty kind of tiraillerie," as one British officer described it.[57] As envisioned in the parlors of London in this age of limited war, foraging was an unfortunate necessity to be carried out, especially in areas where the population had to be assumed to be friendly, with as much discretion and as little disruption to the civil population as possible. Person and property were supposed to be respected, farmers paid for the things taken from them and always left enough for their own needs. That British commanders felt the same way is indicated by their repeated general orders and by the disgusted observation of one Hessian in a letter home that "at the King's express command the troops must treat these folk most handsomely—though we hear they are all rebels—and cannot demand even a grain of salt without paying for it."[58]

The injunctions of the British commanders, however, seldom had any effect. The European regulars, British and German, usually drawn from the outcast orders of society and raised in the hard school, found it convenient, if they needed an excuse, to believe that every American was a rebel, his property fair game for looting and his female family for rape. Despite all the efforts of the commanders, this kind of conduct could never be curbed to any significant extent. Nowhere was this more true than in lower New York and New Jersey in 1776 and 1777. Congressional and other rebel accounts of the outrageous and brutal behavior of the British and Hessian troops toward the civilian population might well need to be discounted to some degree as propaganda, but not by much:[59] they are supported by British and loyalist accounts. Lieutenant Colonel

Stephen Kemble regularly deplored these depredations in his journal. Early in the campaign he noted that "the ravages committed by the Hessians and all Ranks of the Army, on the poor Inhabitants of the country make their case deplorable; the Hessians destroy all the fruits of the Earth without regard to Loyalists or Rebels, the property of both being equally a prey to them, in which our [the British] troops are too ready to follow their Example and are but too much licensed in it." The result was to drive Americans—neutral, apathetic, and even loyal—to the rebels for protection. "No wonder," Kemble noted a bit later, "if the country people refuse to join us." Foraging was the most persistent and continuous form of contact; and the more often the regulars of the British army came into contact with the civilian population, the more enemies they created.[60] Even when they escaped the soldiers, the "country people" were still likely victims for the corrupt practices of British commissaries and quartermasters, a number of whom made fortunes by selling to the army supplies that were confiscated or purchased at ridiculously low prices from civilians.[61]

What this all-too-brief survey of the logistics of the war in America has attempted to show is that, particularly from 1777 on, both the American and British armies were faced with enormous logistical problems that directly and indirectly had considerable effect on the course of the war. Most directly, they greatly reduced the offensive capacities of both armies. A historian once described the fighting in Burma in World War II between the British and the Japanese as a battle between giants who, because of the logistical problems created by climate and terrain, could do no more than tear at each other with their fingertips. The metaphor, with reservations, is not inappropriate to the War of the American Revolution. Each side possessed considerable military potential, but each could seldom bring more than a fraction of that power to bear and then use it only fitfully. The situation was what might be called a balance of weakness. In that balance, however, more advantage lay with the rebels than has traditionally been assumed. The greatest advantage came from the aggressive rebel organizations that gained control of every colony at the beginning of the war and were able to maintain or at least dispute that control except in the face of overwhelming British power. They denied the resources of the country to the British army except where it moved in force. Further, the American army, however weak it became, was never so weak that it was unable to challenge British attempts to pacify extensive areas of the countryside. To obtain the supplies it needed, the British army was forced throughout the war to engage in extensive foraging operations. This allowed the often untrained rebel forces to fight the kind of battles for which they were best suited, and the brutality of those operations drove more and more Americans to the rebel side.

5
AMERICAN SOCIETY AND ITS WAR FOR INDEPENDENCE

John Shy

The British seemed to enjoy celebrating their military disasters more than their victories. A best-selling book on the charge of the Light Brigade was made into a popular film. The Department of War Studies at King's College, University of London, offers as a special subject for advanced students a course on the Gallipoli campaign. And every year the evacuation of Dunkirk is celebrated by BBC television and vacationing British veterans, while the anniversary of Waterloo, not many miles away, is relatively neglected. True to form, the British have celebrated the Bicentennial of the American Revolution as enthusiastically as have the Americans, and perhaps even more effectively. In April 1976 the queen personally opened an outstanding Bicentennial exhibit at Greenwich, and during the previous autumn the British Museum mounted not one but two simultaneous exhibits devoted to the American Revolution.

These two exhibits at the British Museum were especially good and interesting. One, called "The World of Franklin and Jefferson," concentrated on the highest ideals and noblest rhetoric of the Revolution; its subject matter was very edifying. The other concentrated on the War of American Independence; while many items in the latter exhibit were delightful to look at—beautifully drawn and colored maps, fine portraits —its subject matter, dealing as it must with death and destruction, was less than edifying. And so, in effect, the British Museum split the American Revolution into two parts: the constructive part of the political revolution upstairs, and the revolutionary war downstairs.

Splitting the Revolution into two halves—one political and social history, the other military history—is not peculiar to the British Museum;

rather, it has been a characteristic tendency for a long time of almost everyone who has studied the subject. However, this characteristic tendency of historians is essentially false to the historical event, because people living through the long, hard years from 1775 to 1783 made no such artificial division. To cross this dividing line, and to restore some of the unified reality of two hundred years ago, is the self-imposed task of this essay. In particular, it explores the ways in which the nature of American society on the eve of the Revolution shaped the armed struggle and affected its outcome.[1]

Because much of what follows has to be stated in generalities, it may be useful to begin with two very concrete bits of revolutionary history. In 1775-76 General Washington was criticized because he had let the British evacuate Boston without attacking the town. Washington was defended by Charles Lee, his third in command and an able if highly eccentric ex-British officer who would eventually ruin himself by engaging in open controversy with Washington. But in the beginning Lee strongly backed Washington against his critics, contending that they simply failed to understand the American soldier. If Washington had commanded an army of Russians, Lee wrote, he would have assaulted Boston's fortifications. But Americans were not Russians, and Washington correctly did not try to misuse the excellent human material that comprised his army. Lee did not bother to defend American courage; instead, he implied that American soldiers, fresh from their farms and their families, were not stupid enough, or docile enough, to assault strong field works in close-order formation.[2]

The other concrete bit of revolutionary history happened later in the war and takes us to the other side of the hill. In 1780 the British had virtually conquered Georgia and South Carolina. One American army had surrendered at Charleston in May, and a second had been destroyed at Camden in August. As British forces deployed through the lower South and tried to restore royal authority, Lord Rawdon, a very able young British officer, was given command in the South Carolina back-country. Rawdon's own regiment was the Royal Volunteers of Ireland, a tough, well-disciplined unit, made up almost entirely of Scotch-Irish deserters from the American Continental army. Rawdon decided to post the Royal Volunteers of Ireland in the Waxhaws district, on the border between North and South Carolina. The inhabitants of the Waxhaws district were recent Protestant immigrants from Ulster in Ireland, and Rawdon expected that his regiment, with a similar ethnic and religious background, would win the civilians over to the royal cause. But the opposite actually happened. Within a short time, desertion among the Royal Volunteers of Ireland had risen sharply, and Rawdon felt compelled to issue an exceptionally harsh manifesto. In it, he threatened to flog or ship to the West Indies any civilian who aided a British deserter, and he offered a reward for the return of any such deserter—£5 if brought in alive, £10 if only the head were turned in.

This extraordinary document soon reached Washington, who used it to embarrass the British government and high command. When Rawdon's commanding general demanded an explanation, Rawdon tried to pass the matter off as a joke—a bluff intended only to frighten, not a serious threat. But he also complained that the Waxhaws district people had been "universally disaffected," that he had hoped to pacify them by stationing the Royal Volunteers of Ireland among them, but that the people had done everything "to debauch the minds of my soldiers" and had succeeded to "a very alarming degree." He pleaded with Cornwallis, his commander, to recall how the army had been "betrayed on every side by the inhabitants," how people who acted like friends in camp were firing on the British an hour later, and how supposedly "loyal" American militia actually supplied the enemy with arms, horses, and information. Clearly, the matter was no joke.[3]

These two incidents illustrate a very simple point: the military operations of the American Revolution make sense only when they are placed in their political and social context. The nature of American society profoundly affected the character and the outcome of the Revolutionary War. Let us turn to a more systematic examination of this simple but neglected point.

The first step is to look at American society on the eve of revolutionary troubles, in about 1760—not at political conflicts with Britain, which usually get most of the attention, but at the people, how they lived and what was happening to them. Colonial America was highly diverse, with little natural unity before the Revolution. Only our knowledge that the United States would soon emerge from these diverse and disunited colonies leads us to see an artificial unity where in fact there was very little, except the common, though tenuous, bond to London. But it is possible to identify certain social characteristics, common to most or all colonies, that would strongly affect the armed struggle for independence during 1775-83.[4] At least six of these characteristics can be specified.

First, the population of colonial America grew very rapidly during the first three-quarters of the eighteenth century, more rapidly perhaps than any other society had ever grown up to that point in recorded history. It had grown tenfold in only seventy-five years, from about 250,000 in 1700 to 2.5 million at the outbreak of the Revolutionary War. As might be expected, this rate of growth caused some problems, which are discussed below.[5]

Second, the availability of a virtually unlimited supply of land eliminated the periodic starvation, chronic malnutrition, and much of the epidemic disease that were still evident in Europe and kept the European population growth rate close to zero. For example, it is estimated that 400,000 people died during the Irish famine of 1740-41.[6] Although colonial America occasionally suffered the effects of epidemic diphtheria or yellow fever, an adequate food supply made an enormous difference; by cutting infant mortality to a fraction of the European rate, it explains most of the spectacular growth of the American population before 1700.[7]

Third, and closely related to rapid population growth and natural prosperity, was a very high rate of immigration after 1700. Not only did thousands of immigrants, attracted by American land and prosperity, increase the population, but they made it much more diverse. To the relatively homogeneous English population of the seventeenth century were added 200,000 Scotch-Irish and 100,000 Germans in the four decades after 1715, while as many as a quarter of a million black Africans were forced to migrate to the Continental colonies between 1700 and 1775. By 1760, British North America was a very different society from what it had been at the turn of the century. Blacks, who had done so much to solve the chronic labor shortage, caused a growing fear of bloody insurrection, especially after about 1740, when New York City and South Carolina had felt of the terror of slave uprisings. The Scotch-Irish, hardly distinguishable from other English-speaking people today, were widely regarded in the eighteenth century as dirty, lazy, disorderly, and generally undesirable. And Germans, more orderly and diligent, were disliked for being non-English-speaking, remaining clannish, and practicing some of the more bizarre forms of Protestantism.[8] Immigration, as well as increasing and diversifying the population, was a primary factor in spreading people over the land; if population increased tenfold from 1700 to 1775, a rough guess is that the area under settlement increased fivefold in the same period.

Fourth was an emergent social elite. Prosperity naturally gave a minority of early settlers the chance to acquire wealth and status, so by 1760 there was a clearly recognizable group of families in every colony who, in effect, ruled. This was as true of New England as of the middle and southern colonies. But the position of this colonial elite was precarious, for several reasons. It ruled only by consent; the right to vote was widespread in the America of 1760, so most voters simply "deferred" to their social and economic superiors. Too, it depended on British government *letting* it exercise power, in the elective provincial assemblies and in local government. And, finally, it was threatened by the rapid growth, the diversification, and the dispersion of population; the traditional face-to-face methods, so effective earlier in the century, simply ceased to work when people became too numerous, too distant, and too different, as they were by 1760.[9]

Fifth is a negative characteristic that may be labeled "institutional weakness." Underscoring the increasing problems of controlling this exploding society and the precarious position of its governing elite was the lack of European-type structures for the maintenance of order. The elite itself was simply the wealthier and better educated people, not in any sense a legally privileged aristocracy. The colonial militia was simply a universal military obligation, but not a standing army—there was no specialized armed force. The churches, even where they were legally established (like Anglicanism in the South and Congregationalism in New England), were themselves unable to impose their will on people: the Anglicans looked like Congregationalists in practice, and the Congregationalists were split by the great mid-century revival. All churches by 1760 were in considerable disarray. There was no governmental bureaucracy. Even slavery, presumably a strong institution, was looser in practice than in law; the tightening of slavery came *after* the Revolution. In other words, American society was much freer than contemporary European societies. But to many it looked not as much free, in any positive sense, as dangerously anarchic. And there was ample evidence for fear of anarchy; there were outbreaks of violence after mid-century from present-day Vermont to the back-country Carolinas, making civil war seem more likely than a war for independence.[10]

Sixth and last, there was something special about late colonial American society that may be called "provincialism." It was a basic attitude, toward themselves and the outside world, that set Americans off from European societies. Although filled with contradiction, this attitude is characteristic of people who are weak and dependent, yet also energetic and troubled by the internal effects of dynamic growth. Very simply stated, "provincialism" meant a love-hate relationship with Britain and with European civilization generally. Americans, especially the colonial elite, admired Britain and Europe, taking them as models for their own lives and seeing them as standards against which to measure a more primitive America. But Americans also feared and resented European strength and superiority. Americans felt morally superior to Europe and never tired of saying so; but they also knew that America was inferior. Nothing better illustrates American "provincialism," with love increasing at least as rapidly as hate during the early eighteenth century, than George Washington's vain efforts to get a regular commission in the British army.[11]

These, then, were the peculiar and defining characteristics of colonial American society on the eve of the Revolution: (1) rapid population growth, (2) basic prosperity, (3) increasing diversity and dispersion, (4) an emergent social elite in a precarious position, (5) institutional weakness, and (6) provincialism. The question is how these characteristic features of late colonial American society impinged on the waging and outcome of the Revolutionary War. What impact did the society have on the war?

At the outset—from the crisis of 1774 caused by the Boston Tea Party, through the outbreak of fighting in April 1775, to the end of 1775, when the British decided to evacuate Boston—it was the sheer size, prosperity, and energy of American society that shaped the war. Moreover, new British policies after 1763 had directly threatened the economic and political position of the American elite, and that elite—itself so heavily dependent on popular support—had skillfully mobilized public opinion behind it and against British authority. In New England towns, in seaboard cities where most people were dependent on the merchants, in the southern colonies where a single crop united the interest of all white men, and in the Scotch-Irish settlements of New Hampshire, western Pennsylvania, and the Carolina back-country (where hostility to Britain came naturally), the elite had mobilized whole communities, first to offer a wall of unified resistance and then to fight a war. Towns, not individuals, decided to fight, and almost every male over sixteen headed for Boston.[12] The lack of any specialized military organization meant that virtually everyone went to war. And "everyone" meant a great many; within days after Lexington and Concord, 20,000 armed Americans had penned the British army inside Boston. This was possible in 1775, when the population of New England was over 600,000; it would have been impossible in 1700, with less than 100,000 in the same area. Numbers as much as anything were the backbone of American strategy in the beginning.[13]

Considering the problems Britain had in operating at the end of a 3,000-mile-long line of communications, as well as the sheer volume of Americans, mobilized and led by the colonial elite, one might see in this situation a surefire social formula for waging and winning a revolutionary war. But two other social factors soon began to create a new strategic picture.

First, the "provincialism" of American leaders, especially Washington, led American strategy away from reliance on popular military forces—on militia—and toward the organization of something like a regular army. From the outset, Washington said that the militia was worse than useless, and that the creation of a European-style, long-service, tightly disciplined force was essential.[14] Maybe so; historians still argue the question. But one shrewd, experienced British officer thought American rebels would have been *less* dangerous if they had had a regular army; and it was ex-British officers in American service (Lee, Gates, and Montgomery) who seemed to have the best appreciation of what popular forces might accomplish in an unconventional war.[15] Washington and other native American leaders stressed a regular army, I suspect, because they felt a need to be seen as cultivated, honorable, respectable men, not savages leading other savages in a howling wilderness. So a Continental army was formed with enlistments for three years or the duration, harsh discipline, and Prussian drill as modified by Steuben. It was never a very good army by European standards, it never won a battle in open field, and it was never very large because most Americans simply would not join that kind of un-American institution. In this respect, Lee's observation that Americans were not Russians (who in 1776 could be—and were—marched off to serve in the czarina's army whether they liked it or not) takes on a new meaning. But the Continental army did keep the British army pinned down and concentrated, leaving most of the country free to be contested between Americans; it did give the Revolution a kind of respectability that was politically valuable; and it created a chance for men, as officers, to achieve a reputation on a national scale. Out of the Continental army officer corps would come much of the cadre of what would a decade later be the Federalist party.[16]

The second thing that happened to the original American strategy was that the popular enthusiasm of 1775 began to give out rapidly in 1776 and became hardly visible by 1777. The internal divisions and conflicts of late colonial America reemerged to weaken the war effort. Everyone was suspicious of New England; domestic instability kept both New York and Pennsylvania from mobilizing anything near their full potential; and southern states, fearful of slave insurrection, had trouble recruiting men to fight in the North. The lack of any effective institutional mechanism to mobilize manpower for war, once local and popular pressure had begun to weaken, forced the Revolutionaries to fall back on other means— mainly economic incentive.

Though revolutionary America had what looks like a military draft system, operating through the militia, in fact, down at the grass roots, men were almost never drafted; instead, the town or the militia unit, faced with the need to fill a quota, found some way to hire men to do it.[17] The men hired were in general those most in need of money, that is, at the economic bottom of society, like the poor Scotch-Irish deserters from the Continental army who made up the Royal Volunteers of Ireland. The process over a period of years was one of economic differentiation between those who served actively for long periods in war and those who did not. Thus, prewar social differences were reflected in the way the war was fought, and in turn the war sharpened those social differences.[18] This method of raising an army had several important effects: it further weakened the role of higher kinds of motivation in waging the Revolutionary War; unlike World Wars I and II, most men were not serving because it was their unavoidable duty to do so imposed on (almost) all alike, but because they were the ones least able to resist a crass economic appeal. It contributed significantly to the bankruptcy of the war effort so evident by 1778. The financial demands of a centralized army recruited in this way were simply too great for the fiscal system to handle; it was *not* a problem of war being too much for available resources.[19] And, finally, weak personal motivation and governmental bankruptcy combined to produce the real crises of the latter part of the war: the mutinies, the high rates of desertion, the defection of Arnold and others, and the virtual collapse of the war effort from central control back onto state and local levels.

All in all, it was not a pretty picture, and it was not militarily very effective; battles were lost, and fear grew of the collapse of the Revolution itself. The method of waging war seemed a perversion of revolutionary ideals.

To sum up: the sheer size and wealth of late colonial America, plus the ability of its leadership group to mobilize the society, made initial resistance possible. But the "provincialism" of most leaders, plus the lack of strong institutions and the prewar weaknesses and internal social conflicts, led to a serious degeneration in the quality and strength of the war effort. This begins to sound as if the Americans could not possibly have won the war; and yet they did. To understand why they did, we must once again cross to the other side of the hill and consider the effect of social factors on British strategy.

Throughout the war, the nature of American society caused British leaders to misread their strategic problem, misread it so badly that it became a major factor in the way the war turned out. In the beginning, British leaders saw clearly enough certain characteristic features of American society, but they drew the wrong conclusions. What they saw especially was the colonial elite, which made America look like England with its aristocracy and gentry. They also saw the prosperity; from this, as well as from their experience during the colonial wars, they concluded that the American population was "soft," like the more prosperous farmers and artisans of England and Europe, little inclined to active military service. In other words, they saw that the American masses were not Russian peasants. From this one-sided social analysis the British concluded that it ought to be possible to neutralize the leaders of rebellion, causing the enthusiasm of the people to subside quickly. This kind of thinking lay behind the attempts at Boston in 1775 and behind the conventional warfare waged in 1776 and 1777. The British badly underestimated the degree to which broad-based public opinion sustained the initial rebellion, more or less independently of leaders who had mobilized it, making Americans better fighters than they had been in colonial wars. The British failed to think through the way in which their military strategy could be *politically* effective; they simply assumed armed force could "work" in America as it did in Europe or in Ireland.

In the latter stage of the war, British leaders overcorrected early errors;

they tended to see and emphasize other characteristic features of American society and to build a new strategy on these. What they saw and stressed were institutional weakness, internal conflicts, and "provincialism" (which often looked to them like pro-British feeling). The British by 1778 tried to exploit these features to create a loyalist base on which to build a pacified America, and their effort was informed by reports of extensive loyalism (that is, dislike of, or resistance to, revolutionary leaders) everywhere. Building such a base was what Rawdon and his commanders were doing in the South in 1780; Rawdon's interest in the political situation around the Waxhaws was typical of this new strategy.[20]

It is more difficult to say what was wrong (or went wrong) with the new British strategy based on this analysis of American society. But what happened is that instead of restoring law and order, Britain fomented a civil war—not only a civil war, but a war their side (British and loyalist) seemed never able to win. Perhaps the main reason they could not win was that it was too late—too many Americans were already disillusioned by the previous lack of British success. But they also could not win because those Americans who *would* fight for them were bitterly angry people, bent on vengeance, not on restoration of law and order. Moreover, these loyalist allies were often minorities who turned to the British side, not out of principle, but because they were socially and numerically weaker. As soon as British military support was withdrawn, the loyalists were usually overwhelmed by an armed majority.[21] For example, Rawdon failed to pacify the Scotch-Irish in the Waxhaws district at least in part because of British *success* in arming and organizing some neighboring areas, settled by Germans—a back-country minority intensely disliked by the Scotch-Irish.[22] British arming of the Cherokee Indians, and calls for Negro slaves to turn against their masters, had the same kind of ultimately counterproductive effects. In other words, British leaders and army may have stepped into the middle of a major issue in American history: Tocqueville's "tyranny of the majority." Nothing did more in the later stages of the war to keep the Revolution alive than the British effort to arm and activate militarily these "loyalist" minorities.

To reach some sensible overall conclusions about how American society shaped the Revolutionary War, something must be said of French intervention. Without a French army and navy, and without France turning a colonial war into a global war for Britain, the Revolution could not possibly have ended *when* it did and in the *way* that it did. In the long run, politically speaking, French intervention may have made the difference between Americn success and American failure. But it did not make the difference between Britain's winning and losing; American society itself almost guaranteed the military outcome and powerfully affected the political outcome. The size of the society, combined with an elite running scared from American public opinion as well as from British interference, explains massive initial resistance; Britain functioned beautifully as a scapegoat against which to focus otherwise centrifugal social energies. Lee saw it: if Americans fought, it could be only because they wanted to fight—they were not Russian peasants. The "degeneration" of the American war effort from 1776 onward—a predictable process if the social situation is understood—encouraged the British to exploit the internal weaknesses of American society. After fatally underestimating the importance of public opinion in 1774-75, the British went to the opposite extreme, thereby providing the motivation for continued American resistance when the initial enthusiasm seemed to have burned out. Rawdon failed to see that the positive persuasion of one Scotch-Irishman by another had become much less important than the negative effect of Indians, Blacks, and some "Dutchmen" (that is, Germans) fighting for the king. And finally, the "degeneration" of the American war effort produced a new realism, almost a cynicism, about human nature that is one key to American *political* survival after 1783: the harsh realities of a protracted war, more than anything else, explain the difference between the euphoria at Philadelphia in 1776, when Congress declared independence, and the hard-headedness of many of the same men, when eleven years later, in the same city, they hammered out a federal constitution.[23] It is at just this point that Upstairs at the British Museum—the ideals and ideas of the Revolution, the constructive achievement of the Founding Fathers—comes Downstairs and there confronts the grim but instructive experience of a long, dirty war.

6
THE AMERICAN MILITIA: A TRADITIONAL INSTITUTION WITH REVOLUTIONARY RESPONSIBILITIES

Don Higginbotham

"There, my lads, are the Hessians! Tonight our flag floats over yonder hill, or Molly Stark is a widow."[1] Those were the famous words of General John Stark to his militiamen on the eve of the Battle of Bennington, and thanks to them Molly Stark did not lose her vain and volatile husband. For on August 16, 1777, Stark's New Hampshire and Vermont followers smashed a column of Germans from General John Burgoyne's British army, a little gem of a triumph with far-reaching consequences.

Before we sing Stark's praises, other more sobering facts are in order. The Continental Congress had recently rebuked Stark for failing to unite his band with the American northern army and place himself under the jurisdiction of its commander. If we are inclined to agree with the historian who commented that this was one occasion when insubordination achieved splendid results,[2] we might look ahead to October 7 of that same year: Within minutes of General Horatio Gates's climactic battle of the Saratoga campaign against Burgoyne, Stark departed from Gates's camp with his entire militia because their enlistments had expired. These episodes illustrate the complexity of analyzing the performance of militia in the War of Independence.

My purpose in examining the militia is several-fold: to put in historical perspective the approach of previous generations to this subject and, more importantly, to weave together recent strands of scholarship and to add something of my own—to achieve, all told, a kind of overview. Some conclusions advanced are no more than tentative, for, to my knowledge, no one so far has attempted a comprehensive reassessment of the militia; and that undertaking would surely involve more than a single essay or article. My own emphasis is in large part that of examining the militia as an institution. A key institution in the colonial period, it remained structurally much the same in the Revolution, although it was saddled with greater burdens and responsibilities than ever before.

There is a decidedly negative image of the militia in most of our historical literature. Taking as a prime case in point Stark's irresponsibility at Saratoga, C. H. Van Tyne, in his Pulitzer Prize-winning account of the war, declared that "few events . . . so proved the utter failure of the militia system."[3]

When did this view originate? One must commence with Washington and his generals of the Continental army who labored strenuously and for the most part futilely to secure a long-term professional army modeled in important respects after contemporary European systems. Only such a formidable, well-structured military arm could exchange blow for blow with the legions of Gage, Howe, and Clinton. The militia were seen as poorly trained, ill-disciplined, and unreliable. They were, complained General Nathanael Greene, "people coming from home with all the tender feelings of domestic life" and "not sufficiently fortified with natural courage to stand the shocking scenes of war. To march over dead men, to hear without concern the groans of the wounded, I say few men can stand such scenes unless steeled by habit or fortified by military pride."[4]

The temporary soldiers were wasteful of supplies and weapons. General John Lacey of Pennsylvania, himself a state-level officer, conceded in 1777 that departing militia "had left their camp equipage strewed everywhere—Muskets, Cartouch-boxes, Camp kettels, and blankets—some in and some out of the huts the men had left, with here and there·a Tent—some standing and some fallen down."[5] Local units made off with so many Continental weapons that Washington implored "that every possible means may be used to recover them [for] the public and no more delivered to Militia."[6]

Small wonder, given these attitudes, that serious friction erupted between Continentals and militia. To Joseph Reed, president of the Executive Council of Pennsylvania, "the jealousy which has taken place in this State, between the Continental troops and them, very much" resembled "the behaviour of the [British] Regulars and our Provincials" in the French and Indian War. Reed cautioned Nathanael Greene that, if the Rhode Island general had in fact been guilty of criticizing militia (as was reported in Philadelphia), he might be more guarded in his future comments.[7] More openly contemptuous was a Colonel Jackson of the Continental line, who, in sending a detachment of regulars to Dorchester, Massachusetts, in 1777, instructed the captain in charge to take no orders from Colonel Thomas Crafts of the militia. Later, in Crafts's opinion, Jackson added insult to injury. As Jackson himself told the story to General Henry Knox:

Last week Coll. Faneuil dy'd—and Coll. Crafts, myself and other Officers were sent for as pall holders—the Coll. and myself were the two oldest Officers—Just before they carr'd the Corps out, I took the Coll. aside in the room and told him I supposed we might walk according to Rank and I must take rank of him—he paus'd a moment, and then told me . . . we should walk as was always customary in the Town—that was the Oldest man the eldest Pall Holder. . . . I told him I appeared there as Coll. of a Regt. . . . and that I must take rank of him being a Continental officer. He told me he would not submit to it and took himself off and all the officers of his Regt. followed him.

Jackson added that Crafts sought to retaliate by trying to persuade the state legislature to promote him to brigadier general "so as to take rank of all Continental Colls." in Massachusetts.[8] Perhaps the episode has something of a democratic flavor to it. For Crafts, who had been a member of Boston's Loyal Nine—a middle-class resistance group during the Stamp Act crisis—was an artisan, a skilled painter of fine things (as opposed to a housepainter).

In any case, Jackson was scarcely the only Continental colonel who looked askance at taking orders from a militia general. "I have the fullest confidence that you will not put me in a Situation to be commanded by General Herkimer" of the militia, pleaded Colonel Goose Van Schaick, a regular, to Governor George Clinton of New York in 1777. These sentiments were echoed in 1780 by Colonel Daniel Morgan of the Continentals, who warned General Gates that he would find it humiliating to take orders from Virginia militia brigadiers.[9]

Such condescension seemed so well founded that in the postwar years the militia were all but totally excluded from a rightful place in the revolutionary firmament. Histories of the period focused upon the Continental army, commanded by Washington, who quite understandably drew the spotlight to events associated with him. Furthermore, the narrator's task was simplified by staying center stage, avoiding the briars and brambles of the wings or peripheral areas where the militia usually operated. Finally, much of our military history was penned by professional soldiers, like Emory Upton, with an ax to grind for a professional military establishment.[10] In our day, however, this traditionally harsh portrait of revolutionary militia is being challenged. The impact of guerrilla or irregular warfare in the post-1945 world has spawned a desire to understand the place of nonregulars in the winning of independence.

Let us now turn to three somewhat interrelated questions. Who were the militia? What were their functions in the war? And which of those functions did they handle best? The first query sounds easier than it really is. To be sure, the English colonies had included virtually all free white males within the militia structure, and this near universal requirement did not change in 1775 or 1776. Several current researchers have stated or implied that the actual composition of the state militias and the Continental army was considerably different; that the productive citizens preferred service in the local military outfit, which would normally remain fairly close to home; that the Continentals came substantially from the lower echelons of American society—indentured servants, paid substitutes, farm laborers, unemployed persons, and transients, to say nothing of Blacks and British deserters.[11]

These configurations have led to the conclusion that the long-suffering Continentals at Valley Forge and elsewhere were, rather than freedom fighters, mercenaries not much unlike those in European armies. Perhaps so; there is no need to sugarcoat our history. Still, if enlistees counted the monetary features of shouldering muskets as the overwhelming attraction, why were American armies always so short of manpower? Maybe in fact they realized the declining value of the congressional dollar—"not worth a Continental," as the saying goes. We nevertheless might wonder when the social historians are telling us these days that the revolutionary era witnessed a growing disparity between the have and have-nots in America, that more and more men had to struggle to eke out a meager existence.[12]

Once again a fresh interpretation—that of militiamen as having been more stable and upstanding citizens than congressional soldiers—generates a problem. Why, if this were so, did contemporaries describe the militia as so wasteful, so destructive, so generally irresponsible? Surely there must be more to the explanation than their having been short on training and discipline. This occasion is hardly propitious for extended speculation; but it is safe to say that although statistical methodologies have opened fruitful vistas, such as affording us data on the socioeconomic composition of armed forces, they have as yet not proved themselves wholly reliable avenues to the probing of human motivation, of the workings of the mind. One would not claim, for instance, that Thomas Sumter, the famous South Carolina "Gamecock," held his militia band together simply because he paid them in slaves captured from the British; nor that North Carolina's offer to her militia frontier defenders of £10 for every Indian scalp taken was a sufficient inducement to fill her garrisons.[13]

Undoubtedly motivation for service—both militia and Continentals— must be examined in several contexts, including time and place. The patriotic response early in the war tended to be enthusiastic, especially that of the New England militia; but at the same time the Continental rifle companies to be raised in the frontier counties from Virginia to Pennsylvania were quickly filled, with many would-be volunteers left behind. Recruiting for Continental and state establishments as well probably suffered in areas—Philadelphia and parts of Maryland for example— where the dominant political elites were unpopular and where class divisions worsened as a result of economic friction over war profiteering and the hoarding of goods.[14]

Militia officers too are worth some analysis. Colonial Americans had actively sought commissions in the militia, as much for reasons of prestige as anything else. Even Jefferson, of all people, was a county lieutenant in Virginia. Whereas in New England there was a tradition of electing militia officers, the conflict with Britain saw the extension of that practice, especially below field grade, to New York, New Jersey, Pennsylvania, Maryland, and southward. The demand for officers was infinitely greater than ever—than for any of the colonial wars or, quite obviously, for the periods of peace, since militia organizations had deteriorated or become virtually extinct between imperial conflicts. Then, too, some former officers declined to serve in the revamped patriot forces because they were loyalists; while others, accused of being on the king's side, were squeezed out. Consequently, the officer ranks were opened dramatically, as in Maryland. After scrutinizing a list of 403 newly commissioned officers in that colony, David Skaggs explains that "the largest number of commissions went to men representing either the lower half of the landowners (approximately 200 acres or less), or those who apparently owned no land at all."[15]

Expanding the social range of militia officers had significant democratic implications in Maryland and elsewhere. Because local tensions engendered uneven support for the war, Maryland officers at times found their men extremely difficult to control, and officers themselves, willingly or through duress, took positions held by the rank and file. On the other hand, in New England, with its strong Whig fervor, militia companies not only picked their officers, but sometimes members of a company adopted a document—a kind of covenant—stating their concerns and principles, their rules of behavior, and their limits or restrictions upon their officers' authority. "What you have," writes Alfred F. Young, "is not quite Cromwell's soldiers debating around the campfires (although maybe some of that) but a democratic soldiery with all the implications of that word."[16]

The election of officers scarcely ever resulted in elevating the ablest men to leadership positions. Thus the New York provincial congress urged in December 1775 that militia officers be picked subsequently "according to their true merit and ability to serve the public."[17] Few newly chosen officers were as self-effacing as a Mr. Beeker of Tryon County, New York, who, it was reported, "modestly declined" appointment to command a company, "alleging his want of education and experience for a station involving so much responsibility." Instead, Beeker proposed a Mr. Luke, who evidently had some military background and who was then "elected by a large majority." Once the training began, so our informant continues, French and Indian War veterans "were particularly engaged in giving instruction and advice,"[18] as was also true in Philadelphia and elsewhere.

As for field-grade and general officers, a batch of appointees were rewarded for political reasons. That practice, no innovation, had been common in the dependency decades, and it has been the case, more or less, with volunteer and local forces ever since. The refreshing candor of Mr. Beeker's captain-designate in New York was equaled by Richard T. Earle of Maryland, an Eastern Shore planter. Earle kept his commission, but he confessed his inadequacies and tried to do something about them.

He plaintively inquired of a Philadelphia friend: Where could he secure a manual "with some instructions, particularly with respect to dress"? "How are the colonels, majors and captains when in regiments to distinguish themselves"? "Some wear shoulder knots on the right, and some on the left. Some wear small swords and some cutteaus. Some carry fuses and cartridge boxes. Do any above the rank of captain do this?"[19]

Officers with the most extensive experience in earlier wars often accepted Continental commissions. Later the leadership of the militia was bolstered by officers who resigned from the regular army, returned home, and took rank in the militia, as did Thomas Sumter, Francis Marion, William Lee Davidson, and John Stark—to mention a handful of celebrated militia stalwarts. The reduction and consolidation of Continental units freed men for a return to state service, as it did Colonel Peter Gansevoort of the 3d New York, whose command disappeared as the state cut its regiments back from five to two in 1780. Occasionally an officer moved back and forth; Ezekiel Cornell, lieutenant colonel of Hitchcock's Continental Rhode Island regiment in 1776, became the next year a brigadier general of that state's local forces, although in 1782 he was back in Washington's army as inspector general.

But, for the most part, such individuals came home to continue their military careers in the state constabularies. And that, not infrequently, brought political gain from their militia exploits. Historians have always had an interest in the relationship between acclaim on the battlefield and triumph at the polls in our history, in the tendency of the American people to elect their military heroes to office. Most of the examples that come most quickly to mind are the professional soldiers—the Taylors, Grants, and Eisenhowers.

It may be, however, that an in-depth study would uncover that—with the major exception of Washington—the officers who gained the biggest political boost from drawing swords in the Revolution (and possibly continuing through most of the nineteenth-century wars as well) were those persons most closely associated with military achievements in the militia or volunteer units.[20] One of the earliest was Colonel Richard Caswell of North Carolina, who fought at Moore's Creek Bridge in 1776 and the following year was elected the first governor of his state. Caswell's critics grumbled that his inordinate ambition had driven him to steal the laurels of another, Colonel Alexander Lillington, the true hero. They sang of

> Moore's Creek field, the bloody story
> Where Lillington fought for Caswell's glory.[21]

When Virginians replaced Jefferson as the state's chief executive in 1781, they tapped General Thomas Nelson, head of the militia since 1777; and Nelson was elevated principally because of his military reputation.[22] Another governorship appears to bear militia-versus-Continental overtones: the 1777 election in New York of Brigadier General George Clinton of the militia over Major General Philip Schuyler of the Continental line, with Clinton projecting the image—synonymous with the militia—of being a man of the people, militantly anti-Tory.[23]

Now for our second question: the function of the militia in the War of Independence. It is abundantly clear what that institution could not do: namely, carry the brunt of the conflict. Militia units, John Shy reminds us, had done relatively little fighting as regular formations in the colonial wars. Their previous responsibilities were more "a hybrid of draft board and modern reserve unit—a modicum of military training combined with a mechanism to find and enlist individuals when they were needed."[24] Therefore, the Continental Congress opted to wage war by means of a Continental army, whose generals favored minimal reliance upon militia. From the army's camp at Cambridge in 1775, Nathanael Greene asserted, "With regard to the Militia we have no occasion for them. We have here as many of the Province Militia as we know what to do with." Greene's feelings had not changed, only deepened, when he vowed some months later that "all the force in America should be under one Commander raised and appointed by the same Authority, subjected to the same Regulations and ready to be detacht where ever Occasion may require."[25]

Even if Congress and the states responded by raising a formidable army, Washington was a realist; his own forces would hardly be able to contest British regulars and to defend the colonies against their internal enemies as well. "The Militia," he counseled, in explaining his unwillingness to respond to various local crises, should be "more than competent to all purposes" of internal security.[26] Actually, he probably intended to alert colony leaders that they would have to fend for themselves against loyalists, potentially hostile Blacks in their midst, and Indians on their frontiers. To scatter his regiments, to be at all places at all times, would have reduced the Virginian to small-unit operations. Unable to openly contend with General William Howe and his successors, Washington would have had no alternative to guerrilla warfare, or what was known then as partisan war, or *la petite guerre.*

Washington instead advocated a response to the enemy that, in modern terminology, is known as the principle of concentration, or mass. ''It is of the greatest importance to the safety of a Country involved in a defensive war,'' he explained, ''to endeavor to draw their Troops together at some post at the opening of a Campaign, so central to the theater of War that they may be sent to the support of any part of the Country [that] the Enemy may direct their motions against.''[27]

His thinking made sense. To divide his own army would invite his adversaries to defeat it in detail. Besides, a guerrilla conflict had other disadvantages. One might harass and annoy the enemy effectively without its being beaten decisively or driven from the country. That kind of aggressiveness was a tall order, but Congress wanted it. The lawmakers wished the army to stand and fight; and Washington was combative by instinct, although after 1776 he became more cautious, endeavoring to choose the moment and the place that would provide him the greatest advantage and the smallest risk. Then, too, a guerrilla struggle would pose internal dangers to the cause: such physical destruction, such savagery and bloodletting, that the internal institutions of the country, along with the political and legal processes, might fall sacrifice to the war. And in the main, the Revolution's leaders were conservative in both political and military outlook; their principal aims were to preserve and build rather than to tear down and destroy. Finally, the presence of the Continental army intact offered Americans a symbol of unity and an object of national feeling, just as it was to the outside world—where the patriots hoped to get tangible support—a sign of conventional military strength.

So, in Washington's view, the Continentals and militia had separate, although mutually supportive, roles to play. To improve the militia's effectiveness and to create a degree of uniformity everywhere, Congress made recommendations to the colonies as to the size and organization of regiments. If these proposals were disregarded, they were still definitely in order; for although the patriot militias were to resemble closely their colonial predecessors, the Revolutionists encountered problems in reviving that military instrument. Initial laws were enacted in such haste that they had to be amended or superseded with more comprehensive statutes.

Maryland is a case in point. In December 1774, the Maryland convention passed a resolution for establishing "a well regulated" militia. While the convention instructed the inhabitants between the ages of sixteen and fifty to form themselves into sixty-eight-man companies and to elect their officers, it made no provision for the machinery of mobilization, for officers of field grades, or for specific civil oversight. Was the militia to receive orders only from the convention, the colony-wide council, or the local committees of observation—or might all exercise a controlling and perhaps overlapping and conflicting hand? Following Lexington and Concord, the convention provided the answers and called for artillery units and minute companies. Minute companies there and elsewhere did not work out in actual practice to be satisfactory, and after a time many simply faded out of the picture or, as in New Jersey and New York, were expressly abolished.

Likewise, most of the elite or independent companies, usually composed of the better sort of society and popular in the beginning, evidently did not survive long beyond the initial burst of enthusiasm that saw their creation in 1775 and 1776; and probably their demise was just as well, for they not infrequently fell outside the structure of the regular militia. Curiously, one such company, the Kentish Guards of East Greenwich and Coventry, Rhode Island, may have made a minimum contribution as a unit; but the guards provided a remarkable galaxy of future Continental officers—two generals (Nathanael Greene and James Varnum), three colonels (including Christopher Greene, the hero of Red Bank), and various lieutenant colonels, majors, captains, and lieutenants.

As an institution, however, the militia proved deficient. The lawmaking bodies of the colony-states were never able to bring these military organizations up to meeting their responsibilities. The reason in part is that, as time passed, those responsibilities were vastly enlarged—to the point of embracing just about everything of a military nature. If we are mindful of this all-encompassing role they were asked to play, then we can better understand their limitations and their failures. If, as Washington said, the militia were best suited to control the home front, the problem was that the pressures of the war never allowed them to so restrict themselves.

Only initially, in the first year or so, were the militias able to confine the scope of their duties—to enforce the 1774 Continental Association of Congress on non-importation, to compel people to take sides, to put down loyalist uprisings, to seize military stores from royal governors, and to keep the slave population under control. Increasingly thereafter the state forces were involved in repelling Indian incursions, taking the offensive against the red men, and engaging British coastal raiding parties. Besides, wartime demands, especially the manpower deficiencies of the Continental army, prompted drafts—usually of short-term duration—to flesh out the ranks of the regulars; they also resulted in drafts, on a large scale, from existing militia units, which then were reorganized into new regiments; and, unlike the trend of the colonial wars, already established militia regiments were sometimes thrust into service. All of these various contingents were not infrequently asked to fight next to Washington's soldiers in formalized engagements. When required to stay for extended lengths in the field far from home, when mixed closely with sizable bodies of Continentals, and when performing against redcoats in open combat—the militia were at their worst. Nothing in their modest training, not to mention their normally deficient equipment and supplies, prepared them for these duties.

If Washington against his better judgment had to throw militia on the front lines with Continentals, there were also situations when part-time defenders had to oppose the enemy alone, particularly when British raiding parties descended upon the coast of a state and, now and then, penetrated inland. So it was in Virginia, which between 1779 and 1781 reeled from a succession of blows. British Generals Edward Mathew, Alexander Leslie, Benedict Arnold, William Phillips, and Lord Cornwallis roamed and pillaged over sections of the tidewater and even into the Piedmont. Time and time the counties were urged to turn out their militia, of whom—wailed Jefferson—"there is not a single man who has ever seen the face of an Enemy."[28] Simultaneously, the state's resources were being drained southward, for it was serving as a troop-and-supply center for American operations in the Carolinas.

The greenness of the defenders and the repeated demands upon their services, combined with shortages of weapons, equipment, and transportation in an overwhelmingly rural, agricultural society, made it impossible to keep the militia in the field for protracted periods. In early 1781, for example, 9 of 104 militiamen from Virginia's New Kent County responded to an appeal to once again shoulder arms. So deranged were the affairs of the state, so desperate were its authorities, that two of the state's most radical politicians, Patrick Henry and Richard Henry Lee, advocated the appointment of a dictator for the Old Dominion, a legislative motion that lost by a narrow margin.

At the same time, the militias in several states suffered from repeated British-loyalist-Indian raids on the frontier areas. Here too there was depressingly small help from Continental sources. After the Cherry Valley massacre in November 1778, Governor Clinton of New York warned that "Fatal Experience has more than sufficiently taught us the Impracticability of defending our extensive Frontiers by the Militia."[29] There were too many mountain passes to guard, and the white population was too widely scattered to be brought together quickly to repel the invaders.

Even so, in Pennsylvania, New Jersey, New York, and other states the civilian leadership made repeated efforts to make the militia more resilient.[30] No one labored harder at this task than Virginia's Governor Thomas Nelson in 1781. Nelson advocated for some of the militia "constant training, notwithstanding the expense." Here was the notion of a kind of "standing" militia, well trained and ready to go anywhere on sudden notice. Nelson's scheme never gained acceptance, but as chief executive he received from the legislature an enlargement of the governor's powers over the militia. With the consent of his council, the governor could assemble as many of the militia as he thought necessary and could hasten them to any part of the state; he could also employ them to impress supplies and to act in various other ways. Deserters could now receive the death penalty, while others who failed to come forward could be given six months' additional service.[31]

In a more limited way, both Washington and Congress sought to invigorate the militia without appreciably weakening the regular forces. The most common form of succor was to detach Continental officers for duty with the militia in their home states in times of alarm, as, for example, when Generals George Weedon and Peter Muhlenberg returned to Virginia in 1780. North Carolina's only active brigadier general during the last three years of the conflict, Jethro Sumner, directed the state's militia in harassing the enemy. To keep the militia in arms at crucial moments Congress might even offer to pay the militia and maintain their upkeep, as it did for New York detachments garrisoning Fort Schuyler.[32]

All these endeavors did not dramatically change the performance of the militia. When we seek to find what was revolutionary about the American Revolution, as scholars have done since the days of J. F. Jameson, there is no reason to look to the militia, which institutionally remained very similar to what it had been in the colonial period. Yet, as we have seen, its duties in a sense were revolutionary: it was expected to perform virtually every military function imaginable. Indeed, for this very reason—that so much was demanded of the local contingents—I believe the overall impression of the militia should be one of admiration, not derision.

Where specifically did the militia earn their highest marks? We find that answer in their own backyards, in operations within their own immediate districts, and sometimes in colony- or state-wide endeavors. These activities were always exceedingly important, but in the months before and after the outbreak of hostilities at Lexington and Concord they were absolutely essential to the launching and the continuation of the Revolution as a war. The militia's use of muscle guaranteed that the patriots would maintain control of the political and law-enforcing machinery in every colony. Therefore, from a military point of view, these months were quite likely the most crucial period of the Revolution. If one result of this militia-backed take-over was that the loyalists were to remain permanently on the defensive, surely another consequence was that virtually everywhere British armies landed they encountered a hostile environment. That circumstance helps explain why enormous quantities of supplies and provisions for royal regiments had to come from the mother country, 3,000 miles away, rather than from the mainland colonies. These were the same provinces, according to Lawrence H. Gipson, in which Britain had won the earlier Great War for the Empire (or French and Indian War) in large measure because of the availability of essential resources.[33]

Both propositions invite closer scrutiny, although the first one has been expressed on several occasions of late. It was probably Walter Millis in 1956 who initially stressed the local role of the militia in the opening rounds of the struggle: "the much despised and frequently unwarlike" militia's choking off any chance of a loyalist "counter-revolution," as he phrased it.[34] Whatever their methods—and they ranged from intimidation to violence—these home guards did the job. Most of those who publicly spoke or acted against the edicts of the community committees, provincial congresses, or Continental Congress were punished or else they recanted, as did Robert Davis of Anne Arundel County in Maryland. When Whig militiamen sought to interrogate him, he shouted from behind closed doors, "You damned rebel sons of bitches—I will shoot you if you come any nearer." When his tormentors prepared to storm his house, Davis's threats turned to hollow rhetoric. He meekly consented to come before the committee of safety, where he apologized for his verbal indiscretion.[35]

The second proposition, concerning the British army's inhospitable surroundings, needs more extended commentary. British columns, except for Burgoyne's, usually advanced relatively unimpeded from one fixed point to another. But the redcoats and their loyalist allies had minimal accomplishments outside or beyond those fixed points, which were the cities and occasional towns and fortified geographical locations. One accomplishment that historians, however grudgingly, have conceded to the militia as irregulars is their hit-and-run activity against British patrols and outposts *behind the lines,* with the South Carolina trio of Marion, Sumter, and Pickens receiving most of the limelight. But, as the observation about fixed points suggests, the areas of effective British control were scarcely expansive enough for the expression *behind the lines* to have much meaning. In any event, we might well examine more closely sectors that are clearly *between the lines*: broadly speaking, between the contending armies or not completely in the hands of either side. It was there that the loyalists were most aggressive; there, too, that the British sought to obtain supplies, with forage generally the most sought-after commodity. In seeking to checkmate the enemy in these broad zones, the American militia made a most substantial contribution, second only in magnitude to their sustaining local and provincial Whig governmental machinery at the onset of the Revolution. (And we may add, because of their early strong-armed tactics, which were repeated later in the war whenever necessary, there was generally a somewhat secure, stable behind-the-lines region for Continental armies.)

There were Whig-Tory clashes large and small between the lines, so many, in fact—they number in the hundreds—that the London-published *Annual Register* predicted that "by such skirmishes . . . the fate of

America must be necessarily decided."[36] Sizable, well-publicized encounters included Moore's Creek Bridge in 1776, where 1,400 North
Carolinians killed or captured virtually an entire force of roughly the
same strength, and King's Mountain in 1780, where again the opposing
bands numbered over a thousand and again scarcely a soul among the
king's friends escaped. Lesser known struggles also involved numerous
participants, such as Kettle Creek near the Georgia-Carolina border in
1779, where 700 Tories scattered before a much smaller Whig party, or
Ramsour's Mill in North Carolina in 1780, where another 700 loyalists
were dispersed, although there were heavy casualties on both sides.

For illustrative purposes these encounters merit further comment. In
all four instances the crown's followers, previously cowed by threats
from local patriots, had mustered their courage because they foresaw the
protection of British regulars. Moore's Creek Bridge was such a devastat-
ing setback for England in North Carolina (the loyalists had come forth in
the belief they were to be aided by a royal expedition on the coast) that the
Tories kept their peace for over four years, that is, until they again saw the
prospect of a British invasion of the state in 1780, when Lord Cornwallis's troops appeared in upper South Carolina. But after their premature
rising and reversal at Ramsour's Mill, only thirty of them united with His
Lordship at Camden. Also important were the results at Kettle Creek;
most of the Tories of the upper Savannah River region were fearful of
showing their true colors for over a year, until the British capture of
Charleston in 1780. And as for King's Mountain, the royalist defeat was a
blow from which the cause of Britain in the western Carolinas never
recovered.

If these battles were all in the South, there were obviously others above
the Mason-Dixon line, most of which were less spectacular and involved
fewer numbers, a remark that holds true for the between-the-lines skirmishing during the British occupation of New York and Philadelphia.
Describing "a five-year war of neighbors" across from Manhattan Island
in the Hackensack Valley (of Bergen County, New Jersey, and lower
Orange County, New York), a local historian declared that while the
"militia daily risked brushes with . . . raiders from New York," all too
many Continentals remained in their cold-weather encampments and
"did not hear a gun fired in battle from one year to the next."[37]

The statement, if exaggerated, is not without some validity, although
militia units themselves were often dazed and demoralized by initial

British invasions. Yet they did revive, particularly after the crimson-clad regiments settled into winter quarters or congregated at fixed points.

At times the tenacity and staying power of the militia were amazing. From 1775 to 1781 William Lenoir, a company-level officer from western North Carolina, was almost constantly in the field or on alert. ("I slept with my wife on one side and my rifle on the other," he recalled.) The war was never far removed from Lenoir and his fellow settlers of Surry and Wilkes counties. Initially Indians posed a threat, but throughout the conflict the Tories were a menace. Scarcely a month passed in those years that Lenoir's militia obligations did not take up much of his time, be they celebrated campaigns against the Cherokee, Patrick Ferguson's force at King's Mountain, or Cornwallis's invading army; or actions against local loyalist cadres; or operations in support of Whig civil government, such as administering loyalty oaths, securing drafts for the Continental army, and protecting the sheriff in his tax-collecting and law-enforcement responsibilities.[38]

By the fall of 1778 part of the Bergen County, New Jersey, regiment had been continuously in action or on standby duty for two full years. "Many of them," lamented Colonel A. Hawkes Hay, "have not sown any winter grain this season, and none have cut their buckwheat, which is now spoiling."[39] General John Lacey, whose Pennsylvania state regiment prowled about the outskirts of Germantown and Philadelphia following Washington's twin defeats in the area, complained at year's end in 1777 that he had been constantly on the go. He had "slept in a bed for the first time since I joined the Regiment, nearly two months before . . . having [previously] had only blankets spread on the ground." Lacey was not the only militia commander who put in overtime during the winter that Washington's tatterdemalions shivered at Valley Forge. So did Pennsylvania's General James Potter and New Jersey's Generals Nathaniel Heard and Philemon Dickinson; this was the same General Dickinson who cannonaded his own home near Trenton after he found a German *jäger* detachment posted there, the same General Dickinson who, during the Monmouth campaign of 1778, provided Washington with valuable intelligence as Clinton's army proceeded across New Jersey on its trek from Philadelphia to New York.[40]

British and German diarists say not only that the rebel militia harassed and bloodied the Tories, but that the American amateurs made it necessary for their foraging parties combing the countryside to be escorted by anywhere between several hundred and several thousand regulars. It was such a scavenging expedition—detached from Burgoyne's army in search of food and horse—that was crushed by Stark at Bennington. The preponderance of these encounters were only skirmishes; but to the British they were nasty affairs, expensive in time and matériel and successful in limiting the effectiveness of the foragers. British Lieutenant Colonel Charles Stuart complained that the conflict over forage "kept the army the whole winter [of 1776-77] in perpetual harassment, and upon a modest computation has lost us more men than the last campaign."[41]

To John Ewald, a German officer serving in the middle states, this "partisan war," as he termed it, "was carried on constantly in full force." The finest troops were deployed against the Whig marauders, whom he variously described as "the country people" and "uncivilized mountaineers." But the best—"the Jager Corps, the light infantry, and the Queen's Rangers"—were themselves bedeviled by the intruders, were compelled to get their rest at midday "because rest can seldom be enjoyed at night and in the morning."

What of a remedy for these raids, ambushes, and nocturnal intrusions? Ewald felt that when the British entered an area, large segments of the army, not just the light units, should be sent out: search and destroy missions, in the language of recent warfare, against roving rebel bands.[42] That was a doubtful cure. In any case, a solution was never found, not by Howe or Clinton in the North, not by Cornwallis in the South. "I will not say much in praise of the militia of the Southern Colonies," confided Cornwallis, "but the list of British officers and soldiers killed and wounded by them . . . proves but too fatally that they are not wholly contemptible."[43]

So we have looked at the highs and lows of the militia system in the Revolution. But even in the categories in which local fighters were so deficient and unreliable, there were pleasant surprises—instances when, contrary to expectations, the militia, the amateurs who were expected to do it all—performed valiantly. Not the least of these unpredictable contributions was their coming forward in the winter months to hold the lines, to join Continental encampments, in the interim between the expiring of regular enlistments and the recruiting of new regiments for the spring.[44]

Outside of New York and Pennsylvania the part-time soldiers held their own against the Indians. In 1776, state-supported columns from

Virginia and the Carolinas devastated the settlements of the Cherokee, who were never again a serious threat. And the expeditions of George Rogers Clark, if they did not win the West as his biographers have claimed, did save Kentucky. Even in standardized confrontations with British veterans, the militia occasionally provided much needed help: at Princeton, Savannah, Cowpens, Eutaw Springs, and Springfield.[45] Why did militia stand tall in some battles and not in others? It depended on how they were employed and how they were led. There is an old axiom that civilian-soldiers would go just as far on the battlefield as their officers would take them. Officers like Daniel Morgan and Andrew Pickens would take them quite a distance.[46]

Today, quite properly, the pendulum has swung back toward a more favorable image of the militia and their contributions to American independence. But we may wish to halt its movement before it swings too far, before it denies Washington's Continentals their just desserts. John Shy has accurately spoken of the "triangularity of the struggle," of two armed forces contending "less with each other than for the support and control of the civilian population."[47] Generally, as I have argued elsewhere, I think the Continentals did a reasonably good job—better than the British army—of behaving with propriety, even sensitivity, toward the noncombatant elements. Generals like Washington, Greene, Gates, Schuyler, and Lincoln recognized this delicate dimension to the conflict.[48]

Not so the militia. Nothing so reminds us that the Revolution was also a civil war as certain activities of the home-front defenders. Their very éclat as a constabulary and enforcer of conformity posed a threat. As the war dragged on and as animosities increased, the ruthlessness of the Whig militia—and their careless lack of discrimination between friend and foe—to say nothing of their dabbling in local politics—alarmed both state and congressional authorities.[49] The Reverend James Caldwell of Springfield, New Jersey, a staunch patriot whose wife was killed in a British raid, was himself shot down by a trigger-happy militiaman; the minister had gone into enemy-controlled country to bring out a young woman and was returning under a flag of truce when his senseless death occurred.[50] Pennsylvania's General Lacey acknowledged the destructiveness of his own men and agreed with a friend who complained that "Numbers of the Inhabitants begin to be more afraid of our own [militia] than the Army of General Howe.''[51] General Greene in the South was equally concerned about the extreme retribution that Whig civilian-soldiers inflicted upon Tories and alleged royalist sympathizers, fearing it would alienate myriad potential friends. General William Moultrie of South Carolina might be correct in his assessment of one Colonel Scophol of the loyalists as ''an illiterate, stupid, noisy blockhead,'' but Greene felt that good treatment might win over the followers of Scophol and other Tory officers.[52]

Greene's concern elicits another observation. Continental officers not only sought to hold down militia atrocities in day-to-day military campaigning; they additionally may have had a strong hand in persuading the patriot inhabitants to accept the loyalists back into the American fold as the war slowly drew to an end. The process of reassimilation, having never received more than passing investigation, warrants careful scrutiny. For despite the deep bitterness in both camps, the patriots, however grudgingly, allowed most of the Tories to return to their own communities. How was this done when state legislatures had enacted harsh laws against those who sided with the crown? No doubt it was accomplished in several ways; but there is one method, which may have been of considerable significance, that is particularly relevant to Continental-militia relations.

It is illustrated by an episode that occurred in New Jersey in December 1779. A group of residents of the Hackensack Valley, upon completing a three-year enlistment in a Tory military unit, returned to their homes in patriot-held territory as if nothing had happened. Sheriff Adam Boyd and resident militia chieftains, amazed at their brazenness, arrested them on charges of high treason. As Boyd reported to General Anthony Wayne, although the returnees swore they had deserted—they had seen the light—there was abundant evidence to the contrary. Wayne, however, ordered the wayward ones released.[53] By accepting the word of the Tories who wished to come home, regardless of the truth of the matter, the state would be saved the expense of legal proceedings and incarceration. If such a policy of repatriation would not necessarily make the state appear too lenient, it would give the disaffected a method of returning, an easy way out for both them and Whig authorities. The Continental army, in short, was a restraining influence on the excessess of the militia. That in itself was a contribution of inestimable value in a conflict that was waged for the minds of men as well as for their bodies.[54]

*   *   *

The experiences of the Revolution indicated that a strong dose of central control was required to upgrade the militias of the states. Although reforms such as those proposed by Washington, Steuben, and others failed to impress the Confederation government of the 1780s, the military provisions of the federal Constitution appeared to represent a triumph of those ideas. The new political instrument contained authority for a radically different kind of militia system. The federal Congress, in the language of the Constitution, "shall have Power" to call "forth the Militia [of the states] to execute the Laws of the Union, suppress Insurrections and repel Invasions." These passages recognized the wide range of militia endeavors in the recent war; but now they might be carried out under federal rather than state control. Whereas the training of the revolutionary militia had been sorely deficient, Congress was to have the power "to provide for organizing, arming, and disciplining the Militia," although "reserving to the States, respectively, the appointment of the Officers, and the Authority of training the Militia according to the discipline prescribed by Congress."

One might assume that the post-1789 militia system was soon infused with fresh life. But let us jump ahead and look in on the militia in the 1790s, or the 1820s, or the 1840s—to the sight of carnival atmospheres on countless muster days, of weapons of various descriptions, of units uneven in size, of regiments of volunteers (rather than existing components) sauntering off to war. Fragmentation still characterized the militia; no two state structures were the same, although all suffered generally from the same deficiencies. One sees an institution not much unlike the militia of the colonial period, and so it remained for years to come.

Why was this so? The relevant constitutional clauses never received vigorous implementation. There were only the pallid provisions of the Uniform Militia Act of 1792, which slumbered on the books until 1903, when with the Dick Act the National Guard, successor to the militia, was put on the road to meaningful national control. Just as the states had sought to maintain hegemony by one design or another, so national leaders increasingly believed—and thought the wars of the nineteenth century bore them out—that the militia as an institution had little value in the defense of the country. Yet the militia tradition, if not the institution, lived on in the concept that citizens should be called upon to fight in times of danger, be they militia or, as was more likely, volunteers under federal, rather than state, control or enlistees in the regular army.

Whatever the later vicissitudes of the militia, that institution, for all its frailties, made its finest contributions to the nation in the Revolution. Seldom has an armed force done so much with so little—providing a vast reservoir of manpower for a multiplicity of military needs, fighting (often unaided by Continentals) in the great majority of the 1,331 land engagements of the war.[55] Surely in retrospect we can be as charitable toward the militia as Joseph Reed, who had watched the semi-soldiers throughout the war and who declared, "In short, at this time of day, we must say of them, as [of the] Price of a wife: Be to their faults a little blind, And to their virtues very kind."[56]

7
AMERICAN GENERALS OF THE REVOLUTION: SUBORDINATION AND RESTRAINT

Richard H. Kohn

In August 1775, as American forces lay surrounding Boston, there came forth from British lines under flag of truce a message addressed to General Thomas Mifflin from one Mr. John Day of Nova Scotia, an old friend and now a contractor victualing British troops. Day asked Mifflin to consider whether independence and war were justified or beneficial to America, and whether Mifflin expected Britain to allow the colonies ever to leave the empire. And Day raised a question troubling many minds in 1775: "Admit you are successful, may you not fly from an imaginary Tyranny to a certain one?"[1]

Day, of course, was asking whether Americans, in casting off a system of government acknowledged on both sides of the Atlantic to be perhaps the freest in the world, could defy history and establish institutions that could assure the liberty they sought.[2] Certainly they would have to raise an army, the one institution that their own experience and heritage taught was the greatest danger to liberty. The fear of a standing army was by 1775 an old and accepted political tradition, bound up inextricably in the Revolution itself. Worries about military subordination began with the creation of an American force in 1775 and continued unabated until the army disbanded. In June 1775 the Massachusetts Provincial Council appealed to Congress to adopt the swelling forces around Boston in part to insure civilian control.[3] At the very time when John Adams pushed desperately for Congress to organize and discipline a regular army, he bluntly informed Horatio Gates that "we don't choose to trust you Generals, with too much Power, for too Long Time."[4] Virtually every discussion of military authority or effort to strengthen the army provoked heated debate, warnings, declarations, fears.[5] Years after the war John Adams recalled Washington's aides and secretaries dictating "Letters, which were not well calculated to preserve the Subordination of the military Power, to the civil Authority, which the Spirit of Liberty will always require and enforce."[6]

Nor was concern for civilian supremacy limited to Congress. Any incident of military arrogation was sure to cause comment—or an explosion. In early 1776 Isaac Sears swept through Queens County administering test oaths to suspected Tories and arresting those who refused, provoking John Jay to remind Colonel Alexander McDougall of the slavery sure to follow displacement of civilian rule by the military.[7] When informed that Colonel Stephen Moylan quartered his regiment of dragoons in Durham, Connecticut, on his *"own Caprice,"* Governor Jonathan Trumbull summarily informed the colonel that preparations had been made at another town and that the state would not "be made subservient to the pleasure of an Individual. . . . [y]ou are but a servant of this Country," exploded the governor, "hired for its Defence, not to trample upon and butcher your fellow Countrymen, but *their Enemies."* If Moylan persisted, "it may become necessary to assure you, in some other mode than by writing, that, in this State, the civil Authority is superior to the military—That I am Commanding Officer, and not you."[8] Patiently and respectfully Moylan defended himself, explaining the circumstances that had caused the change in plan. Washington praised Moylan's restraint: "You will, upon the whole, find many advantages by cultivating a good understanding with Civil authority."[9]

For the most part, the sensitivity and fears of the revolutionary generation have not been taken seriously, either by historians or by the American people generally. Very quickly Washington and the Continental army were elevated into symbols of national glory, which, combined with the denigration of Congress for its divisions and weakness, made any questioning of military loyalty seem ridiculous. To succeeding generations, the fear of a military take-over appeared almost as an oddity of the age, although ironically the suspicion of standing armies and concern for civilian supremacy survived as a central element in the American political tradition.

And yet Americans had reasons beyond ideology for their fears. No citizen or official could be certain that the generals, from Washington down to the most junior brigadier, could be trusted. As a group the generals were gentlemen and officeholders of known ambition—jealous of rank and sensitive to their prerogatives.[10] "I would never give any legislative body an opportunity to humiliate me but once," announced Nathanael Greene in 1776.[11] Government during the war was untested and extremely vulnerable, and history indicated that revolution and civil war usually spawned military strongmen or dictators.

Civil-military conflict existed and some generals were not above abusing their power. In 1775 and 1776, Charles Lee traveled the coast from Boston to South Carolina, intimidating and disarming Tories on his own authority, enraging civilian leaders; on one occasion he ordered the city of Portsmouth, Virginia, put to the torch.[12] Street patrols became necessary to protect citizens and safeguard property after the army arrived in New York. Indeed wherever the Continental army went, especially after 1776, fields were stripped of fences, horses and teams impressed, food and supplies of all kinds commandeered. Washington and the other generals tried their best to prevent wanton destruction; once Nathanael Greene decreed that all soldiers gathered around a fire of fencing would be liable for punishment unless they pointed out the actual culprits. But all acknowledged that violence occurred, and some generals were willing to justify, or even threaten, violence when necessity demanded.[13] According to Greene, the southern army became in 1780 "so addicted to plundering, that they were a terror to the inhabitants," and Washington confessed that same year that "every ounce of Forage that has been used all the latter part of the Campaign, and a good deal of the Provision, has been taken at the point of the Bayonet."[14] (Such conflict worked both ways, of course. Civilians treated the army with derision and contempt as well as fear, abusing the soldiery, refusing quarters, pursuing soldiers for debt, and withholding pay and supplies.) Sometimes individuals and whole units defied their civilian masters. In 1779, after receiving orders to join the Sullivan expedition, the entire commissioned complement of the 1st New Jersey Regiment threatened to resign unless furnished their pay and supplies within three days.[15] None of the generals disobeyed the Congress directly, but many used the threat of resignation and others participated in congressional politics, maneuvering for rank and influence and sometimes fighting savagely with individual congressmen.[16]

Another cause for concern, especially as the war lengthened, was that the Continental army came increasingly to resemble the classic European standing army. At Valley Forge officers began resigning in droves amid cries for half-pay and provision for widows and orphans of those slain in service. Greene thought "one radical cure" was "to put the Army upon the British establishment."[17] Indeed, half-pay was a cornerstone of the British military system, a pension that supported a shadow military establishment for mobilization, but one that in America, where the Continental army was raised only for fighting the war, had ominous overtones. But whatever the disagreements over half-pay (and they were profound), both sides saw the issue admittedly as one of adopting a British, or European, military practice.[18] In 1776 John Adams was even more explicit about such adaptations, winning adoption of Articles of War copied directly from those of the British Army.[19] Moreover, beginning in 1777 the Continental army began to mirror its European relative in social composition: the soldiery a mixed lot of convicted Tories, criminals, British deserters, bounty jumpers, draftees, and drafted substitutes —an army overwhelmingly of the young, of the poor, of rootless laborers and tradesmen, led by officers from the wealthier agricultural and commercial layer of society. Contemporaries well understood this fact. According to one French officer in 1777, the soldiers were "vagabonds and paupers" who "had a bad reputation with the general public."[20]

Even more threatening to civilian supremacy, there grew up in the officer corps almost immediately a sense of solidarity and corporateness that by war's end was pervaded by paranoia and alienation. It was not surprising for group feelings to develop in men from essentially similar backgrounds who entered into the ancient, almost mystical fraternity of arms and who experienced together the danger and privation of life in the field, the camaraderie of camp, and the extremes of elation and despair. But what welded the officer corps together and gave it a special internal cohesion was the sense of being victimized by an ungrateful society. The grievances were many and, as the war grew longer, seemed to grow more galling and more onerous: congressional injustice on appointments and promotions, grudging unwillingness to grant half-pay or compensation for widows and orphans, low pay or lack of payment altogether, stingy rations and allowances, defective or nonexistent supplies. In the winter of 1777-78, incensed over the promotions of Colonel James Wilkinson and General Thomas Conway, officers began resigning, citing also the pay issue and loudly blaming Congress for the conditions at Valley Forge.[21]

Even after half-pay was granted, the depreciation of money and the uneven distribution of funds and supplies robbed the men of the dress and the dignity of their station. Within a short time, officers were banding together to petition for relief, again with threats of mass resignation.[22] "The officers look upon Congress with an evil eye, as men who are jealous of the army, who mean them no good, but mean to divide and distress them," Dr. Robert Honeyman recorded in his journal. "It is surprising with how much freedom & acrimony they declare their sentiments."[23]

By 1780, with American forces near dissolution for lack of money and supplies, the officers had come to view the army as the special repository of virtue and patriotism, especially in contrast to civilian society. "Depreciation of virtue . . . every species of extortion . . . luxury, effeminacy . . . every species of rascality is practised," reported General Knox's aide sourly. "Balls, entertainment, routes, rackets, assemblies, drums, &c., seem . . . to have taken full possession of all Classes."[24] For Colonel Ebenezer Huntington, enraged like most officers by the army's suffering, the worst enemy was the speculators, whom Huntington wanted eradicated—legally or by force.[25] During the latter months of 1780 came warnings to Congress that the anger in camp had reached a point at which civil government was in jeopardy.[26] Clearly by 1782 the army's patience had expired. "From morn to night, and from night till morn you will hear some of the best officers and soldiers (that any nation could boast of) execrating the very country they are risking their lives, limbs, and health to support for their inattention and neglect," lamented Colonel Henry Jackson.[27] By the end of the war, the resentment, the feeling of maltreatment and victimization—the sense of martyrdom— was widespread.[28] The wonder of the officers' near revolt at Newburgh in 1783 was not that it happened, but that it was so long in coming.[29]

Finally, the alienation of the army led to threats against civilian authority that alone justified congressional fears. Rumors about the army seizing control of the government surfaced often enough to indicate that some, in the army and outside, discussed the possibility seriously. In 1779 Alexander Hamilton reputedly declared in public "that it was high time for the people to rise, join Genl. Washington and turn Congress out of Doors."[30] Three times in 1780 generals warned Congress that the army was angry enough to revolt. "Many talk of a Dictator," reported Greene.[31] In Philadelphia, Pennsylvania Supreme Executive Council

President Joseph Reed was "told that some officers of considerable rank have pressed the General to assume dictatorial authority," leading Reed, formerly an aide of Washington and for a time adjutant general of the army, to confess that the "change of sentiment . . . in the army with respect to civil government has for the first time given me apprehensions."[32]

Much of the loose talk, of course, was designed to frighten the states and Congress into providing supplies and other support. But the threats paralleled a growing disgust for Congress and a progressively weakening confidence that republicanism could survive. A few months after the Yorktown victory Colonel Lewis Nicola broached the subject of monarchy indirectly to Washington, admitting his own disbelief in the suitability of republican government and indicating that talk of mutiny over pay and half-pay was common.[33] Others, like Greene and Jasper Yeates, later a Pennsylvania supreme court justice, expressed similar doubts.[34] New Jersey lawyer William Peartree Smith was the most explicit: "All the inferior wheels will run into confusion, and by and bye, some Master Hand will seize it. So did a Cromwell; and if this should become necessary, as (inter nos et sub rosa) I think it will, God grant it may be the man who merits from the Country he has rescued—a DIADEM!"[35] In two hundred years of celebrating the genius of their political institutions, Americans have forgotten that other alternatives existed during the American Revolution, among them military dictatorship or some form of one-man rule imposed or installed by the military. The Revolution could have ended, as Thomas Jefferson put it, "as most others have . . . by a subversion of that liberty it was intended to establish."[36]

Although the generals of the Continental army were never a unified group, they, like the rest of the officer corps, came to see the army as a special community. They grew to hate Congress for its weakness and its arrogance. For civilians, wallowing in luxury, they felt nothing but contempt. And some of the generals considered the possibility of rule by force. The great testing time for the generals—and for the Revolution— came in 1780 when the currency collapsed and the army nearly disbanded for lack of support. Indeed, in 1778 the entire war effort began to wind down, stricken by protracted political bickering, economic troubles, administrative chaos, and sinking morale. That year bitter fights erupted in Congress over foreign affairs—the Lee-Deane struggle, differences over peace terms, diplomatic appointments—followed by spectacular scandals over the use of public money and official position for private aggrandizement. Equally vicious struggles broke out in the states, the political leadership fractured over issues of loyalty and economics. In 1779, Continental and state currencies began their dramatic plunge to eventual worthlessness. Local committees failed to control skyrocketing prices. Popular rage at speculation and profiteering boiled over. In the army each successive winter seemed to bring on worse conditions—short rations, inadequate clothing, lack of munitions. Beginning in 1779 the army lived off impressments, with authorities at all levels expropriating the needed goods by force. With governmental treasuries near empty, the army, too, hit bottom in 1780. "[A]las what is our Situation," exclaimed New York delegate William Floyd. "Our Treasury nearly Exhausted, Every Department out of Cash, no Magazines of provision laid up, our army Starving for want of Bread, on the Brink of a General Mutiny, and the prospect of a Spedy Supply . . . very Small."[37] Two weeks later, three feet of snow buried the main camp at Morristown.

At the very time when the Revolution was about to founder from internal weakness and exhaustion, the British went on the rampage. In May 1780, Charleston with its 5,000 defenders fell to a besieging British army. In August, the remaining American army in the South under Horatio Gates was erased at Camden, leaving Georgia and South Carolina under occupation and the entire region at the mercy of enemy forces. In September, Arnold's treason was exposed, and soon after the Pennsylvania and New Jersey lines mutinied. At the time many believed the Charleston debacle marked the nadir.[38] But the situation had sunk to such desperate straits that some talked of negotiating a peace short of victory, others of sacrificing liberty to keep the cause alive. Pennsylvania and Delaware teetered on the brink of martial law and an extraordinary convention of New England states, meeting at Hartford in November, formally recommended investing George Washington with dictatorial powers to support the army.[39] It was then that generals and civilians alike spoke of military rule, and while all thought in terms of specific and temporary grants of authority, the implications were all too clear—and all too frightening. In 1780 French minister Luzerne recounted the congressional debate over sending a special committee to camp to reconstitute the army: "It was said . . . that his [Washington's] influence was already too great; that even his virtues afforded motives for alarm; that the enthusiasm of the army, joined to the kind of dictatorship already confided to him, put Congress and the United States at his mercy; that it was not expedient to expose a man of the highest virtues to such temptations."[40]

What made the situation so dangerous was that by 1780 the generals of the Continental army, individually and as a group, had come to labor in their own minds under a vast set of grievances against Congress and the nation. Over and over again during the war they had bridled at what they considered unwarranted political interference with the army, at the seeming indifference, irresponsibility, and irrationality of Congress on military policy, at civilian prejudice against the military generally, and at a variety of personal insults inflicted by their superiors. For years they had been predicting disaster. In 1777, Henry Knox noted the rapid increase of "*impiety*," and Philip Schuyler out of despair for winning the war even considered some kind of compromise peace.[41] At that time many named finance as the chief danger, calling for taxes on the population heavy enough to support the struggle.[42] Through 1778 and 1779, the generals grew more disturbed and more cynical about the political wrangling and the unwillingness of government to act. "What are Congress doing— why is the Establishment of the Army put off to this late Season," lamented Anthony Wayne in April 1778, "why this torpor—why this supine[ne]ss when the Season for action has Arrived?"[43] "Where are our men of abilities," cried Washington; "why do they not come forth to save their country?"[44] General Alexander McDougall asked similar questions of Elisha Boudinot, a leading New Jerseyite, attacking that legislature for "nibling" at taxes. "One would imagine by their Conduct the members were all corrupt Lawyers, staving off sufficient Taxes, till the war is over, when your money will go . . . for fine things for the Girls, and spirits &c." "What is your press about? Why dont some able . . . pen, sound the Alarm?"[45] McDougall had long believed that the chief threat to the Revolution was the weakness and corruption of the American people themselves. In reply, Boudinot agreed that internal weakness posed more of a danger than the British. But he blamed political institutions more than the people and thought the most fundamental problem was a Congress so lacking in power and authority that the Confederation might not survive the war.[46] Within another year, most of the American generals would echo almost exactly McDougall's and Boudinot's sentiments.

At the same time, many of the generals had grown contemptuous of Congress and began to view themselves as the victims of some special rack of political torture. Late in 1777 North Carolina congressman Thomas Burke openly accused General John Sullivan of incompetence for his performance at Brandywine. Sullivan responded in kind: "I am not Clearly convinced that a member of Congress has a right to Take . . . Liberties . . . with the Character of an officer and I think I can never be brought to believe that he can have a Privilidge of writing to any Gentleman *Accusing* him of want of Capacity & Every thing that would make him contemptible in the Eyes of the World & the other be Barred from replying with Spirit because his Accuser was a member of Congress. . . . I therefore considered myself at full Liberty at Least to return Acrimony for Acrimony."[47] Promotions also convulsed the generals: first the major generalcy offered to Phillip DuCoudray, which stimulated a resignation threat from Knox, Greene, and Sullivan and a congressional rebuke in return; then the elevation of Wilkinson and Conway, which led the brigadiers to consider resigning together. Instead they filed a formal protestation with Congress.[48] A few months later, Congress granted half-pay, but according to General James Mitchell Varnum, the army was angry because the grant was limited to seven years and generals were to receive only a colonel's portion.[49]

Indeed the long years of service at modest pay and benefits, eroded by depreciation, impoverished almost all of the generals. Samuel Holden Parsons told Congressman Jesse Root that the generals had "used our utmost exertions to calm the fears" of officers and to "instill sentiments of patriotism and respect to our Superior Council," but the generals themselves had gained no pay raise and were now "as far sunk as our brethren" and near "total ruin."[50] Benedict Arnold was denied credit for his contributions to several victories and also denied promotion. In 1778, Pennsylvania authorities brought him to trial on charges of abusing his position as military governor of Philadelphia. One solution for such difficulties was resignation, which Philip Schuyler, bruised after years of infighting over the northern command, finally exercised in 1779. But even that could prove difficult. Congress delayed honoring Schuyler's request for six months and in other cases simply refused to let a general leave service. It took Massachusetts Brigadier John Glover—impoverished and worn out from years in the field—three years of badgering and agitation before Congress and the commander in chief allowed him to retire.[51]

Personal treatment aside, even more provoking to the generals as military commanders responsible for winning a war was the refusal of Congress and the states to authorize a regular army or to support adequately the forces authorized. Constantly the generals called for drafts, for long enlistments—for anything that might fill up the ranks and make the army more lasting. What most wanted was a regular force led by an officer corps stablized by the inducement of half-pay and enlisted for the duration of the war. The reliance on militia struck most of them as absurd.[52] Washington in 1780 attributed "all the misfortunes we have met with in the Military line" to short enlistments.[53]

From 1778 onward, generals lamented the shortages, confusion, and mismanagement of military affairs. For Quartermaster Nathanael Greene, however, the vacillation of Congress combined with his own personal treatment to make the Rhode Islander as soured as any general officer in the army. Accused of profiteering, blamed for waste and for the supply troubles, Greene spent the last sixteen months of his three-year tenure trying by resignation to escape a savage running battle with his political superiors. "The great body of the People you know are contracted, selfish and illiberal," he told a fellow officer.[54] "Administration is torn to pieces by factions," he confided to Sullivan; "False pride and secret enmity, poisons our Councils and distracts our Measures."[55] Describing in disgust another change in the Commissary Department, Greene observed that "Before any one system can be digested & improved to advantage, a new one is introduced. Never was the politics of a nation governed so much by the spirit of novelty."[56] Greene reacted to the accusations and criticism with a mixture of anger and self-pity. From the start he had been "a greater slave to public business" than anyone; he had not wanted the job and now worked "to pave the way for others glory"; he "studyd aconomy" and ran his department with "little wanton waste of public property"; and his "emoluments" were "far less than the Commissary Generals" though his duties were "infinitely more perplexing & troublesome."[57] By the time he left office to command in the South, Greene's dislike of Congress and politicians was extreme: "They have such a desire to please one another, and such a thirst for popularity, that all their measures are of the servile kind. God preserve us, for I am sure they will not."[58]

In 1780, exactly the kind of anger and exasperation expressed by Greene and earlier by McDougall overcame the rest of the generals. As their sense of isolation within a hostile and unworthy society grew stronger, their rhetoric grew more severe and their hatreds more explicit. They blamed the people for a loss of virtue, and many even concluded that a party or group was eating away from within, purposely trying to unhinge the Revolution. Jedidiah Huntington would not "pretend to say" "where the Blame lies," but Brigadier General John Paterson told superior William Heath that if the loss of Charleston would not "rouse the country to exert its natural strength . . . I must conclude they have lost all their virtue (or never had any) and that the cause is tottering on the brink of ruin."59 Two months earlier, Paterson wrote an impassioned letter to Heath worrying that the Massachusetts officers might resign in a body. He described the Massachusetts line as so wasted away as to be useless militarily.

"Where is the public spirit of the year 1775," Paterson continued. "Where are those flaming *patriots* who were ready to sacrifise their lives, their fortunes, their all for the public? I can point some of them out in the [General] Court, telling the people that the army are the only persons they have reason to fear, throwing their weight . . . against those who have fought, bled, and eaven the widows of those who have been killed in the service of their country."60 Heath quoted the letter at length to the assembly, but edited out the most inflammatory portions. Heath was perhaps the most moderate of the generals in 1780, at least in private correspondence.61 Henry Knox was not so restrained: "Great God! is it possible that a people . . . should be so inattentive . . . through supi[ne]ness, to be on the verge of ruin. . . . Have we not been dreaming . . . the most enert beings on earth. The army . . . . have been permitted, nay, stimulated to decay; . . . the mass of America have taken a monstrous deal of opium."62 Acidic Anthony Wayne had never liked Congress, but on the march through Philadelphia to the South in early 1781, he was forced to scrounge for clothing and arms because state and national officials could not furnish him money—"the same supi[ne]ness & stupidity that pervades most of our civil Councils," he concluded.63

The most extreme was McDougall. Two years earlier his anger over criticism from Congress had exploded. "I drew my sword," he told a legislator, with civil supremacy over the military as "one of the first wishes of my heart. . . . But he must be a stranger to history . . . who expects the full enjoyment of his civil Liberty in a war with a Cruel and

Arbitrary Enemy. . . . Rome in the most virtuous & jealous of her Freedom, had her Dictators,'' he continued. ''The American Generals . . . are subject to the most illiteral Athenian Caprice and abuse and . . . their reputations Caluminated by many who have not spirit to take the Field, or if they did have not understanding enough to lead a Corporal's Party. . . . It is time for the American genls to be on Guard; and not to be made the scape goats of any Public bodies, however dignified or reputable they may be.''[64] In January 1779, Nathanael Greene and Washington spent a month in Philadelphia. Greene was both repulsed and charmed by ''Splendid entertainments . . . Large Assemblies and Evening Balls''—up early and out so late that he could not get his work done.[65] McDougall, ''nailed to the Chair and Table'' with duties, took a month to reply. ''Can the country expect Spartan Virtue in her army, while the people are wallowing in all the luxury of Rome in her declining State,'' he asked. ''The present Manners and forms of Government ['democratical Constitutions'] will not long exist together.''[66] In 1780 McDougall well understood the alternatives. Informed by Greene of the abuse meted out by Congress, he replied that ''if the General officers had not Halters about their necks, they would not have been so often insulted and neglected. To be exposed to the Calumny incident to our office, at the same time unsupported slaves, is a condition too much for Human Nature to bear.''[67] Significantly, the generals chose the summer of 1780 to petition Congress as a group about their pay and half-pay. Not by accident, McDougall carried the petition to Philadelphia. He minced no words with Congress's committee. ''Indeed I have explicitly told Mr. Adams that our Army no longer Consider themselves as fighting the Battles of *Republics in Principle* but for Empire and Liberty to a People whose object is Property and that the army expect, some of that Property which the Citizen seeks, and which the army Protects for him.''[68]

Knox, Greene, McDougall, and other officers believed that the answer lay in political reform;[69] tampering with human nature struck them as futile. In early 1780, Congressman and former Brigadier John Armstrong wrote long letters to friends in Congress and outside, arguing that the crisis was based on finance and that the solution—to avert a more radical cure—was price regulation.[70] Armstrong's former comrades viewed the crisis and the remedy in far more fundamental terms: Congress's powers.

The solutions had to come from that body—a regular army enlisted for the duration, half-pay, executive administration in military affairs and in the government generally, and a rearrangement of the entire financial system. In September many of the officers detailed to friends in the government the very same program recommended later by the Hartford convention of New England states, the very same program being sought (and later instituted) by Robert Morris and the nationalists and made permanent by the Federalists within another twenty years.[71] Former General Philip Schuyler, who was in the thick of the movement as a congressman and New York lawmaker, went so far as to move in the state senate for the eastern states to call a convention, settle their boundaries, form a new (and permanent) union, devise a fund for their common debts, and invite other states to join. Schuyler wanted some ''permanent and uniform system for drawing out the resources of the country'': in his mind, a ''Congress with powers . . . [so] extensive as to oblige each State to do its duty.''[72]

Revolution was in the air in 1780. Officers at the highest levels in the army were discussing military dictatorship, and other alternatives were rapidly running out. Of all the generals, Benedict Arnold should have been soft-spoken in September 1780, but even he felt free to lambast civilian authority. ''It is . . . to be lamented that our army is permitted to starve in a land of plenty. There is a fault somewhere. It ought to be traced up to its authors, and . . . they ought to be capitally punished.''[73] To fellow Connecticut General Samuel Holden Parsons, Arnold claimed, ''The Army . . . are fully convinced that [Congress's] wish and intention is to disgust and disband us in detail. . . . I have [been] recommending a thousand or fifteen hundred men of all ranks to [visit] Congress to present a spirited but decent memorial setting forth their claims.''[74] Arnold said and wrote nothing that other generals were not thinking and writing to each other at the time, although he hedged carefully his most explosive proposal. But Arnold had his own special alternative.

Doubtless in every war the leaders of America's armies at one time or another have registered similar complaints about politicians, military policy, or the willingness of the civilian population to sacrifice for the cause. But the Revolution, because it was a civil war and a struggle for national existence, occurred at a time when political institutions were only partly formed and republicanism was not yet firmly rooted. And in 1780, the America generals as a group expressed an extremely dangerous rage and personal resentment. The question that remains is why they never moved, either in unison or singly, against Congress or civilian government. When the American Revolution turned to the right, why did it not swing violently; why did no Cromwell, no Napoleon, nor Stalin emerge to ride the whirlwind unleashed by war and revolution? An answer, of course, would require a much broader analysis of the character of American political history and institutions, the structure of society, and perhaps the very nature of the Revolution itself. Perhaps the turn rightward in 1780 simply was sufficient, for through a combination of internal reorganization, French aid, and the lucky circumstances that produced the Yorktown victory, the war was won. A brush with internal political crisis, however indirect, did occur at the Newburgh cantonment in early 1783. And a strong man did emerge, but in the guise of faithful republican general, symbol of national unity, patriarch and president—"first in war, first in peace, and first in the hearts of his countrymen," in Henry Lee's entombing phrases.

George Washington never succumbed to temptation. To the end he remained, as characterized in 1775, "Discreet and Virtuous, no harum starum ranting Swearing fellow but Sober, steady, and Calm."[75] He seemed to sense from the beginning that any bid for supreme power would shatter the Revolution and ultimately fail. Whether by chance or design, the generals who could have rivaled his power or position had been silenced, discredited, or driven from the army by 1780—Charles Lee, Gates, Mifflin, Conway, Schuyler. Nor could Congress, which seemed to sink in public esteem as the war lengthened, really compete in prestige or veneration. Necessity might beckon, but already by 1780 George Washington found himself, in the words of a British spy three years later, "elevated to a pitch of grandeur he never dreamed of, & would not even now grasp at the supreme power, if to obtain it, he must as Cromwell surround the state house and tell them: 'begone; the Lord you seek has left this place.' "[76]

The rest of the generals never had Washington's opportunity. The few who ever gained command of an independent army—Gates, Greene, or Lincoln in the South; John Sullivan, Gates, and Schuyler in the North—never controlled the entire Continental army, much less the various state forces also. Any coup would have required American generals to cooperate without the commander in chief's knowledge and against his authority. No such possibility existed after 1777 because the generals as a group were rent by jealousy and suspicion. Greene, Sullivan, and others accepted the existence of a "Conway Cabal," and as late as two years afterward, Sullivan insisted "not from Conjecture, but from certain knowledge" that "the Faction Raised in 1777 . . . are waiting to Collect Strength & Seize Some favorable moment, to appear in force."[77] After Washington eliminated or isolated his rivals, those remaining in 1780 were almost all "Washington men." Greene revealed the atmosphere in confiding to Joseph Reed that "the great man is confounded at his situation, but appears to be reserved and silent," then cautioning Reed not to "let the least hint drop . . . of the information I give, as it may prove ruinous to me. I have difficulties enough, God knows, without adding to them."[78]

Although from essentially similar social backgrounds and united in their resentment of Congress and their devotion to Washington, the army, and the Revolution, the generals came from different states, had different loyalties, and differed in age, religion, and education. More important, throughout the war, they struggled viciously among themselves over rank and prestige. McDougall complained in 1777 when Stirling, whom McDougall outranked, was jumped to general. William Smallwood's promotion to major general provoked Samuel Holden Parsons to refuse to serve longer as a brigadier. Moses Hazen suffered five years as a colonel until finally asking General Sullivan in Congress openly for promotion. Robert Howe and George Weedon battled with Congress over their status. At one point, Virginia Generals Peter Muhlenberg, William Woodford, and Weedon all resigned over their relative rank and the dispute dragged on for years.[79] Some of the hatreds were famous: Gates and Schuyler, Gates and Arnold, McDougall and Heath in 1782. Ambition for glory also split the group. On the Sullivan expedition in 1779, Edward Hand had a battle plan rejected by a council of other generals. "This was the first time I found my . . . Comm[an]d of the Advance corps had given jealousy," he noted in his diary, "or that it was possible that men engagd in their Countrys Cause would oppose salutary measures because the Honor of a Brilliant Action could not be immediately Attributed to themselves or to favourites."[80] Some in Congress encouraged the competition either out of friendship or for political purposes, but within a short time the situation was totally out of hand. "They Quarrell like Cats and Dogs,'' sighed John Adams in disgust at the "Wrangles between military officers, high and low. . . . They worry one another like Mastiffs, Scrambling for Rank and Pay like Apes for Nuts.''[81] Significantly, the only time the generals acted together to confront Congress was over the issues of their own personal pay and half-pay.

Even had they united, the generals must have realized that overturning civilian government was both unnecessary and impossible. Most of them came from the same local and provincial elite that ruled in Congress and the states after independence, and many had held political office before the war. Indeed at the beginning, general officers were appointed precisely because of their social and political importance.[82] Many were related by blood, marriage, or friendship to prominent officials: Greene's brother was governor of Rhode Island; James Clinton's brother was governor of New York; Jedidiah Huntington's first wife was the daughter of Connecticut's Governor Jonathan Trumbull; and New Jersey Governor William Livingston was Lord Stirling's brother-in-law. Samuel Holden Parsons spent three years at Harvard with John Adams "upon terms of familiarity.''[83] Many generals moved freely from the army to positions of political authority. Joseph Reed turned down a generalcy in 1777 to enter Congress and later became president of the Supreme Executive Council in Pennsylvania; Colonel (and later Brigadier General) Elias Dayton, on the other hand, refused election to Congress in 1778.[84] In 1780 alone, five former Continental army generals sat as delegates in Philadelphia. In fact the line between civilian and military was on occasion blurred completely. Governor George Clinton retained his general's commission through the entire war.[85] And in 1781, Alexander McDougall sat in Congress while still on active duty, wearing his uniform and viewing his "civil capacity but a secondary one" to his military position.[86] As a group the generals already possessed power and influence; what motivated most of them, if Wayne and Greene were at all typical, was glory and the benefits that flowed from it.[87] John Adams, who helped to place Washington in command in 1775 and lived to see Napoleon explode across the face of Europe, admitted to the cadets at West Point in 1821 that "military glory is esteemed the first and greatest of glories.''[88]

To stage a coup in 1780 would thus have required sending armies up and down the country, turning out Congress and state administrations peopled by relatives, friends, and former officers. Such action was not only impractical and dangerous with a British army on American soil, but unnecessary except to strengthen government and to replace a weak Congress with some sort of executive rule. With the emergence of Robert Morris and the nationalists in late 1780, exactly the kind of political revolution desired by the generals and the rest of the army occurred. Within a year, national finances were reformed and invigorated, a bank chartered, half-pay for life instituted, the army reorganized and put on a permanent footing for the duration of the war, the supply system reformed, executive departments established to administer congressional programs, and the Articles of Confederation finally ratified. "I find that Congress & [the] assemblies begin to Rouse from their Slumber & Individuals are now alarmed . . . who have for years past been Employed in amassing wealth," reported John Sullivan.[89] Morris's program gave the army hope. "Indeed we already feel the good effects of his administration," observed Adjutant General Edward Hand in mid-1781. "The army is better fed at present than it has been for years."[90]

Finally, with few exceptions the generals came to understand that any military revolt would backfire on its authors, destroy the Revolution, and eradicate a tradition that lay at the very foundation of American liberty. As much as they might rant against weak government or loss of public virtue, most understood, as McDougall put it, that "the General officers had . . . Halters about their necks."[91] Time and again they closed their letters with a rhetorical shrug of the shoulders, expressing a trust in Providence and a belief that they had done their duty and could do no more. McDougall committed the outcome in 1780 to "that God, who has hitherto extricated America out of various difficulties, apparently insurmountable. It is . . . a consolation to us," he told Greene, "that we have done our duty to her."[92] Greene agreed and, like the rest, accepted the inevitable. "Was our government compact, a Dictator might draw out the forces and resources of the Country with greater dispatch than any other mode that can be adopted," he speculated. "But as the Government is wide, and as the people are jealous and will be more and more so if the Military departments get the reins of civil government, I am in great doubt whether there would be as prompt obedience from the people at large under a Dictator as under a Congress with full and ample powers."[93]

The final crisis for the generals came in early 1783, when the war was won but when many feared that the union and American liberty might not endure. Until 1780 the generals had always, in spite of their own bitterness, intervened to calm the officer corps and to avert or suppress mutiny in the enlisted ranks.[94] Throughout, the generals had mediated between the army and civilian authority, representing each to the other and maintaining the form and substance of military subordination. The crisis of 1780 changed their role. Half-pay for life and their successful effort for added compensations for themselves wedded the generals to the rest of the officers in a community of self-interest.[95] And in their resentment and their desire for reform of the army and the central government, the generals became allied with the nationalists in Congress, thereby politicizing the army.[96] The result was the Newburgh conspiracy in 1783.

While animosity toward Congress as an institution and toward politicians lessened after 1780, the generals remained cynical and suspicious. Like the rest of the army, they focused more and more on their personal treatment, and especially on pay and half-pay, both of which they wanted settled before demobilization robbed the army of its leverage. As early as January 1781, Benjamin Lincoln suggested commutation to a lump-sum payment so that Massachusetts officers could avoid the shame and guilt of "pensioner[s] on public alms," whom antimilitary New Englanders would surely label half-pay officers.[97] A year later, when agitation over pay began in the Massachusetts line, Generals Heath and Knox stepped in immediately to join and direct the movement.[98] By late 1782 with peace a certainty, the entire army was in uproar over half-pay. "Some people talk of coercive measures," reported Maryland Brigadier Otho H. Williams from Philadelphia.[99]

Once again the army joined the nationalists in Congress. This time, however, in order to win the nationalist program for reform of the central government and pay and half-pay for the officers, the generals were asked directly to mutiny. McDougall, again the army's representative to Congress, agreed.[100] In February 1783, Assistant Financier Gouverneur Morris broached the subject to Knox, the leader of the officers in Newburgh, and to Greene, commanding the army in the South.[101] One last time both men stared into the abyss and considered the implications of revolt. Both drew back. "I consider the reputation of the American Army as one of the most immaculate things on earth," Knox informed McDougall. "We should . . . suffer wrongs and injuries to the utmost verge of toleration rather than sully it in the least degree." The army's influence could "only exist in one point, and that . . . is a sharp point which I hope in God will never be directed than against the Enemies of the liberties of America.''[102] Greene, too, saw only ''a critical business, pregnant with dangerous consequences. . . . When soldiers advance without authority, who can halt them? We have many Clodiuses and Catalines in America,'' he told Morris, ''who may give a different direction to this business, than either you or it expect. . . . I have done my duty, and wait events.''[103]

In the end, the nationalists turned to Horatio Gates. And yet even Gates, ruined by Camden and by politics in Congress and the army, was only a tool.[104] His only son recently dead, his wife dying, his career a shambles, Gates allowed himself to be tricked by the nationalist leaders in Philadelphia and to be used by the young hotheads around him at Newburgh. And aide John Armstrong lived to regret his authorship of the address that brought the army to the brink: ''a millstone round my neck during the whole of my political career,'' he reflected in 1816, and ''more than once gone near to sink me.''[105] Ranged against the small band that toyed with coup were the generals of the Revolution. They stood with Washington, rejecting the bloodshed and civil war sure to follow any attempt to displace civilian rule.[106]

Even Gouverneur Morris—according to contemporary historian William Gordon's information, ''a person of no principle, a downright Machiavelian Politician''—had not wanted military dictatorship.[107] ''I entirely agree with you in Sentiment as to the Consequences which must follow from any unconstitutional Procedure of the military,'' he replied to Greene. ''The Boundary between their humble Petitions and their most forcible Demands is shadowy and indescribable. I did hope from *their influence* and . . . if Congress had taken *manly and decisive Measures,* America would have been united and happy. I was content on his Ground *again to labor and to hazard,* but neither Time nor Circumstances will permit any *Thing now.*''[108]

At Newburgh, the generals had in their own minds weathered their worst crisis.[109] In spite of their anxiety over half-pay and imminent demobilization, they had intervened again to protect civilian authority. They sensed that by their own restraint, subordination, and sacrifice, they and the nation had defied history and maintained liberty through the great test of revolution and war. Back in 1780, young David Humphreys, who through the war served four generals including Washington and Greene, had expressed their thinking perfectly. ''Heaven be thanks I am not a

General," he had written, "and never shall be, for . . . they . . . have more ability, fortitude, perseverence and integrity, than ever mortals had before."[110] In 1783 the generals considered the survival of liberty a personal triumph that they wished somehow to perpetuate. When they met at Steuben's headquarters to form a society to keep alive the friendships formed in the officer corps and to assure their interests after the war, they chose for their model "that illustrious Roman Lucius Quintius Cincinnatus," a citizen-general who had achieved supreme power but relinquished it voluntarily to return to his plow. The generals "resolved to follow his example, by returning to their citizenship."[111]

The subordination and restraint of the Continental army was one of the great legacies of the Revolution, too often forgotten or attributed to George Washington alone. It was the gift of the first group of American generals, and it is ours still today, preserved intact through two centuries of American history. It remains, as it was in 1783, the sacred trust of the United States armed forces.

8
TIME: FRIEND OR FOE OF THE REVOLUTION?

Richard Buel, Jr.

It is a truism that historians view the past in the light of the present. The suggestion that the Vietnam War may be causing a shift in perspective on our Revolutionary War should not then shock anyone. I believe such a shift is taking place. Until Vietnam, the question about the Revolutionary War that American military historians most often asked was, "How did Britain manage to lose?"[1] Since Vietnam we are more inclined to ask, "How could Britain possibly have won?"[2] This change has come about because we suddenly see the analogy between Great Britain in eighteenth-century America and the United States in Vietnam. In both wars, a power with apparently unmatchable military resources failed to achieve its objectives against an adversary who looked hopelessly weak by comparison. The parallel in these two experiences has led us to reassess the relative strengths and weaknesses of the protagonists and to gain a more sophisticated understanding of what military potential is. It has made us sensitive to the question "Which power stands to gain most from a war of attrition?" and to the advantages always enjoyed by the side best able to keep political control of the territory in dispute.

When we focus on these two points it becomes possible to see that, despite the unquestionable superiority of the British in terms of conventional military resources, they suffered from a chronic disadvantage in fighting the American war. The Americans started out with a more or less complete political hold on their territory, a hold the British could never break except by force of arms. From the outset, the ministry saw that its main chance lay less in the army's ability to destroy the hard core of

Revolutionaries, who could always retreat to the interior, than in its own power to create an environment where loyalists could regain political control of the most valued parts of the continent.[3] But this they could never achieve, perhaps because the Tories tended to be a self-selecting group who identified with Britain precisely because they did not feel at home with or in control of their surroundings. Though every British victory produced new loyalists, they usually came from the part of the population least able to execute Britain's larger aim of bringing the colonies back into the empire. Consequently in most places political ascendancy belonged to the patriots, who could usually keep nominal control by force of arms where there was no concentration of British troops.[4]

The prime example of Britain's problem in maintaining effective political control over the rebellious colonies is found in South Carolina. There everything seemed to be working for Britain. Large concentrations of slaves along the coast coupled with scattered settlement in the interior allowed an invading force to move about without fearing a spontaneous gathering of rebels such as that which forced Burgoyne to surrender at Saratoga. The virtual destruction of the southern army at Charleston and Camden in 1780 left the British apparently in firm control there. Yet they found it impossible to garrison so vast a territory in such a way as to protect collaborators against roving partisans unless they divided their force. And if they divided their force, they could be picked off piecemeal. Admittedly, rebel bands could not by themselves have seized political control of these areas from the British. Such a feat would depend on Nathanael Greene's ability to reconstruct a southern army using Virginia as his principal base.

But unless Britain garrisoned the entire continent, which even she could not do, there would always remain an enclave from which a Greene could draw men.[5]

Several consequences followed from the Revolutionaries' continuous hold on all but small stretches of coastline and the islands. Britain had not only to raise her armies abroad and transport them to America but also to provision them from Europe. Though the British could recruit some North American manpower, the patriots had an advantage in this respect, which made casualties less costly to them than to the British.[6] And, as Arthur Bowler has shown, provisioning from Europe proved both inadequate and expensive.[7] The patriots had seen from the start that they would enjoy these advantages[8] but they did not set much store by them, probably realizing that they were not decisive. To win a war of attrition takes more than the power to conduct operations of similar scale on better terms. One must also be able to exhaust the enemy before one's own resources fail. Consequently, the colonists put more stock in two other factors, which they thought made Britain vulnerable.

First, the mother country groaned under a staggering debt. Indeed, the colonists thought, rightly or wrongly, that the debt had prompted Britain's steady efforts since 1763 to raise a revenue from America.[9] Secondly, the colonists held an exaggerated opinion of the part they played in Britain's political economy. The non-importation associations of the 1760s and 1770s rested on the belief that Great Britain so depended on America for supplies and markets that she could be brought to terms without a fight. Some even asserted (and the disturbances plaguing British society in these years seemed to bear them out) that the use of force against America would lead either to political revolution or to civil war and national bankruptcy. For if the colonies were indeed the principal source of Britain's wealth and power, as the parliamentary opposition continually assured them, then any attempt to subdue them forcibly would simultaneously increase the demand on the public revenue and cut into its source.[10]

A more sober view of the consequences to be expected from Britain's economic difficulties was that they would set limits on her military options that might help the Revolutionaries. If financial and political prudence led the ministry to keep down the level of forces deployed in America, the colonists could easily outnumber and defeat them.[11] If the British mounted a massive attack, they could not sustain it for more than one or two campaigns. If the Revolutionaries could only withhold a decisive victory from Britain for that short time, the day would be theirs. Therefore the colonists saw little reason to fear that the principal gains to be expected from victory, namely full title to the vast western lands and a thriving commerce freed from imperial restrictions, would not be sufficient to secure whatever public debt the war incurred. And after all, they started out debt-free.[12]

Long after the disastrous defeats of August and September 1776 the colonists still cherished these beliefs, which indeed had much to do with the decision of Washington and his staff to settle for an essentially defensive strategy. They did not have much choice, of course, given the clear superiority of the British army (supported by her navy) to the unsoldierly materials they themselves had to work with. Nevertheless, their optimism in the autumn of 1776 after the bulk of the army had safely evacuated Manhattan represented more than relief that they need no longer fear being enveloped by Howe. It sprang from their conviction that Britain could afford only one or two compaigns on the scale she attempted in 1776. Americans took heart from the little that General Howe would have to show for the huge expense of the campaign.[13] The surrender of Fort Washington and Howe's unchecked advance into New Jersey momentarily shook their confidence, but Trenton and Princeton restored it. So long as they did not risk the army in offensive action—except where it enjoyed a clear advantage or where there were compelling political reasons—so long as they used it mostly to keep hold of as much ground as possible, Britain would soon find the cost of the war disproportionate to the yield.

Looking back, we can see that the colonists deceived themselves. Britain was both richer and less dependent on her North American colonies than they thought, partly because that radical economic change which we now call the industrial revolution had already begun there. But despite their miscalculation it could still be argued that time was on their side since it did give them certain advantages in the fields of diplomacy and international relations. In 1778 France recognized the new nation and formed a defensive alliance with her, bringing Europe's largest nation into the struggle on the side of the Revolutionaries. A year later Spain joined France against Britain, and by the following year all the great maritime powers but Portugal formed a league opposing Britain's pretensions to control such neutral ships as carried strategic supplies to the belligerents. Most historians acknowledge that this expansion of Britain's war in Europe, together with her lack of allies, explains both her loss of naval supremacy in the western Atlantic during the summer of 1781 and Cornwallis's surrender at Yorktown in the following October. For the high price of two armies and seven years of war, Britain had acquired footholds in New York and Charleston, nothing more. The steady success of the Americans in keeping apparent political control over so much of the continent convinced the British that they were pursuing unreachable goals in America and paved the way for peace.[14]

*   *   *

Because all ended well, the casual observer might think the Revolutionaries vindicated in their first belief that time was on their side. But I spoke of *apparent* political control with a reason. I mean to argue that there were other, less dramatic ways than conquest or Tory insurgence in which the patriots might lose their hold over the continent. My thesis builds on the generally accepted notion that the ability of the Revolutionaries to command internal resources dropped sharply as the war went on. I agree with Arthur Bowler that it dropped to the point where, failing decisive help from France, the Revolutionaries were faced with a stalemate. But here I part company with Bowler to argue that, in certain areas at least, such a prospect worked not for America but for Britain. I suggest that far from being a friend to the revolutionary cause, time became a potential enemy. I suggest that but for a combination of extraordinary exertion and good luck in 1781 the Revolutionaries could have ended up with something that, though they might have called it independence, would not have been worth the price they had paid. And it is not impossible that as the people became ever more disillusioned with the result of their heroic sacrifice, British rule might in time have been restored.

To explain my point I must ask you to look again at how the Revolutionaries gradually lost control of the country's resources because of their economic policy. The decision of the colonies and Congress against using taxation to pay the costs of the conflict as they arose, and to issue credit instruments in the form of paper money, did not at the time seem a reckless, new departure. The eighteenth century accepted the necessity of using public credit to pay for a war. As one ministerial pamphleteer put it, only "by borrowing present capital on the credit of future interests [could] the abilities of several years" be realized in one.[15] And because paper money would enable the Revolutionary regimes to procure with the consent of the suppliers, it looked like a way to finance the war that fitted particularly well with republican objectives. Indeed, the Revolutionaries expected it to confer a military advantage. Just as the Greeks had found their own free citizens the best defense against a numerically superior Persian army of slaves, so American resources freely given would surely outdo an enemy who had to rely for half her soldiery on men whose services had been sold by foreign princes.[16] Lastly, the colonists' previous success with tax-anticipation currency also encouraged them to use it

again in the Revolution.. The colonial economy had always been sufficiently short of currency to make such issues popular and particularly in
the period after 1763, thanks to Britain's restrictive economic policies.[17]
So the revolutionary leaders felt reasonably sure that the same strategy
would work as well in 1775. Nor were they disappointed: Most people
welcomed the issues of state and continental paper at par.

Unfortunately the paper currency began to depreciate rapidly after less
than a year and a half of fighting. In the northern part of the confederacy
during the six months from October 1776 to April 1777 it lost half or more
of its value.[18] So rapid a fall reflected a decline in the demand for the bills
of credit issued by the states and Congress, a decline that has usually been
attributed to excessive supply. But this explanation fails to take into
account that paper money did not have to act as a currency. In October
1776 Congress made provision for its conversion into loan office certificates bearing 4 percent interest, and in 1777 it made the state currencies
subscribable.[19] If we commit ourselves wholly to an explanation stress-
ing the quantity of money, we would have to argue that the aggregate
emissions of the states and Congress had accumulated an unpayable debt
by October 1776. But at the end of the year the indebtedness of all the
revolutionary governments together came to no more than £13.5 million
current money. The British public debt was ten times larger—more than
ten times in effect, since current money had less value than sterling and
the ratio of debt to population was more than two-and-a-half times greater
than in America.[20] Clearly the depreciation did not spring from any
conviction that the continent had already exhausted its resources. Rather,
the decline in the demand for bills of credit was caused by other political
and economic factors.

The principal political factor, of course, was that a series of defeats
beginning in August 1776 generated doubts that the Revolution would
succeed. And since the credit instruments issued by the states and
Congress would be no good if the Revolution failed, people began to
discount the bills as a hedge against this possibility. The depreciation
occurred by common consent in the marketplace. It represented a popular
judgment not so much about America's resources as about the leadership's ability to use them effectively.[21] More than military leadership was
in question. Though most of the states had by then improvised revolutionary regimes, Congress had for several reasons neglected to place the
powers it was exercising on a formal constitutional basis. Dickinson's

draft of the Articles of Confederation had been presented to Congress on July 12 and hotly debated from the last week of July through the first week in August.[22] But Congress could not agree on certain key issues, such as the standard by which the states would divide the common charges of the continent. Reports of the sharp division between North and South about apportionment undoubtedly leaked out and contributed to the decline of the continental currency.[23]

There were equally important economic reasons. The disruption of normal commerce and the closing of state courts to private debt actions had combined to decrease the demand for currency,[24] and the state governments had little means to redress the imbalance. The best way to increase the demand for money would have been a program of taxation, but the states lacked the resolution to pursue this policy vigorously. For one thing, the objections to parliamentary taxation had so dominated revolutionary polemics before the war that the patriot leaders now wondered if the resentment they had once incited against Parliament might not rebound on their own heads. For another, the autumn of 1776 seemed a particularly bad time to press taxation. Not only had the leadership lost prestige in the battles of Long Island and New York, but also Congress had then delegated to them a matter of supreme importance demanding their full attention. Congress wanted the states to implement the congressional resolve of September 16 that a permanent army be raised for the duration rather than continuing to enlist men for short terms of service.[25]

With so much to do, the states understandably, if unfortunately, addressed the symptoms rather than the causes of the economic troubles. To ensure that goods needed by the army would be forthcoming, they passed laws against depreciating the currency, proclaimed embargoes, and decreed that those who engrossed needed supplies might lose them to seizure at fixed prices.[26] Had these laws been enforceable they would have further depressed the demand for currency. But that they proved unenforceable did nothing to halt the depreciation. Once it had begun, anyone who wanted to secure the value of currency received in the few commercial transactions still open had no choice but investment in supplies needed by the army. In other words, the depreciation that followed upon the disruption of the usual trade pattern, the exchange of agricultural surplus for foreign imports, stimulated economic activity where it was least wanted. And declaring the currency legal tender so that debtors could pay their debts in it would bring no more than a temporary increase in the demand for money, though it might make depreciation momentarily more acceptable.[27]

These developments forced those in charge of finding men and supplies for the war to face some unpleasant choices. Either they must modify their reliance on consent in the marketplace or they must yield to its demands for more and more cash. The same factors that deterred them from taxation, namely their loss of prestige and their fear of turning the people against the cause, made them shy of using coercion except as a threat to give the diminishing incentives of the marketplace greater attraction.[28] On the other hand, pumping money into the economy would only speed up depreciation by further decreasing the demand for currency while increasing the cost of goods and services needed by the army. In the end, the leadership decided that they had to opt for printing more money. This would at least allow them to carry on the war for the moment, though they knew it might lead to a disastrous dead end if they could not break the vicious cycle of depreciation. As the country mortgaged more and more of its future for less and less in the present, an unpayable debt was in the making. And the longer the war lasted, the more this danger increased. In other words, as the military prepared for a long war of attrition, the civil leadership embarked on the course that made sense only if they could bring either the war or the depreciation to a quick halt.

One strategy that the leadership might in theory have used to break the cycle of depreciation without either taxing the people or paring down the war effort was borrowing. If people could be persuaded to subscribe the money they received for goods and services to the public funds, the government could stop issuing new money and still procure with consent. But how could the leadership persuade people to lend their money when the value of the principal was depreciating while their interest would be paid in the same medium? The states had less of a problem here than Congress. State governments at least had the power to tax, though wisdom might dictate restraint in the exercise of it. And some of the states did respond to the request of Congress in 1777 that they convert their bills of credit into interest-bearing loans, considerably reducing the quantity of paper money.[29] Yet the problem remained that Congress had no power to tax and could hardly ask the states to assume the burden of interest on congressional loans when some had already agreed to pay interest on the funding of their own currencies. The commissioners in France suggested

a way out of the difficulty. In January 1777, they had obtained a
"commitment" from the French to supply the United States with an
annual subsidy of 2 million livres a year. Why not agree to pay interest in
bills of exchange on France? Wouldn't this give holders of Continental
currency a real incentive to subscribe to the congressional loan, making it
possible to halt the printing of money?[30]

Unfortunately, numerous difficulties beset this good idea. Even assuming that the French would meet their commitment, 2 million livres at
5 livres to the dollar would pay only interest on a loan of $7 million at 6
percent, the rate Congress had adopted in February 1777.[31] If the next
campaign cost no more than the last (unlikely given the rate of depreciation), that still left Congress with a projected shortfall of $12 million. The
obvious remedy would be more European loans, enabling Congress to
borrow Continental money. But unless the Americans could win some
victories to convince the world that they could support their cause against
Britain, permitting the great powers to grant the colonies recognition, and
unless they could establish a constitutional government with some claim
to a revenue and solvency, more loans from Europe were not likely.[32]
Faced with a hard campaign in 1777, Congress did nothing decisive about
the country's deteriorating finances, hoping that the British would tire of
the struggle. Burgoyne's attack from Canada and Howe's advance on
Philadelphia showed that this was unlikely. On the day before Brandywine, as much in desperation as in hope, Congress voted to pay interest
on all "loan office certificates already issued or which shall be issued"
before March 1, 1778, in bills of exchange on Paris at 6 percent.[33] Then
they compromised the differences that had previously prevented agreement on the Articles of Confederation, sending them to the states in
November.[34] And the victory at Saratoga emboldened Congress for the
first time to lay the states under requisition for $5 million.[35]

In late 1777 and 1778 circumstances favored the financial policy of
Congress more than ever before. One historian has calculated that those
taking up the offer to pay interest on nominal dollars with bills of
exchange on France would have netted 30 percent on their capital.[36] Yet
the scheme failed. This need not surprise us if we recall that bills of
exchange on France would be only as valuable as Franco-American trade
was extensive. And except for secret transactions in strategic commodities (conducted largely by Congress), Franco-American trade had
become almost nonexistent. Nor would it revive until France recognized

the United States as an independent nation, or while Britain maintained naval supremacy in the western Atlantic. Therefore, those merchants who would in peacetime have held large reserves of cash to promote the exchange of local goods for imports chose to engross commodities instead, preferring not to hold more depreciating currency than they must. Producers in the interior still held reserves of money because they needed it to discharge their debts, but they were not well placed to deal in transatlantic commerce. In the summer of 1778, news of the Franco-American alliance and the presence of a French fleet off the coast made it look for a moment as though international commerce might be about to resume. This impelled the merchants to go into cash rather than commodities,[37] which briefly halted the depreciation. But by then the loan of the preceding September had been closed.

Though Congress acknowledged that the Franco-American alliance made American independence "morally certain,"[38] it also drove the revolutionary leadership straight into the dead end they had tried to avoid since the currency first began to depreciate. The alliance intensified the dilemma of Congress about whether to scale down the war effort to what the nation could afford or to make one more extraordinary effort in the hope of ending the struggle. To mount another all-out campaign would require that Congress issue yet more bills of credit, which would further damage its ability to procure resources by consent. Before the alliance became known, Congress clearly felt disposed to try for one more Saratoga. Their willingness in March 1778 to appoint Jeremiah Wadsworth commissary-general showed this. Before accepting the office, he had made Congress understand that it must not leave him short of cash, as previous commissaries had been.[39] And word of the alliance helped Wadsworth persuade Congress to discourage state price-fixing laws that threatened his ability to procure supplies for both French and American forces in the marketplace.[40] It also distracted Congress from attending to financial matters until they were completely out of hand. By the late autumn it became clear that not only had the alliance failed to produce the decisive results hoped for, but the nominal value of the Continental debt, which had doubled in the campaign, had reached proportions that made payment at par unacceptable to a growing number of people.[41]

The change of attitude appeared most plainly in a state like Connecticut, which, because the commissary had concentrated its buying there since 1775, had acquired perhaps the biggest per capita stake in Continental currency. It had witnessed a popular movement for price regulation during the early years of the war, a taxpayers' attempt to hold down the nominal value of the debt because they assumed it would ultimately be paid at par.[42] Wadsworth's capacity to break the regulations in 1778, together with the accelerating depreciation caused by the campaign, had aroused political hostility to funding the debt at par; the radical appreciation of the currency that must ensue might beggar large numbers of people. In the late autumn of 1778, when Congress at last faced up to the financial mess, it found new impediments to its freedom of movement. Until then, it had seemed as if Congress could not act too strongly in matters concerning fiscal responsibility. But now it dared aim for no more than halting the depreciation: a policy that went beyond this to start an appreciation ran the risk of backfiring.[43] In its anxiety not to do too much, Congress fell short of the mark. It proposed a plan that put taxation second and that relied mostly on an attempt to draw into the loan office $41.5 million in paper money by canceling the notes emitted between May 1777 and September 1778.[44] Congress explained that the British had counterfeited them, but that was hardly a reasonable excuse, for the enemy had worked from the start to discredit all Continental currency. Congress would have liked to do as some states did in 1777: force the exchange of currency for loan office certificates; but not feeling sufficiently confident, the lawmakers gave the people the option of exchanging them for newer emissions of currency.[45]

It soon became clear that most people preferred exchanging old issues for new currency rather than for loan office certificates. Furthermore the ineffectiveness of the measures Congress had taken seemed partly responsible for the dizzy spiral of depreciation in the Middle Atlantic states in the spring of 1779. Faced with popular unrest in Philadelphia, which led to the formation of popular committees to protect people against the currency's impending fall, Congress took desperate measures:[46] on May 21 it added a $45 million requisition to the $15 million requisition that had accompanied the earlier attempt to withdraw $41.5 million in emissions.[47] The demand for $60 million from the states by the end of the year, together with a grass-roots committee movement that spread northward from Philadelphia in mid-1779, did check the depreciation for the moment. In those jurisdictions that looked as though they would comply, the currency even rose slightly in value.[48] Connecticut tried to comply immediately with the requisitions of January and May, levying 27 shillings on the pound in taxes. This brought the total taxes due to the state in 1779 to 31 shillings and 7 pence, an almost sevenfold increment over the previous year.[49] Such action certainly should have revived the demand for Continental money, eventually permitting the Continental commissariat to use it more effectively in buying supplies. Unfortunately, it did not.

In 1778 a complex series of events produced a grain shortage of crisis proportions. Indian raids on northwestern farms, Hessian fly in the Middle Atlantic and South, problems with transporting wheat surpluses from south to northeast—all contributed.[50] But the major cause was the concentration of four armies east of the Hudson from July to November 1778: Washington's at Westchester, Sullivan's at Rhode Island, Burgoyne's in Massachusetts, and D'Estaing's expeditionary force at Boston. The prospect of joint operations with the French had swelled Sullivan's ranks, and Burgoyne's Convention army included the militia necessary to guard it. D'Estaing's refitting in Boston from September to November demanded a region that had long ceased to be self-sufficient for grain supply to requisition not only present necessities but also provisions to last through a proposed West Indian foray.[51] Washington's army could live off supplies brought in from west of the Hudson, but even then there remained three armies—plus the civilian population of eastern New England—scrambling for the few surpluses that did exist between the Connecticut and the Hudson rivers.

Sullivan's army in Rhode Island suffered most. Even the civilians living on the Massachusetts coast, who in losing the fisheries had lost their livelihood, did better than his men, for they, after all, could usually barter salt for grain along the Connecticut coast.[52] But Sullivan had to depend on the commissary, and the comissary found it virtually impossible to compete with French agents and Convention army buyers. They had specie or its equivalent to offer; Sullivan could pay only in a depreciating currency. Producers under contract to the commissariat either openly broke contracts or demanded prices so high that commissary agents, starved for cash by Congress, could not deliver on time.[53] In the end, to compete in the marketplace, Wadsworth's agents sometimes had to barter salt, imported for packing meat, in exchange for flour.[54] They could justify this only as a temporary expedient since it cut directly into the supply of salt meat, but they assumed that the crisis would soon be over. Congress was thinking of moving the Convention army from Massachusetts to Virginia, while the French would presumably sail for the West Indies before ice closed off the port of Boston.[55] And in fact both the Convention army and D'Estaing did leave New England in November.

Unfortunately their departure did not help much. Though it was more convenient to have the Convention army in Virginia, aggregate demand on Continental supplies did not diminish. In the spring some new developments even increased it: French agents resumed buying for D'Estaing's fleet in the Middle Atlantic states so that it would not have to return to France for revictualing;[56] an expedition against the Iroquois mounted during the summer of 1779 drew on provisions from the western regions;[57] and Massachusetts organized an expedition on her own authority to attack the positions recently established by the British in the Penobscott area.[58] But supply did not rise to meet demand as might have been expected, given the relative decline in military activity after September 1778 (except on the western frontier).[59] British depredations in the Virginia tidewater and along the Connecticut coast during the spring and summer of 1779[60] had less effect than the fact that farmers found the prospect of payment in a fast-depreciating currency no inducement to increase production. By 1779, only the promise of payment in wanted commodities like salt, West India goods, and European dry goods could have stimulated production. The farmers knew that for three years these items had been too scarce to make this likely,[61] so they had no inducement at all either to produce more or to sell what they already had produced.[62]

The grain crisis continued through 1779 until the ability to buy farm produce passed more and more exclusively to those who had what farmers wanted in exchange. In New England these were the merchants who had helped refit the French fleet during the previous autumn and had used the proceeds to buy salt, sugar, and dry goods form the West Indies during the winter. This windfall in commodities, increased by successful privateering,[63] enabled Massachusetts to mount the Penobscott expedition in July. And not even the fiasco that followed could deprive the Boston area of its commercial advantage. At the end of the summer, privateers brought in no less than nine rich prizes from the Jamaica fleet with an estimated £5 million in salt and sugar on board.[64] The possession of such highly valued goods gave eastern Massachusetts the ability to pay outrageous prices far beyond the commissariat's reach,[65] which in turn enabled middlemen to outbid commissary agents in the interior as the French and British agents has outbid them in 1778.

The commissariat had only two options. First, it could continue a course it had thought temporary, of paying for produce in the salt the farmers wanted. Because salt importations on public account in New England had succeeded unusually well early in 1779,[66] the commissariat could more easily barter salt for flour that summer than in the preceding autumn, on the eve of the meat-packing season.[67] On the other hand, barter on so large a scale meant even less demand for currency, which would cause greater depreciation and also threaten to exchange one shortage for another. If the salt for packing meat in autumn were sold in summer to buy grain, the commissaries might later find it impossible to replace on reasonable terms. British cruisers and the weather would more likely disrupt salt imports in the second half of the year than in the first.[68]

There remained one other possible course: to ask that the legislatures exercise control over the market so that eastern Massachusetts would cease to gain at the expense of the commissariat. But this strategy, too, posed problems. So long as Massachusetts hankered to pursue the Penobscott adventure, the states would not pass uniform regulations. In April the commissariat did persuade the Connecticut legislature to enact a law requiring the selectmen of each town to take a census of grain and forbidding anyone to sell a surplus except to public agents. But before the selectmen could complete the census, word of the law leaked out and large surpluses disappeared over the border to Massachusetts.[69] The unpopularity of such attempts to resist the operations of market forces almost always made them unenforceable. If Connecticut had tried to apply the grain census law to the summer harvest of 1779, farmers would probably have refused to thresh any more grain than they needed for their personal use.[70] New York tried to circumvent this problem by passing a law requiring farmers to deliver an assessed quota of grain and peas, but the assessors succumbed to local pressure and returned ridiculously low figures.[71] Laws empowering local officials to seize at the behest of the commissariat suffered a similar fate.[72]

In this unpromising situation, the enormous requisition of May 21, 1779, did not succeed in restoring the currency as a circulating medium. In states like Connecticut, when it became known that the government would comply with the requisition, the prospect of such heavy taxes brought the exchange of "commodities in general" to a temporary halt. Instead of selling, farmers "alarmed about [the] rates" because they supposed "all the cash they can obtain will be required for public demands" held on to their produce.[73] At the same time, popular committees to regulate prices began to form in imitation of those that had earlier appeared in Philadelphia. In the context of the radical depreciation that preceded them, the committees looked to some like a people's movement to defend the currency,[74] but in fact they were as much inspired by a fear that the new taxes would cause a radical appreciation.[75] Grass-roots opposition to appreciating the currency, added to the prevailing commodity shortages, meant that most people wanted no more money than they had to have for paying taxes. Therefore the requisition of May 21, far from restoring a money economy, confirmed it as a barter system.[76]

Currency never quite stopped circulating in 1779, though it became progressively more restricted in its uses. Long after it had failed in most other respects, currency continued to pass in sales of livestock because, between limited pasture and the cost of replenishing depleted herds, farmers had to keep moving one generation of stock off the land to make room for the next.[77] Currency also circulated longer in the interior.[78] Producers there, always chronically in debt to the seacoast, overvalued liquidity, and bartering cost more than it did in the densely settled commercial areas. Nevertheless, by the end of 1779 the currency had collapsed in the northern half of the confederacy for virtually all purposes but the payment of taxes and speculation.[79] Virginia managed to maintain the Continental money and its own currency longer than the other states by accepting it in payment for lands, but at grotesque rates of depreciation.[80]

With the currency went most of the revolutionary governments' power to procure with consent in the marketplace, leaving them no choice but forced procurement. In a healthy economy taxation is the fairest method of forced procurement because it allows each person to meet his obligations in the way that hurts him least, that is, through an exchange in the marketplace. It also gives the government a chance to maximize its assets by procuring goods in the marketplace when and as it needs them. But with exchange reduced to barter, Congress and the states had only two options. They could tax in kind, giving people some choice of the medium of payment; such a policy had the disadvantage that it could exacerbate shortages and gluts. Or they could attempt to reconstitute the marketplace by creating a new medium of exchange. Congress tried this in March 1780, giving the states an incentive to retire the old currency by authorizing them to issue a new one against it at a rate of twenty to one.[81] Though the new notes were supposed to be backed by state taxes that would pay the interest on them, paper money had become so discredited that the new emission depreciated almost as quickly as the old. To sustain the volume of bills of credit, interest had to be payable in specie or its equivalents, and no state as yet had this capacity, despite the benefits derived from French military purchasing in America.

As a result, between the autumn of 1779 and the summer of 1781 the war effort ground almost to a halt. Mobile detachments could still live off the land; Nathanael Greene managed to raise and maintain a small force to defend the South against British incursions during this period. But the lack of a sound currency hampered him and, although he succeeded in turning his weakness into a strength, his strategy remained as fundamentally defensive as Lafayette's in Virginia.[82] Washington, who had to maintain a much larger army to match the concentration of British forces in New York, squandered most of his energies on keeping the army together despite recurrent shortages, shortages that did eventually help to precipitate the mutinies of January 1781. In such circumstances, as Weigley observes, Washington could not consider offensive action. Yet so long as American commanders could deny the British army a political hold in the interior, one might argue that the stalemate worked to American advantage. After all, it still cost Britain more to maintain enormous overseas forces, with little so far to show for themselves, than it cost the Revolutionaries to bide their time until the subsidies and forces expected from France arrived. Those who ask, ''How could Britain have won,'' would certainly so value the years of stalemate.

I hope to challenge this approach through my analysis of the depreciation, which points up the high value attached to commodities in the American economy as the currency failed. The commissariat's disadvantage in competing with the French and the Massachusetts Board of War in 1779 suggests that the British could also exploit the stalemate since they had the goods that Americans wanted. The analogy is not perfect in that every state outlawed trade with the enemy. But, as earlier laws passed to help the commissary demonstrated, it is one thing to enact a law, another to enforce it. The army could not intervene to help. The small size of Washington's force and the nature of eighteenth-century firepower made it impossible to hold extended lines. If Washington had dispersed his men around an enemy stronghold like New York in an effort to stop illicit trading, the British could have picked them off a few at a time.[83] And the states resolutely refused to pass the one kind of law that Washington and Congress thought might stop it, a law making such trade a capital crime.[84]

Because those on both sides had an interest in keeping the traffic concealed, there is little hard evidence of its nature and extent. But one can say a few things about it with confidence. As the currency depreciated and the revolutionary regimes gradually lost the power to procure with consent, the attractions of the illicit trade increased. Connecticut authorities became aware of it early in 1777, and by 1778 they suspected that it had grown great enough to help cause the area's commodity shortages.[85] As the war went on, more and more evidence accumulated that supplies from the patriot interior contributed to stocking the public markets of New York. The reports from spies on provision prices in the city and the suspicious concentrations of stock that appeared along the seacoast and southwestern frontiers of Connecticut formed part of this body of evidence.[86] The town officials of Greenwich even claimed to see a direct correlation between New York prices and the strength of forces stationed there.[87] The flow of supplies to New York does not seem to have freed the British army from the necessity of importing most of its provisions, and indeed Commissary Weir's superiors clearly thought it cheaper to do so![88] But on occasion, particularly in the autumn of 1778, Weir bought in local markets partly supplied from the patriot interior in order to guard against the danger that the enemy might intercept the fleet of victuallers.[89]

The scope of the illicit trade extended beyond supplying the New York market and occasionally the British army. The enemy possessed one asset equal in value to salt. Deprived since 1775 of British dry goods, Americans had come to crave them, and neither trade with the French islands nor privateering had done much to put them back on the American market. Madison acknowledged their powerful lure in his response to a rumor early in 1781 that the ministry was considering "a trade with us in British goods of every kind except Linens and Woolens." "Such a plan,'' he said, ''would open fine prospects to them in a private view.''[90] And some evidence exists that, beginning in 1780, the British promoted the trade at least in the sense of permitting it. Some British exports to the United States—and especially those suited to the illicit trade, such as glass, earthenware, wrought silk, and printed cotton—rose most sharply not after 1783, as would be expected, but after 1779.[91]

Besides obtaining certain necessaries, the British achieved three objectives through the trade in dry goods. First, it raised tensions between France and the United States by showing the French quite plainly that they could never hope to take the place held by British manufactures in our economy.[92] Secondly, it drained the confederacy of what little specie had accumulated from French subsidies, French military procurement, and minor capital flows in response to market conditions.[93] This jeopardized Robert Morris's efforts to establish a credible currency; and so long as Americans lacked a credible currency, they could not revive the war effort to the level achieved from 1775 to 1777, when the consent mechanisms of the marketplace still functioned. During 1782, in fact, Morris found himself unable to do more than maintain Washington's army in a state of graceful inactivity.[94] Third and worst of all, the illicit trade helped to demoralize the revolutionary regimes by forcing them to wage war against their own citizens in order to control it.

Nowhere was this more evident than in Connecticut. The vulnerability of her coastline and southwestern frontier to enemy raids—raids often led by former residents turned loyalist—gradually drove patriots away and left these areas to those disposed to collaborate. As a result, local officials charged with enforcing the laws increasingly protested that they could not possibly stop the trade without large contingents of militia that the state could ill afford to send.[95] By 1781 the situation had become so serious that when Connecticut's government learned the British were stockpiling dry goods the length and breadth of Long Island, it commissioned their seizure.[96] When Governor Clinton of New York protested, Trumbull defended the action by alleging the existence of ''a plan systematically laid'' to introduce British goods into Connecticut. In this manner, he said, the British hoped to give ''inimical, evil & artful men'' the power ''to catch hold of the avarice, luxury, pride and vanity of some persons who are designing and others who are unwary.'' Trumbull feared that economic temptation coupled with the recent proclamation by Clinton and Arbuthnot inviting people within the revolutionary governments to form loyalist associations would undermine what little political control of her frontier Connecticut had left.[97]

The government's failure to stop the illicit trade created a political climate in which no one trusted anyone else. Those caught engaging in the traffic would often implicate those enforcing the laws as well, not always without cause.[98] Some accusations proved true, sometimes because an officer had used the trade for intelligence purposes,[99] but on occasion simply because law enforcement officials had indeed succumbed to temptation.[100] Unfortunately, because it seemed all too likely that someone who could share in the gains would soon abandon principle and do so, such charges often rang true when they were not. Even Trumbull, after ten years of election by popular majorities to the governorship of Connecticut, found himself whispered out of office by a rumor that he had traded with the enemy. In 1782 the legislature succeeded in blunting the force of the rumor by releasing a report exonerating him just before the election. But in 1780, 1781, and 1783 they could maintain him in office only by electing him themselves.[101]

One incident in particular reveals the damage that the illicit trade did to Connecticut politics. In 1782 Richard Smith, a former Connecticut resident who had spent most of the war in Britain, applied to the government for readmission. In January 1783, after censuring one Moses Seymour of Hartford for circulating the rumor that Smith had paid Trumbull a bribe of 100 guineas, the legislature granted Smith's request.[102] A Hartford town meeting immediately protested the action as inconsistent with state laws against trading with the enemy, and an invitation to everyone in British-held territory "to double at once the whole amount of their property by bringing into the State, any quantity of British Goods they may think proper to call their own."[103] When Smith tried to bring his effects across the sound from Long Island to New London, an armed vessel part-owned by Thomas Mumford seized them six miles out and carried them into Rhode Island. Mumford and his associates, who undoubtedly saw themselves as upholding the spirit of the law against trading with the enemy, intended to libel the cargo in the maritime courts as illegal British imports. Supporters of Smith retook the vessel while she rode at anchor in Rhode Island waters and brought her back to New London, where Trumbull intervened to secure her against legal action. Mumford then publicly accused Trumbull of misusing his authority in an attempt to protect Smith's property beyond Connecticut's jurisdiction.[104] Mumford had held many important posts in Connecticut's revolutionary government, including a recent term on the Council of Safety, and he and Trumbull had worked closely together through much of the war. For these two men to have ended up in such conflict showed that the basic trust necessary for any political system to work had indeed reached the verge of collapse.

One can try to dismiss the effect of the illicit trade on Connecticut politics as unique to that state. Only Connecticut had a sheltered, tidal shoreline 618 miles long and contiguous to Long Island and New York,[105] an invitation to smugglers. One can try to term it insignificant, since the leadership did survive, though only because peace came in time. But what if Yorktown had not happened? What if France had lost interest in supporting the costly struggle? Without French naval power could the United States ever have dislodged the British from strong points like New York, Charleston, and perhaps Portsmouth, Virginia? Would the illicit trade then have affected many other states, damaging the prestige of their revolutionary regimes and causing either their collapse or their accommodation with Great Britain? Connecticut's experience strongly suggests the possibility. The revolutionary leadership saw this, too:[106] it goaded them on to heroic exertion at Yorktown. Fortunately good luck and the help of France, who wanted something to show for her efforts, led to Cornwallis's surrender. Otherwise the only force that might have saved Americans from stalemate would have been intervention by the British people against their government's policy. And would they have intervened if Britons had continued to enjoy a growing commerce with America in spite of the revolutionary governments? They would surely have concluded that time had become an enemy to the Revolution and that they need only wait.

9

THE RELATIONSHIP BETWEEN THE REVOLUTIONARY WAR AND EUROPEAN MILITARY THOUGHT AND PRACTICE IN THE SECOND HALF OF THE EIGHTEENTH CENTURY

Peter Paret

What I should like to do in this paper is to compare the war in America with other conflicts of the period, to consider these wars as discrete military episodes—separate entities that combine into a broad stream of military experience—and to ask what these wars attempted to do, how they went about doing it, and how we might characterize the relationship between effort and achievement in each. By comparing the Revolutionary War with other conflicts, we not only fit it more accurately into the overall picture of eighteenth-century warfare, but we may also come to understand some of its unique phenomena more clearly than we would if we were to immerse ourselves in its particulars to the exclusion of what soldiers and governments were doing elsewhere.

Let me begin with two statements that in one form or another pervade the literature: First, in essential respects the Revolutionary War differed from other wars of the period; and, second, the elements that differentiated it from other conflicts were of seminal significance—that is, the Revolutionary War, at least as it was fought on the American side, pointed toward the future. Don Higginbotham, in his book *The War of American Independence,* expressed the idea in this way: ''The American

Revolution did more than prove the validity of Enlightenment ideals; it ushered in yet another revolution—in the aims and nature of warfare."[1] It should be added that the passage in which this statement occurs contrasts wars waged by mercenaries for aims to which they are indifferent—dynastic or state policy—with wars fought by patriots, defending, in Washington's words, "all that is dear and valuable in life." Another scholar, the English historian Piers Mackesy, in his book *The War for America* states that "the struggle that opened at Lexington was the last great war of the *ancien régime.*"[2] That sounds like a contradiction of Higginbotham's statements; but it need not be one. Mackesy may be saying that Great Britain fought the war in a traditional manner, or perhaps he uses the term *ancien régime* not to characterize behavior but to define a period of time—as a synonym for the eighteenth century before the French Revolution. He continues with a statement that certainly seems to be in complete accord with Higginbotham's view: "In the American War there first appeared the fearful spectacle of a nation in arms." But the second part of his sentence immediately qualifies and restricts this assertion: "In the American War there first appeared the fearful spectacle of a nation in arms; and the *odium theologicum*" (which, for our purposes, we might translate as the "bane of ideology") "which had been banished from warfare for a century returned to distress the nations." I don't mean to go on with textual analyses of recent scholarship; I have cited these passages from two admirable works simply to illustrate the difficulty historians face in bringing out the particularity of a specific event while giving an accurate account of its larger context. And furthermore, the second half of Mackesy's sentence points to a not unimportant analytic failing that is frequently encountered in the literature on the American Revolution. Mackesy rightly observes that the bane of ideology, which had been banished for a century, returned. That is, ideologically motivated war, in which many of the participants even at the lowest levels are emotionally involved—rather than detached impassive professionals—was not introduced at Lexington, but *re*introduced.

That suggests that the Revolutionary War should be compared to the European military experience of the seventeenth, rather than of the eighteenth, century: to the Dutch struggle for independence; to certain phases of the Thirty Years' War; to the English Civil War. It might be useful to resist the tendency of bracketing the Revolutionary War with the conflicts of the mid-eighteenth century, a time when Europe had temporarily shed the *odium theologicum,* when many states had achieved relative political stability, and when the European community had devised a nonideological balance-of-power system as the basis for its international relations. Political development proceeded at different rates of speed on the two sides of the Atlantic; and rather than contrast the military behavior of an emerging nation with those of developed states, it might be more appropriate to compare the Revolutionary War with some seventeenth-century episodes and then perhaps compare the Mexican War, which was hardly waged "for everything that is dear and valuable in life," with the War of the Austrian Succession or with some other eighteenth-century attempt at territorial aggrandizement. I am not suggesting that we disregard differences in time in favor of constructing historically disembodied models of civil and military behavior. The passage of time and the uniqueness of the specific event must always be the first determinants of historical analysis; but I do want to raise the question whether comparisons should be based solely on proximity in time or whether stages of social, ideological, and political development should not be taken into account as well.

Let me return once more, briefly, to the statements quoted above in order to trace one or two of their implications further. It is, of course, true that European armies in the eighteenth century were essentially mercenary and professional in character—at least so far as the rank and file are concerned. But many—including the Prussian, Austrian, and Russian armies—were in fact made up of a mix of mercenaries, who might be foreign or native volunteers, and of native conscripts.[3] Certainly the Prussian conscript or the Austrian Grenzer was not a free citizen who fought for a policy that he understood or in some manner identified with: he was a peasant, more likely than not illiterate, who was forcibly enrolled. But there can be no question that he was not only motivated by compulsion and, after a period of service, by *esprit de corps* but also by loyalty to his local environment—the patriarchal conditions of his existence—and by a regional patriotism. Soldiers may not yet have been conscious of fighting for a nation—Frederick the Great's grenadiers thought of themselves as Pomeranians, Silesians, men of the Mark Brandenburg, rather than as Prussians; their peers across the Rhine may already have dimly sensed that beyond their native Normandy or Poitou there was a more comprehensive abstraction called France—but everywhere in Europe the idea of nation was announcing itself, and here and there it was already cracking the shell of the absolute monarchy and of corporate society. Governments and commanders employed the concept of nation to justify their actions, appealed to their men in its name, and in turn were influenced by it. The military institutions of eighteenth-century Europe contained within their native cadres the seed of the future nation in arms.

But just as we cannot regard the armies of the *ancien régime* simply as institutions of uninvolved mercenaries, so we should not assume that the military future belongs wholly to the nation in arms. Once more we must ask what time frame should contain our analysis. Fifty years ago it was easier than it is today to view modern history as a process toward the nation-state and the nation in arms. Now, with separatist movements at work in such ancient political entities as Great Britain and Spain and with the emergence of new multinational empires, we can no longer be quite so certain. And even in the early stages of the process that may now have passed its peak, the trend was far from uniform. In the wars of the French Revolution and of the Napoleonic Age we can, on the one hand, point to what might be called the "sentiment of military nationalism" in the French armies and at least to the force of military patriotism—if not yet nationalism—in the reformed Prussian army and the modernized Austrian army, though to a lesser extent. But such developments scarcely affected the rank and file of the British and Russian armies, which do not differ radically from their eighteenth-century predecessors. The English and German professionals who were defeated in America decisively beat the Grande Armée and the *Grande Nation* in Spain and at Waterloo three decades later. The European military future was mixed; and so, of course, was that of the United States.

I have made these comments, which go over familiar ground, merely to suggest the kind of evidence that ought to be considered when we try to fit the Revolutionary War into its historical environment—that is, place it among the wars that immediately precede and follow it. When we come to analyze the war in America as one conflict among several, we will find it useful to divide our inquiry into two parts: first we must take a closer look at the hypothesis of the war's seminal nature, which on the one hand refers to motivation and organization. Having sorted out the matter of influence, we should then consider some other elements in the war—

number of men involved, size of the theater of operations, the relationship between effort and goal—and compare these with analogous factors
in the three major wars that were waged in Europe between 1756 and the
1790s.

To begin with: motivation. The politico-military characteristics of the
Revolutionary War find no parallel in eighteenth-century Europe. Part
civil war, part struggle against an external opponent, the conflict was
waged by a political authority organized as an assembly representing
states that possessed by themselves a measure of sovereignty. Its army
was composed of state militias and of a central force, the Continental
army, originally made up of volunteers enlisting for varying periods of
time but soon enrolling some men through a compulsory quota system,
which, however, accommodated a range of exemptions. Except for the
ill-conceived Canadian expedition, the policy of the Revolutionaries was
one of enduring, of maintaining an independent political authority and an
armed force in being, regardless of territorial losses. In this they succeeded magnificently; but it is equally impressive that in the course of the
war they consolidated the political resources of their society and created a
new system of government.

Nothing similar can be found in Europe in the hundred years preceding
Lexington: "A revolutionary struggle which involved an armed insur-
gent population was unique in the memory of the age."[4] And, indeed, a
significant element of American resistance consisted not in regular operations but in thousands of episodes of civil disobedience and active
opposition throughout the vast area of the thirteen states—what we today
mean when we use the term "revolutionary warfare" in a generic sense.[5]
And it was entirely appropriate that as a counterstrategy the British
repeatedly chose a policy of pacification—long-range penetrations,
breakup of the rebel infrastructure, reestablishment of a loyal administration and society.

But the War of American Independence was not only highly innovative
in its political features, it was also unique in the sense that it did not set a
trend. It inspired some Europeans, but it was not a model that European
societies followed. The political and military upheavals of the age of the
French Revolution and of Napoleon contained nothing like it. The French
Revolution itself was from the start a highly centralized movement whose
task was not to create a new nation, but to replace one social system and
ideology with another and a relatively inefficient system of centralized

government with a stronger one. After a brief transitional period its military institutions, too, progressed from a lower to a higher level of standardization and uniformity and fought in support of policies that almost immediately changed from the defense of the Revolution to aggressive national expansion on the order of Louis XIV's assault on the balance of power.

Other revolutionary movements, such as the Polish insurrection of 1794, followed a different pattern: they neither possessed America's relative social homogeneity, her economic and diplomatic resources, or her strong, yet flexible, political traditions, nor were they able to pursue a strategy of delay and attrition because of the size of their territories and the distance separating them from the enemy base. The occupation of one or two of their urban centers meant the end of the struggle. Nor, finally, can we trace similarities in the popular movements against French imperialism during the second half of Napoleon's reign. Resistance in Spain, in the Tyrol, in Russia was characterized not by democratic tendencies but by traditional loyalties and hatred of the foreigner. In 1823 the Spanish peasant, who had helped make life unbearable for the French between 1808 and 1813, welcomed a French expeditionary force, which occupied Madrid with the blessing of the other major powers and overthrew the constitutional, mildly liberal, anticlerical system that had gained power by a coup d'état.

Probably the closest European parallel to the American Revolutionary War was provided by the anti-revolutionary movements in France during 1793 and 1794: the insurrection of Lyon, that of Toulon, and the uprising in the Vendée.[6] These were true armed insurrections, incorporating a significant proportion of the population, fighting for such traditional liberties as freedom of worship and freedom from conscription against the double tyranny of centralization and a hostile, activist ideology. The comparison doesn't bear too much weight, but in passing let me refer to the difficulties England experienced in supporting her allies in the French civil war of the 1790s. The troubled course of naval operations off Toulon and in Quiberon Bay, both relatively near to major British bases, suggests that waging a war across the Atlantic posed almost insuperable obstacles to the command structure and technology of the period and to the social and economic preconceptions on which all eighteenth-century logistic systems were based.[7]

Let me now turn to the area of tactics and of operational organization.

The view that in the Revolution Americans pioneered a new type of warfare that influenced the next generation of European soldiers, once widely accepted among American historians, is no longer tenable today.[8] Again we must look both at what came before and what followed the Revolutionary War. The assertion of American tactical and operational innovation rests almost entirely on the issue of infantry tactics. But it is a misconception to hold that eighteenth-century armies fought only in tightly packed linear formations. Since the beginning of the century each major force had units trained for reconnaissance—and combat patrols, raids, ambushes, outposts—for the so-called war of detachments, or the little war, and the relative proportion of these units increased in each generation. A crucial element of the military revolution that occurred in the 1790s was the fusion of these specialists of the light service with specialists of the line, the heavy infantry, so that henceforth at least in some armies—first in the French, then particularly in the Prussian army—the same men could fight in line, fire volleys, form attack columns, and skirmish. Integrated infantry tactics were not the result of American stimulus, but a development that occurred throughout. It might be added that rifles were introduced as military equipment in the middle of the eighteenth century in Europe. Elite light infantry units, *Jäger,* in the Prussian and Hessian services were armed with rifles and acted as tactical models for other light infantry, equipped with the cheaper and in some respects more efficient smoothbore musket. Here too the campaigns in America at most confirmed a trend that was already well under way.

Infantry tactics were only one area of war that saw significant development at the end of the *ancien régime.* Leaving aside the introduction of universal conscription in some societies, we see at least four other vital changes that occurred to varying extent in the European services. Army structure was recast into divisions or brigades, relatively self-sufficient, standardized operational commands. In 1812, for instance, the reformed Prussian field army consisted of six brigades, each of which permanently combined two infantry regiments, a grenadier battalion, three cavalry regiments, engineer, supply, and reserve units, and a small staff. Restrictions imposed by France and the poverty of the state prevented the organization of artillery and light infantry units in sufficient number to permit their permanent integration in the brigade structure; they were assigned according to operational needs. But basically the former haphazard assemblage of regiments and battalions into ad hoc commands, whose composition was constantly changing, had given way to permanently integrated combat groups, whose components had learned to work together and which, as a whole, could be part of the line of battle one day and perform an independent mission the next. The gain in flexibility and rapidity of operations, as well as in their more securely articulated overall control, is obvious.

Second, the traditional system of fixed supply-points was modified in favor of greater logistic flexibility. Third, artillery was made more mobile and powerful, the number of guns was increased, and new tactics were evolved to exploit the army's new potential. Finally, the Napoleonic period witnessed significant changes in strategic doctrine. They were made possible by some of the developments just mentioned—the division organization, for instance, and the development of a more comprehensive and authoritative general staff. The essential characteristics of the new strategic style—which, of course, was by no means universally understood or followed—may be summarized as speed, the effectively coordinated action of sometimes widely separated commands, and a greater readiness to risk battle—a belief that destroying an army might bring greater advantages than outmaneuvering it.

The war in America contributed little or nothing to these developments. There is no evidence of standardized divisional organization on either side, though it can be argued that independent commands, which were more significant than in Europe, point in that direction. In logistics, too, the war in America taught the use of improvisation. On the other hand, the scarcity of roads and the great expanse of the theater of war increased the value of depots and forts. So far as artillery goes, overseas influence on its design, manufacture, and tactics did not exist. Finally, operations in America were not distinguished from wars on the Continent by greater speed or a more urgent insistence on physical decision. They did, however, include coordinated actions of a kind that had no true parallel in central Europe. An extensive strategic pattern such as that formed by British operations in 1777 was determined by geographic factors and the location of bases to which no equivalents existed in Europe; nevertheless it might be interpreted as a harbinger of the coming cooperation of divisions and army corps. But on the generation of commanders of the Revolution and the Napoleonic Age, who were brought up on the campaigns of Maurice de Saxe and Frederick, the American campaigns made little impression. In the military education of

Napoleon they appear not to have figured at all. And in general that holds true of every military aspect of the war in America. The war does not figure prominently in the professional literature of the 1780s and 1790s. Even the numerous publications that now deal with the little war, partisan warfare, or the war of detachments rarely draw on American experiences; most of their tactical examples are taken from the Seven Years' War and, after 1792, from the Wars of the French Revolution.

If this still seems surprising, it may be useful to ask what the concept of influence can and cannot mean in relation to our subject. Similarities of doctrine, equipment, actions need not be the result of one society or army learning from another; they may be determined by attitudes general to the times or by its technology. The point might become clearer if we reverse the direction that influence is conventionally assumed to have taken in the Revolutionary War and look at instances of Americans referring to European patterns. I suppose that the adopting of Steuben's simplified drill could be interpreted as exerting a Prussian influence on the Continental army; but really all that is at work here is a commonsense response to fundamental conditions imposed by the basic infantry weapon of the time, the smoothbore musket, which requires volleys—in short, linear formations—to be effective. For Washington to be concerned about precedence in the order of battle, about ceremonial, the correct manner of mounting guard in camp, and other paraphernalia associated with the forces of European absolutism is no more than to think in the common military idiom of his generation—and perhaps also to respond, as leaders of revolutionary forces often do respond, to the attraction of regularization, of demonstrating of one's legitimacy by appearing as much like the enemy as possible. Similarly, for Washington to read Bland's *Treatise on Military Discipline* and Guibert's *Essai général,* and to be stimulated by these works to think about organizational and tactical issues in his command and reach his own conclusions, is not to become a link in a chain of influence—especially since these authors had nothing startlingly new to say to him. On the other hand, if Wellington had chosen the Battle of the Cowpens as model for a new defensive doctrine, or if Scharnhorst had based the training of Prussian skirmishers on American patterns, we could realistically speak of an American influence on Europe.

To have meaning in our context, "influence" must be a process leading to the adoption of something significantly different from prevailing ideas or methods. It must mean more than similar actions determined

by common economic and technological conditions and more than the
gradual accretion of professional expertise. Every war, after all, affords
lessons; they may be the result of observing one's own forces at work and
of recognizing that this or that aspect could be improved—logistic ar-
rangements, promotion policies, for example—or they may be learned
from the enemy, which in the Revolutionary War could mean no more
than confirmation of matters that were already known. But this process of
experience and of learning, which certainly occurred on both sides, has
no relation to the hypothesis that Americans fighting for their independence necessarily fought in a manner different from that of traditional
European societies and that subsequently these societies adopted the
more modern style of the patriots. To sum up, European armies acquired
very little that was new to them from the American War—in some areas
because social and political conditions differed too greatly and remained
too dissimilar, even after the French Revolution, to make borrowings
possible; in others because every European army already contained
significant innovative elements, which enabled each service to adapt—
sometimes with great reluctance—to new military challenges.

Let me now proceed to the second and final part of our analysis: a
comparison of numbers of men involved, size of the theater of operations, and the relationship between aim and achievement in the Revolutionary War and the three major European wars of the second half of
the eighteenth century. No more than the most fragmentary outline of the
opening phases of these conflicts can be given here, but even that may
prove enlightening. While I trace events in Europe, the reader may want
to keep in mind the first stages of the war in America, beginning with the
engagements in April 1775 between 4,000 patriots and 1,800 British
troops at Lexington and Concord and during the British return to Charleston. On May 10, Fort Ticonderoga surrendered. Five weeks later the
Battle of Bunker Hill was fought between 2,000 patriots and 2,500
British soldiers; after this no significant confrontation between land
forces occurred until November, when the British surrendered their post
at St. Johns in Canada.

When we consider the outbreak of the Seven Years' War, we must first
of all dismiss the common half-truth that wars in the eighteenth century
were always limited wars. That belief is due in large part to a failure of
clearly distinguishing methods of fighting and reasons for fighting and

also to the tendency of forgetting that "limited," "unlimited," and "total" are relative terms. Total war meant something quite different in 1812 from what it was to mean in 1917, let alone in 1944. Actually these terms are not very useful as analytic devices unless they are combined with a study of the relationship between effort and aim. It would certainly be difficult to interpret the Seven Years' War as a limited war. The aim of the anti-Prussian alliance was to destroy Prussia as the second major power in Central Europe, which, though not the same as destroying her altogether, is far more than depriving her of some relatively insignificant territory.[9] Prussia's aim was the maintenance of the status quo, and the method that Frederick employed to achieve it was a preventive attack. Between June and August 1756 he mobilized a field army of 120,000 men. On August 29 he invaded Saxony, the weakest member of the hostile alliance. On October 1 the opening battle of the war was fought between 28,000 Prussians and 33,000 Austrians, resulting in a Prussian victory at a cost to both sides of some 5,600 casualties. Two weeks later 18,000 Saxons surrendered to Prussian forces. The main result of the campaign was that Frederick gained Saxony as an operational base for the war. During the winter he increased his army to 180,000 and the following April opened the new campaign in a theater of operations about the size of Massachusetts.

In contrast to the Seven Years' War, the second conflict in our sample, the War of the Bavarian Succession, was a limited war. Very little fighting took place—most of it small-unit actions in hilly and wooded terrain, raids, ambushes, harassment of marching columns and transport. But while the intensity of violence, in Frederick's words, was insipid, the limited war actually settled a major political issue.

In the last days of 1777 the elector of Bavaria died. He left no direct successor, and Austria used the occasion to claim the country. If the coup succeeded, it would alter the European balance of power by significantly strengthening the Austrian empire. Consequently Frederick objected, mobilized, and, when his threat was dismissed as a bluff, invaded Bohemia and Moravia in July 1778. In effect that spelled the end of Austria's coup, which was predicated on the absence of serious opposition. Austria was not prepared to fight a major war and eventually withdrew from Bavaria.

This brief and uneventful episode provides an illuminating contrast to events taking place at the same time in America. The theater of operations measured about 220 miles by 60 miles. Two Prussian armies of some 160,000 men advanced into this area and were opposed by an equivalent Austrian force, which adopted a fairly passive defense. Prussian strategy was to push both armies forward; the one that met major resistance would fix the enemy, permitting the other to maneuver. For a time Frederick hoped to swing his left flank through Moravia and to threaten Vienna. But supply difficulties, epidemics, and the absence of the need to seek a military decision caused the Prussians after some months to withdraw through the Bohemian mountains, retaining only a few bases for operations in the coming year, which turned out to be unnecessary.[10]

Finally, the Wars of the French Revolution opened in April 1792 when France declared war on Austria and Prussia largely for internal political reasons. The Girondins, the party for the moment dominating the revolutionary government, believed that a war would unite the nation behind their leadership. The allies, on the other hand, hoped that by invading France they would strengthen the domestic opposition to the Revolution and pressure Paris to modify its policies. To achieve these goals they were prepared to commit only a fraction of their strength—Prussia mobilized no more than one-fourth of her field army—and the 170,000 men that the allies deployed along a 300-mile front proved to be insufficient.

What conclusions can we draw from our survey? It seems apparent that the War of American Independence and the three contemporary European conflicts are of entirely different character, different not only in their political features but also in the fundamental elements of space and of force. In America small armies operated over a very large area that lacked a single center of crucial administrative and social importance, such as Paris or Vienna. In Europe far more powerful forces operated in a fraction of that space. The difference is of a magnitude that has qualitative significance. Staff-work, logistics, strategic and operational concepts, even tactics—all functioned in different ways on the two sides of the Atlantic.

That is the basic reason why neither really affected the other. The concentrated battle-tactics of Europe lost much of their validity in the territorial expanse and among the political dispersion of the thirteen states. The few thousand soldiers moving back and forth between Canada and Georgia, whose climactic encounters would hardly be considered battles in Europe, could not teach the commander much that would be of value in Germany or France. Or so, at least, Europeans thought. And that, obviously, explains what would otherwise be the puzzling absence of thorough treatment of the American War and its lessons in the European literature.

Of all European services, the British was best suited by experience, doctrine, and understanding of naval power to fight overseas. But England was hamstrung by the impact that domestic opposition to the war had on strategic planning and by the political and social character of her army's and navy's command structure and organization. Besides, her efforts and her aims were never fully in accord. No doubt at the beginning it was expected that a show of strength would restore order, but even if the policy of pacification had succeeded, it would not have brought back the political conditions of the 1760s. After the first two years of fighting, England could hope only that a military victory would enable her to treat from strength and to conclude a settlement that would have denied the thirteen states total independence, but surely would have granted everything short of it. That was perhaps not a sufficiently compelling motive to help her overcome the obstacles to fighting a war across 3,000 miles of ocean.

In this respect, incidentally, the American War is like the others to which we have compared it: in each case, the side whose interests were most profoundly affected emerged as the victor. That holds true for the Seven Years' War, in which Prussia's political autonomy was at stake; for the war of 1778, fought to prevent a shift in the balance of power that would have damaged Prussia more than it would have benefited Austria; and for the campaign of 1792, in which the allies, like the British before them, hoped that a show of force would bring the other side to its senses.

And it is crucial to remember that the stronger political motive of the American Revolutionaries was held not by a small elite; it expressed attitudes, a sense of what was possible and desirable, that could be found throughout society. Furthermore, these feelings and ideas had been shaped by their having developed in a unique environment—the American environment, which was defined by remoteness from Europe and by territorial expansiveness. It was this setting that made American political ideals very different, not only from European concepts of the centralized state, but also from European republican ideologies in the 1770s and 1780s (as well as in the two centuries since then). And it was the same remoteness and openness of the American military environment—so unlike that of the community of European states, smaller, far more densely developed, immediately abutting, pushing against each other—that in the final analysis enabled the patriots to succeed in their political experiment and also to triumph in its defense.

AFTERWORD
Don Higginbotham

What do these essays tell us about the state of Revolutionary War scholarship? That the field is much alive and doing well is perhaps only a statement of the obvious, just as it is equally true that the authors here show no desire to return to drum-and-bugle history—there are no flanks turned, no heroic charges, no spine-tingling battlefield orations, although all do have their place in the human drama we call history. Our investigators instead have sought to explore the deeper meaning of the Revolution as a war, with the "whys" taking precedence over the "hows." For the most part, their papers are designed to stimulate our thinking, to indicate neglected areas of research, and to suggest new approaches and conclusions, which they freely admit often require additional scrutiny.

These essays reveal that the War of American Independence was an exceedingly difficult struggle for both Britain and America. If one were pressed to uncover a comprehensive theme or underlying thread for the accumulative efforts of these scholars, I think it would be that the American Revolution was a war of attrition.

As for Britain, it is probably ahistorical to refer to the Revolution as her Vietnam, as some historians have done. But it is hard to escape the conclusion that post-World War II events in Southeast Asia have added influential dimensions to the way in which most of us have looked at Britain's obstacles in putting down her colonial rebellion. Indeed, few, if any, reputable historians raised serious doubts about the mother country's ability to win before Eric Robson did so in the aftermath of France's collapse in Indochina in the early 1950s.[1] More recent scholarship has explained in detail the restraints and limitations England experienced in fighting 3,000 miles from her own shores against an opponent whose territory was vast and whose people were in arms.

Actually, there were also contemporaries who were skeptical that either side could impose a clear-cut military solution. Major General von Lossberg of George III's German forces declared, even prior to the Franco-American alliance, that "we are far from an anticipated peace because the bitterness of the rebels is too widespread, and in regions where we are masters the rebellious spirit is still in them." To Lossberg, the land was "too large, and there are too many people. The more land we win, the weaker our army gets in the field." He felt "it would be best to come to some agreement" with the rebels.[2] So did Russian Foreign Minister Nikita Panin, who sought to mediate a peace between the belligerents. He believed the fighting would wind down without any decisive outcome, as had been the case in the Spanish-Dutch war that finally resulted in the inconclusive armistice of 1609.[3]

Part of Britain's problem was in the nature of her military leadership, which scarcely saw the war in its totality and complexity. Weigley and Gruber are of one mind that generals were scarcely professionals in a modern sense. They lacked a body of strategic doctrine from which to choose alternatives for practical application; that kind of breadth in military education lay in the future.

But even if strategic alternatives were not clearly recognized and systematically analyzed, there were implicit options, according to Gruber, who finds them present in military literature, the influence of which has led to considerable debate, as has the word *strategy* and how we should use it. There was the then-prevailing philosophy of circumscribed war, especially strong on the Continent itself, of Vegetius and Saxe, with its advocacy of avoiding decisive engagements and draining the enemy by an assortment of undertakings. But there was also another tradition stemming from antiquity, from Caesar in particular, which spoke of mobile, aggressive operations leading to the destruction in combat of one's adversary. The result, claims Gruber, is that the British drew upon a total tradition that was dual or ambiguous. Thus Gruber, by implication, and Paret, more explicitly, have warned us not to push too relentlessly the old concept of the eighteenth century as an Age of Limited Warfare. Likewise, these two authors stand together in the view that of the European military establishments of the period the English was most likely to achieve success in an overseas war.

All the same, Gruber contends that British strategy remained ambiguous, swinging back and forth between exertions to exhaust the rebels and schemes to fight climactic battles. It was, however, the more conservative of the two strategies that predominated among the king's generals in the provinces. Was this situation the conscious choice of the commanders? Or was it the result of other factors, such as the failures of the supply services? Certainly, as Bowler demonstrates, armies do move on their bellies. The British army was usually well fed; only very infrequently did supplies have to be cut. Nevertheless, the problem of building adequate reserves—the six months' stores recommended by the generals —did evidently influence offensive operations. Of course, one may be cynical of their really requiring such enormous reserves; the point is they thought so, be it a rationalization or not, and they acted accordingly. That is, Bowler discerns "an interesting correlation between those reserves and offensive operations."

Yet it might be maintained that Britain's extraordinarily unique circumstances cried out for entirely new principles, that neither of her strategic traditions was viable in this imperial civil war fought in the New World. Doubtless, too, there are those who will argue that British strategy—however defined—was inadequate because the policy of seeking a military decision was poor or unrealistic. If so, the fault would belong more with the London politicians than with the generals in the field.

In any event, the longer the conflict lasted, the more Britain found it necessary to turn to a war of attrition, all but writing off—temporarily, at any rate—much of the northern and middle theaters after 1778 as her emphasis shifted southward, as increasingly the maxims of Saxe prevailed over those of Caesar.

A consequence of Britain's war of attrition was the growing attention that the home government gave to the military potential of the loyalists. We are reminded of Paul Smith's observation that "in dealing with the Loyalists, Britain made two palpable errors: she turned to them for assistance much too late, and then relied upon them much too completely."[4] Still, she had small choice but to rely more heavily upon the king's friends, whatever her errors in dealing with them earlier. Moreover, in doing so, Britain, according to Shy, hoped to exploit notable weaknesses in American society, to undermine the Revolution from the inside. For the old internal divisions in colonial America reemerged to weaken the patriot war effort as popular enthusiasms of 1775 and 1776 diminished. Yet the loyalist strategy failed, possibly, as Shy speculates, because "it was too late—too many Americans were already disillusioned by the previous lack of British success." Those who did respond—the religious and cultural minorities—were "bitterly angry people, bent on vengeance, not on . . . law and order." One recalls that the threats and depredations of these aroused loyalists drove Andrew Pickens of the Long Canes neighborhood in South Carolina to arms, just as the burning of Thomas Sumter's up-country plantation aroused the "Gamecock" and drew him into the field. It was assuredly a high price that Britain paid for the services of these loyalists. In fact, Shy goes so far as to guess that "nothing did more in the later stages of the war to keep the Revolution alive than the British effort to arm and activate . . . these . . . minorities." Since British leaders failed to evaluate the possible repercussions from the use of Blacks, Indians, and loyalists, an observation of Gruber's is timely: namely, that the British military tradition "was also quite narrow—primarily because it was created by . . . men who did not as yet presume to consider more than the military dimensions of a campaign or war."

If Britain steadily, though not always consciously, moved toward a war of attrition, it is equally evident that the same may be said of the Americans—even more so; from the beginning they never envisioned, save fleetingly, the prospect of vanquishing the invader by means of a Caesarean test of arms. And as the war progressed, they were even less inclined to risk the big battle, as they had risked it at Long Island and Brandywine, both really defensive in nature. In fact, the Americans had no sensible alternative to a war of attrition, given their absence of a strong central government, their inveterate hostility to standing armies, and their own logistical and economic difficulties outlined by Bowler, Buel, and Shy.

Perhaps these elements help explain why Weigley is more impressed with Captain's Frothingham's summation of Washington as a defensive strategist than he is with Colonel Palmer's picture of the Virginian as a bold warrior. In *The American Way of War,* Weigley asserts that the "preservation of his army" was Washington's overriding ambition. If the army lived, so would the Revolution. He hoped that ultimately Britain "would lose patience and abandon the war."[5] I doubt that Bowler would find fault with any of this. He declares that "the American army of the

Revolution was small, far smaller than the military situation demanded. It was kept small and was hamstrung in its operations in very considerable measure by inadequate logistics and administration. For most of the war it remained, of necessity, on the defensive. When it did undertake offensive operations, they were usually on a relatively small scale and of short duration.'' Let us add a pertinent comment from Shy: "It was not a problem of war being too much for available [American] resources" (human, material, and financial), but it was too much for the methods of mobilizing and distributing those resources.

In some respects, the Americans were very successful with their war of attrition. Washington did hold his army together, and that army, as well as its chief, became important symbols of the respectability of the Revolution and of emerging nationalism. Furthermore, Washington, a fighter by instinct, lashed back on selected occasions, sometimes skillfully, in actions that had as much psychological as military value—Trenton, Princeton, and Monmouth are examples.

Other American operations, away from Washington's immediate jurisdiction, also witnessed a fruitful strategy of erosion, against Burgoyne in the North Country and against Cornwallis in the Carolinas. And for all the militia's shortcomings, they often blended nicely into the American scheme of warfare; they complemented the role of the Continentals, who could scarcely devote their full energies to the home front and endeavor to control the Revolution's internal opponents. The militia as an institution was never significantly reformed during the war; structurally, it remained much the same as it had been in the colonial period and as it would be in the nineteenth century. But—except when called upon for assignments beyond its capabilities—it contributed substantially to the patriots' defensive struggle. As James Simpson, the loyalist attorney general of South Carolina, saw it, the militia's chief value to the rebels was in helping to erect and sustain civil governments, for it was "from their civil institutions that the rebels derive the whole of their strength." His conviction was, in Piers Mackesy's words, "that royal institutions had been overturned so totally that they were extinct and past reviving."[6]

In spite of the numerous benefits that Americans derived from a defensive strategy—and there was probably no viable alternative, neither a wholesale guerrilla conflict nor an all-out formal offensive manner of fighting—this war of attrition did take its toll on the American side. At times, the excesses of the militia, in dealing with loyalists and Whigs as well, wrenched the Revolution toward the left, threatened to turn the war into a guerrilla contest, and posed a danger to republican institutions.

The Continental army itself was a potential danger, possibly an ever growing one, to the ideals and institutions of the new nation, observes Kohn. He believes that "the sensitivity and fears of the revolutionary generation have not been taken seriously" on this subject. The army's unhappiness rose with the length of the war as complaints mounted over appointments, promotions, adequate pay, future half-pay, compensation, rations, and supplies. To Kohn "the wonder of the officers' near revolt at Newburgh in 1783 was not that it happened, but that it was so long in coming." In the last analysis, he sees the "subordination and restraint of the Continental army" as remarkable, "one of the great legacies of the Revolution." When we read in his essay of those in and out of the service who questioned the suitability of republican institutions, we are reminded of the recent study by Pauline Maier, who finds it somewhat surprising that the colonists, with their political heritage drawn from an English monarchy, should have ever turned to republicanism.[7] But, in light of Kohn's work, perhaps a better question would be this: Why, after constructing republican forms, did the Americans, especially those in the army, display a willingness to keep them?

Economic travail, the cause of so much of the army's bitterness, may well have brought the Revolution itself to the verge of collapse. That is the contention of Buel, who argues that this was the actual case in 1781 in Connecticut, a state that had been flooded with Continental paper partly because of the presence of the American commissariat and a state that witnessed an expanding trade between its citizens and the British in New York City. What appeared to be happening in Connecticut would quite possibly have occurred everywhere had the war dragged on much longer. The explanation, which Buel spells out in some detail, is basically that the Americans had lost control of their economic resources because of their economic policies.

Were there alternative fiscal programs that the patriots might have undertaken? While he is not certain, he does maintain that the Americans —to say nothing of countless historians—wrongly concluded that they stood to gain, rather than to lose, from a war of attrition against England. In short, time was a foe, not a friend, of the Revolution, which was in danger of crumbling from within. "And it is not impossible," Buel continues, "that as the people became ever more disillusioned with the result of their heroic sacrifice, British rule might in time have been restored."

Possibly so. "One must not allow the events of the past twenty years in Asia to push one into treating their lessons as valid for the whole of human history, and surrendering to the conviction that the counterinsurgent can never win."[8] Of course, we shall never know what the outcome would have been had the conflict dragged on for several more years. Still, it is not farfetched to speculate, as Buel does, that American conditions on the home front would have gone from bad to worse. Would Britain therefore have outlasted America? Granted, she had the resources, but she had not done her utmost to mobilize them. Was she likely to engage in unprecedented methods as the years ticked by, to harness by sweeping, twentieth-century means, the wherewithal to win a remote eighteenth-century war? Finally, as to motivation, I consider intriguing, and worthy of further reflection, Paret's statement that of the eighteenth-century conflicts he surveyed, "the side whose interests were most profoundly affected emerged as the victor."

In any event, France's presence in the struggle eventually explained, if not the outcome itself, at least how and when the fighting would end. Prior to that time, the War of Independence does seem to fit Bowler's metaphor, borrowed from a description of the Burma theater in World War II, of two opponents who "could do no more than tear at each other with their fingertips." Ironically, it was not the British but the Americans and their French allies who won the climactic battle—or, in this instance, a siege—at Yorktown.

With the hindsight afforded us by Paret's essay, it now seems obvious that there was small fare in these transatlantic skirmishes and campaigns for future European military thinkers and planners. This was true not only because, broken down into its components, much of the North American warfare had antecedents in European light infantry, thin skirmish lines, and so on; but also because no European nation thought that it would have to engage in the kind of war that Britain faced in America between 1775 and 1783. If that is what outsiders thought, then they were correct. As Piers Mackesy has pointed out: "Unique characteristics explain the uniqueness of the [English] failure. England was maintaining nearly 60,000 soldiers beyond the Atlantic, most of them in a hostile country: a feat never paralleled in the past, and in relative terms never attempted again by any power until the twentieth century."[9]

Weigley uncovers still another explanation of why the Revolutionary War was passed over: it took place before the study of strategy was a very serious business. Besides, Napoleon, who captured the imagination of soldier-scholars everywhere, was a practitioner of the offensive, the strategy of annihilation—not the defensive, as was Washington. At this juncture we may bring Paret and Weigley together, with Paret showing that Europeans ignored the War of Independence and with Weigley revealing that Americans—except for the popularizers and the romantics—turned their backs on it as well. Not only did they eschew a careful and appreciative investigation of Washington as a strategist; they also neglected the study of the militia and saw no value in that force as a military institution in the nineteenth century.

Despite the attitudes of past generations, both Paret and Weigley recommend the Revolutionary War as a rewarding field in the here and now. Yet Paret urges us to break out of the bind of always comparing the revolutionary outburst in America with eighteenth-century conflicts in Europe, to instead contemplate stages of social, political, and ideological development of the people who seek to alter their status through violence, and to be mindful of other neglected factors, such as space and numbers. As for Weigley, he speculates here (as he does in *The American Way of War*) that the strategy of annihilation, which dominated American military thinking from the Civil War era onward, may now be a thing of the past. In an age when a vigorous, offensive-minded strategy may no longer be appropriate to the nation's objectives and interests, the strategy of Washington and his colleagues—the strategy of a war of attrition—may be more timely and relevant than ever before.

That in itself was a flexible or multifaceted strategy, or perhaps a series of strategies, varying in some measure according to time and place and including both the concentration approach of Washington and the dispersal approach of Greene and the militia. If, as some claim, not only has the big war been discredited because of inevitable nuclear holocaust, but so has the so-called limited war—the Koreas and the Vietnams—then we must ask what will be the future role of the military in the nation. Let us hope, among other things, that our reexamination of the War of Independence may cast some small ray of light upon this and other questions about the past, present, and future.

NOTES

Chapter 1

1. Don Higginbotham, *The War of American Independence* (New York, 1971), p. 1.

2. Even the timing is instructive: from Hemispheric War I to decisive British success in Hemispheric War II was twenty-three years; twenty years later came the humiliation of the Peace of Paris that sealed American independence, so the entire development took forty-three years in all. From 1917 to our decisive victory over Germany and Japan in 1945 was twenty-eight years; and our defeat in Vietnam came nineteen years later, or forty-seven years in all.

Chapter 2

1. Troyer S. Anderson, *The Command of the Howe Brothers During the American Revolution* (New York, 1936), pp. 5, 21-22, 244, 329-31; Eric Robson, *The American Revolution in its Political and Military Aspects, 1763-1783* (London, 1955), pp. 99-101, 129-34; Maldwyn A. Jones, "Sir William Howe: Conventional Strategist," in *George Washington's Opponents,* ed. George A. Billias (New York, 1969), pp. 53-67; John Shy, "The American Revolution: The Military Conflict Considered as a Revolutionary War," in *Essays on the American Revolution,* ed. Stephen G. Kurtz and James H. Hutson (Chapel Hill, 1973), p. 138.

2. For an explicit statement of this idea see Eric Robson, "The Armed

Forces and the Art of War,'' in *The New Cambridge Modern History: The Old Regime, 1713-1763,* ed. J. O. Lindsay (Cambridge, 1957), 7:163-90.

3. There is abundant evidence of the king's concern for his officers. See Sir John Fortescue, ed., *The Correspondence of King George the Third From 1760 to December 1783,* 6 vols. (London, 1927-28); his interest in books on the art of war is reflected in the King's Library at the British Museum, which includes such contemporary authorities as [Samuel Bever], *The Cadet: A Military Treatise,* 2d ed. (London, 1762); and his enthusiasm for maneuvers and demonstrations may be glimpsed in Edward Barrington de Fonblanque, *Political and Military Episodes . . . from the Life and Correspondence of the Right Hon. John Burgoyne* (London, 1876), p. 15; Franklin B. Wickwire and Mary Wickwire, *Cornwallis: The American Adventure* (Boston, 1970), p. 203; and Bellamy Partridge, *Sir Billy Howe* (New York, 1932), p. 12.

4. Sandwich's early experience with the army is mentioned in George Martelli, *Jemmy Twitcher: A Life of the Fourth Earl of Sandwich, 1718-1792* (London, 1962), pp. 25-26; in 1768 he subscribed to Bennett Cuthbertson, *A System for the Complete Interior Management and Oeconomy of a Battalion of Infantry* (Dublin, 1768).

5. Gerald S. Brown, *The American Secretary: The Colonial Policy of Lord George Germain, 1775-1778* (Ann Arbor, 1963), pp. 1-15. Alan Valentine, *Lord George Germain* (Oxford, 1962), pp. 34-35, 45, 42; and J. C. Long, *Lord Jeffery Amherst: A Soldier of the King* (New York, 1933) sketch Germain's connections with Ligonier, Wolfe, and Amherst.

6. Long, *Amherst,* chaps. 2, 4-9. Notwithstanding his experience, Amherst's strategic recommendations were usually ignored during the American War (ibid., chaps. 19-21).

7. John R. Alden, *General Gage in America . . .* (Baton Rouge, 1948), especially chap. 17; and A. G. Bradley, *Lord Dorchester* (New York, 1926).

8. Partridge, *Sir Billy Howe,* pp. 9-12; Ira D. Gruber, *The Howe Brothers and the American Revolution* (New York, 1972), pp. 56-58; and William B. Willcox, *Portrait of a General: Sir Henry Clinton in the War of Independence* (New York, 1964), pp. 10-35.

9. Fonblanque, *Burgoyne,* chaps. 1-3; Wickwire and Wickwire, *Cornwallis,* pp. 24-29.

10. Inventory of General Robert Murray, May 6-15, 1738, British Public Record Office; London, Probate Records 3 37/69 (hereafter cited as PR); inventory of Alexander Mullin, Dec. 10, 1741, PR 3 40/127; inventory of Brigadier Thomas Pagett, June 1, 1741, PR 3 41/22; inventory of Thomas Harrison, Oct. 22, 1763, PR 3 60/32. Catalogue of books of Captain Robert Seton, Mar. 14, 1732, CC 8/12/8(2), Scottish Record Office, Edinburgh (hereafter cited as CC); inventory of Major William Howe, Jan. 29, 1734, CC 8/12/8/1; catalogue of

books of Colonel John Steward, Sept. 22, 1752, CC 8/12/10; inventory of Captain David Maitland, Nov. 26, 1764, CC 8/12/11; inventory of Sir William Maxwell, Mar. 1, 1769, CC 8/12/12; cataglogue of books of Captain Thomas Cuthbert, Feb. 17, 1785, CC 8/12/13. *A Catalogue of the Entire and Valuable Library of the Learned Capt. Winde* . . . (n.p., [1740]); *A Catalogue of the Genuine and Elegant Library of the Late Sir Clement Cottrell Dormer, collected by Lieutenant General James Dormer* . . . [London, 1764]; *A Catalogue of the Library of a General Officer Lately Deceas'd* . . . [London, 1773]; and *A Catalogue of the Library of His Excellency John Earl Ligonier, Field Marshal* . . . (n.p., [1783]). All of the printed catalogues are now in the British Museum.

11. The six libraries assembled in whole or in part after 1740 were those of Thomas Harrison, David Maitland, Thomas Cuthbert, Sir William Maxwell, an anonymous general officer, and John Earl of Ligonier. Earl of Orrery (Roger Boyle), *A Treatise of the Art of War* . . . (London, 1677) was cited by such authors as Humphrey Bland, *A Treatise of Military Discipline* . . . , 8th ed. rev. (London, 1759), preface [to 1727 ed.]; and Campbell Dalrymple, *A Military Essay Containing Reflections on the Raising, Arming, Cloathing, and Discipline of the British Infantry and Cavalry* . . . (London, 1761), pp. 210-11. An annotated copy of the *Catalogue of the Library of a General Officer,* p. 7, now in the British Museum, shows that Orrery was not bought when offered for sale in 1773.

12. [Bever], *The Cadet,* chap. 13; Dalrymple, *Military Essay,* pp. 210-11.

13. Fonblanque, *Burgoyne,* p. 19.

14. [Antoine de Pas] Marquis de Feuquières, *Memoirs Historical and Military: Containing a Distinct View of all the Considerable States of Europe* . . . 2 vols. (orig. pub. 1711; reprint ed., West Point Military Library, New York, 1968), was regarded by Dalrymple, *Military Essay,* p. 212, as the most sensible of foreign authorities.

15. Maurice de Saxe, *Reveries on the Art of War,* trans. and ed. Thomas R. Phillips (orig. pub. 1753, reprint ed., Military Classics, Harrisburg, Pa., 1944); both Bever and Dalrymple cite Saxe more frequently than any other contemporary authority.

16. Flavius Vegetius Renatus, *The Military Institutions of the Romans,* trans. John Clark, ed. Thomas R. Phillips (orig. pub. 1767; reprint ed., Military Classics, Harrisburg, Pa., 1944).

17. Orrery, *Treatise,* p. 2; Gaius Julius Caesar, *The Commentaries of Caesar* . . . *To which is prefixed a Discourse concerning The Roman Art of War,* ed. William Duncan (London, 1753), dedication. The three English translations were those of Clement Edmonds (1604), Martin Bladen (1705), and Clarke (1712); these three translations had run to total of twenty-six editions by the outbreak of the American War.

18. James W. Hayes, "The Social and Professional Background of the Officers of the British Army, 1714-1763" (M.A. thesis, University of London, 1956), chap. 5.

19. This interpretation is taken from C. Julius Caesar, *Commentaries of His Wars in Gaul and Civil War with Pompey. . . ,* trans. Martin Bladen, 8th ed. rev. (London, 1770), the most popular translation in England on the eve of the American War.

20. Vegetius, *Institutions,* pp. 71 (quoted), 85, 106, 113.

21. Quoted in Robert S. Quimby, *The Background of Napoleonic Warfare* (New York, 1957), p. 15; Feuquières, *Memoirs,* 2:2-4. Quimby emphasizes the aggressive characteristics in Feuquières.

22. Saxe, *Reveries,* pp. 97-98, 117, 121-22 (quoted).

23. Orrery, *Treatise,* pp. 127-32, 135-39, 149 (quoted), 197-205.

24. [Bever], *The Cadet,* pp. 175-76 (quoted), 182-89.

25. Orrery, *Treatise,* pp. 15, 205.

26. The ministry's strategy was set forth in Earl of Dartmouth (William Legge) to Gage, Jan. 27 (quoted), Feb. 22, Mar. 3, Apr. 15, 1775, British Public Record Office, London, Colonial Office Papers (hereafter cited as CO). The background of that strategy is discussed in Bernard Donoughue, *British Politics and the American Revolution* (London, 1964), chaps. 10-12; Alden, *Gage,* chaps. 12-15.

27. Dartmouth to Gage, July 1, 1775, CO 5/92; Lords of the Admiralty to Samuel Graves, July 6, 1775, British Public Record Office, London, Admiralty Papers 2/1332; Dartmouth to Josiah Martin, July 5, 12, 1775, CO 5/318.

28. Gruber, *Howe Brothers,* pp. 25-31, 82-83.

29. Howe to Dartmouth, Apr. 25, 1776, CO 5/93.

30. Howe to Lord George Germain, Aug. 6, 1776 (quoted), CO 5/93; Gruber, *Howe Brothers,* pp. 104-07.

31. Howe to Germain, Jan. 20, 1777, private, CO 5/94; Gruber, *Howe Brothers,* pp. 109-57.

32. Brown, *American Secretary,* pp. 86-105; Gruber, *Howe Brothers,* pp. 174-88, 230-32; Willcox, *Portrait a of General,* pp. 138-60.

33. Gruber, *Howe Brothers,* pp. 192-94, 199-201, 207-08, 224-67.

34. Germain to Clinton, Mar. 8, 1778, most secret, CO 5/95; Paul H. Smith, *Loyalists and Redcoats* (Chapel Hill, 1964), pp. 82-99.

35. Germain to Clinton, Mar. 21, 1778, most secret, and secret instructions for Clinton, Mar. 21, 1778, CO 5/95; Germain to Clinton, Aug. 5, 1778, CO 5/96.

36. Germain to Clinton, Jan. 23, 1779, secret and confidential, and Mar. 31, 1779 (quoted), CO 5/97.

37. Germain to Clinton, Dec. 4, 1779, CO 5/98; Jan. 19, 1780, CO 5/99; Sept. 6, 1780, CO 5/100; Feb. 7, May 2, 1781, secret (quoted), CO 5/101.

38. Clinton to Germain, Nov. 8, 1778, CO 5/96; Clinton to Duncan Drummond, Mar. 2, 10, 1779, Clinton Papers, William L. Clements Library, University of Michigan, Ann Arbor; Clinton to Germain, Apr. 4, 1779, CO 5/97; P. H. Smith, *Loyalists and Redcoats,* pp. 93-94, 106-08.

39. Clinton to Germain, May 3, 1779, CO 5/97; Clinton to Germain, June 18 (nos. 57, 58), July 25 (nos. 60, 61), 1779, CO 5/98; Clinton to Henry Fiennes Clinton, Duke of Newcastle, Aug. 14, 1779, Newcastle Papers, University of Nottingham Library, Nottingham; Willcox, *Portrait of a General,* pp. 270-71, 274-79.

40. Clinton to Germain, Aug. 20, 21, 1779, CO 5/98; Willcox, *Portrait of a General,* pp. 289-310.

41. Clinton to Cornwallis, June 1, 1780, and Clinton's "Instructions to . . . Cornwallis," June 1, 1780, Clinton-Cornwallis Letterbook no. 1, Clinton Papers; Henry Clinton, *The American Rebellion: Sir Henry Clinton's Narrative of His Campaigns, 1775-1782,* ed. William B. Willcox (New Haven, 1954), pp. 186 (quoted), 183-87, 213, 221-24; Wickwire and Wickwire, *Cornwallis,* pp. 133-35; Willcox, *Portrait of a General,* p. 321. Recapitulation of the army under Sir Henry Clinton, July 1, 1780 (enclosed in Clinton to Germain, July 4, 1780), CO 5/100.

42. Clinton to Germain, July 4, Aug. 14, 30, Sept. 3, 20, Oct. 11, Nov. 28, 1780, CO 5/100; Clinton, *American Rebellion,* pp. 189-92, 195-96, 214-18, 221; Willcox, *Portrait of a General,* pp. 322-43.

43. The redistribution of British troops may be traced in Clinton's returns of Nov. 1, 1780 (enclosed in Clinton to Germain, Nov. 10, 1780), CO 5/100; of Jan. 15, 1781 (enclosed in Clinton to Germain, Jan. 25, 1781), CO 5/101; and of May 1, 1781 (enclosed in Clinton to Germain, May 13, 1781), CO 5/102. Clinton's attitude on making Virginia the seat of the war is clearly expressed in Clinton to Phillips, Mar. 10, 1781 (enclosed in Clinton to Germain, Mar. 1[-16], 1781), CO 5/101; Clinton to Germain, Apr. 23, 1781, CO 5/102; Willcox, *Portrait of a General,* pp. 347-91.

44. Distribution of the Army under . . . Clinton, May 1, 1781 (enclosed in Clinton to Germain, May 13, 1781), CO 5/102; Willcox, *Portrait of a General,* pp. 392-444.

Chapter 3

1. Dave Palmer, *The Way of the Fox: American Strategy in the War for America* (Westport, Conn., 1975), pp. 3-24. The best introduction to the history

of modern strategic thought, especially to the impact of Jomini and Clausewitz, remains Edward M. Earle, ed., *Makers of Modern Strategy* (Princeton, 1943).

2. D. H. Mahan, *An Elementary Treatise on Advanced-Guard, Out-Post, and Detachment Service of Troops* . . . (orig. pub. 1847, rev. ed. New York, 1864); H. Wager Halleck, *Elements of Military Art and Science* . . . (New York, 1846).

3. John Bigelow, *The Principles of Strategy: Illustrated Mainly from American Campaigns* (orig. pub. 1894; 2d ed., revised and enlarged, New York, 1968), pp. 159-61 for the Trenton-Princeton campaign, pp. 105-09 on British strategy largely in the Hudson Valley, pp. 234-58 on the southern campaigns.

4. Matthew F. Steele, *American Campaigns*, 2 vols. (Washington, D.C., 1901).

5. A. T. Mahan, *The Influence of Sea Power upon History, 1660-1783* (Boston, 1890).

6. B. H. Liddell Hart, *Strategy*, 2d rev. ed. (New York, 1967); J. F. C. Fuller, *A Military History of the Western World*, 3 vols. (New York, 1954-56), 2:271-340 (p. 312 quoted).

7. Theodore Ropp, *War in the Modern World*, new rev. ed. (New York, 1962), pp. 86-97 (pp. 88-93 on "The Continental Army and Navy"); Richard A. Preston and Sydney F. Wise, *Men in Arms*, 2d rev. ed. (New York, 1970), pp. 172-78.

8. Field Marshal Viscount Montgomery of Alamein, *A History of Warfare* (Cleveland, 1968), pp. 320-21 (p. 321 quoted).

9. Emory Upton, *The Military Policy of the United States* (Washington, D.C., 1912), pp. 2-67. A recent expression of Uptonian views on the Revolution can be found in C. Joseph Bernardo and Eugene H. Bacon, *American Military Policy: Its Development since 1775*, 2d ed. (Harrisburg, Pa., 1961), pp. 1-46.

10. Walter Millis, *Arms and Men* (New York, 1956), p. 37.

11. Peter Paret, *Yorck and the Era of Prussian Reform, 1807-1815* (Princeton, 1966), especially pp. 204-08 on the British army.

12. Thomas G. Frothingham, *Washington: Commander in Chief* (Boston, 1930); Dudley W. Knox, *The Naval Genius of George Washington* (Boston, 1932).

13. The multivolume biographies of Washington by Douglas S. Freeman and James T. Flexner cited below have much information on Washington's relations with Congress. See also Jennings B. Sanders, *The Evolution of the Executive Departments, 1774-1789* (Chapel Hill, 1935), especially chaps. 5, 6 on the administration of the war. Page Smith, *John Adams*, 2 vols. (Garden City, N.Y., 1962) has much material on the Continental Congress and the army because John Adams played a major role in military matters. A recent work on the political relationships between congressmen and generals, dealing mainly with the north-

ern army, is Jonathan G. Rossie, *The Politics of Command in the American Revolution* (Syracuse, 1975).

14. Carl von Clausewitz, *On War,* trans. Col. J. J. Graham, new and rev. ed. with an introduction and notes by Col. F. N. Maude, 3 vols. (New York, 1968), 1:86.

15. Frothingham, *Washington,* pp. 88, 92, 104.

16. Ibid., p. 107.

17. Ibid., pp. 105-07.

18. Ibid., pp. 107-08.

19. Ibid., p. 108.

20. Ibid., pp. 43-44, 107-11, 199-202, 325-27.

21. Ibid., pp. 326-27.

22. Mao Tse-tung, *Mao Tse-tung on Revolution and War,* ed. with an introduction and notes by M. Rejai (Garden City, N.Y., 1970), p. 254.

23. Frothingham, *Washington,* p. 109.

24. Ibid., especially pp. 109, 186, 280.

25. Ibid., p. 278.

26. Ibid., p. 267.

27. Ibid., p. 210.

28. Ibid., p. 277.

29. Knox, *Naval Genius,* chap. 5, "Sea Power Baffles Washington," pp. 29-38.

30. Ibid., p. 77.

31. Lee to Washington, Apr. 5, 1776, in John C. Fitzpatrick, ed., *The Writings of George Washington. . . ,* 39 vols. (Washington, D.C., 1931-44), 4:45ln.

32. Knox, *Naval Genius,* p. 76.

33. Ibid., p. 77.

34. Ibid., pp. 72-74.

35. Ibid., p. 127.

36. Ibid.

37. Don Higginbotham, "American Historians and the Military History of the American Revolution," *American Historical Review* 70 (1964):30, referring to Willard M. Wallace, *Appeal to Arms* (New York, 1951).

38. Francis V. Greene, *The Revolutionary War and the Military Policy of the United States* (New York, 1911).

39. Lynn Montross, *Rag, Tag and Bobtail: The Story of the American Revolutionary Army* (New York, 1952); Christopher Ward, *The War of the Revolution,* ed. John R. Alden, 2 vols. (New York, 1952); John R. Alden, *The American Revolution, 1775-1783* (New York, 1954). Montross was a historian with the Historical Division, U.S. Marine Corps.

40. Higginbotham, "American Historians," pp. 30-31. The two additional overall treatments are George F. Scheer and Hugh F. Rankin, *Rebels and Redcoats* (Cleveland, 1957), and Howard H. Peckham, *The War for Independence* (Chicago, 1958).

41. Don Higginbotham, *The War of American Independence* (New York, 1971).

42. Douglas S. Freeman, *George Washington,* 7 vols. (New York, 1948-57); *R. E. Lee: A Biography,* 4 vols. (New York, 1934); *Lee's Lieutenants: A Study in Command,* 3 vols. (New York, 1942-44). Vols. 3-5 of *Washington* concern the Revolutionary War.

43. Freeman, *Washington,* 5:480-83 summarize Washington's strategy, while 5:478-501 summarize his Revolutionary military career more generally.

44. Ibid., p. 480.

45. Ibid., p. 481.

46. Ibid., pp. 480-81.

47. Ibid., pp. 481-83 (p. 481 quoted).

48. James Flexner, *George Washington,* 4 vols. (Boston, 1965-72).

49. Marcus Cunliffe, *George Washington: Man and Monument* (London, 1959), pp. 70-113.

50. Marcus Cunliffe, "George Washington's Generalship," in *George Washington's Generals,* ed. George A. Billias (New York, 1964), pp. 3-21, states briefly the salient points of the longer study of General Washington.

51. Theodore Thayer, *Nathanael Greene* (New York, 1960); and, "Nathanael Greene," in *George Washington's Generals,* ed. Billias, pp. 109-36.

52. Cunliffe, *Washington,* p. 89.

53. William B. Willcox, "Rhode Island in British Strategy, 1780-1781," *Journal of Modern History* 17(1945):304-31; "British Strategy in America, 1778," ibid. 19(1947):97-121; "The British Road to Yorktown: A Study in Divided Command," *American Historical Review* 52(1946):1-35; "Why Did the British Lose the American Revolution?" *Michigan Alumnus Quarterly Review* 62(1956):317-24; "Too Many Cooks: British Planning Before Saratoga," *Journal of British Studies* 2(1962):56-90; "Arbuthnot, Gambier, and Graves: 'Old Women' of the Navy," in *George Washington's Opponents,* ed. George A. Billias (New York, 1969), pp. 260-90; ed., *The American Rebellion: Sir Henry Clinton's Narrative of His Campaigns, 1775-1782* (New Haven, 1954); *Portrait of a General: Sir Henry Clinton in the War of Independence* (New York, 1964).

54. Eric Robson, *The American Revolution in its Political and Military Aspects, 1763-1783* (New York, 1954).

55. Piers Mackesy, *The War for America, 1775-1783* (Cambridge, Mass., 1964).

56. Ira D. Gruber, *The Howe Brothers and the American Revolution* (New York, 1972).

57. Palmer, *Way of the Fox,* p. xvi.

58. For example, see Palmer, *Way of the Fox*, pp. xvi-xix.

59. Ibid., p. xvi.

60. Cunliffe, *Washington,* p. 109; but note that Cunliffe writes not of Fabian strategy but of tactics, which reflects part of the problem in dealing with Washington as a strategist.

61. Palmer, *Way of the Fox,* p. xix, citing Higginbotham, *War of American Independence,* p. 88.

62. Palmer, *Way of the Fox,* p. xvii, citing Freeman, *Washington,* 5:481.

63. Palmer, *Way of the Fox,* p. xviii, citing Freeman, *Washington,* 5:481.

64. Dave R. Palmer, "General George Washington: Grand Strategist or Mere Fabian?" *Parameters: The Journal of the U.S. Army War College* 4(1974):4. This article, pp. 1-16, is a convenient summary of Palmer's main arguments. Palmer's *Way of the Fox,* chap. 7, pp. 95-114, also deals with this period.

65. Palmer, "General George Washington," p. 7; see *Way of the Fox,* chap. 8, pp. 115-43.

66. Palmer, "General George Washington," p. 12; see *Way of the Fox,* chap. 9, pp. 144-78.

67. Palmer, "General George Washington," p. 14, citing Fitzpatrick, *Writings of Washington,* 24:124; see *Way of the Fox,* chap. 10, pp. 179-99.

68. Palmer, "General George Washington," p. 14.

69. Frothingham, *Washington,* p. 97.

70. Freeman, *Washington,* 3:529.

71. Aug. 9, 1776, in Fitzpatrick, *Writings of Washington,* 5:405.

72. Sept. 2, 1776, ibid., 6:6.

73. Sept. 8, 1776, ibid., 6:28.

74. Palmer, *Way of the Fox,* p. 139.

75. Ibid., p. 125.

76. Palmer, "General George Washington," p. 12.

77. I have attempted to make my own beginning toward such a reexamination in another place, in chapters on Washington and Greene as strategists in Russell F. Weigley, *The American Way of War* (New York, 1973), pp. 3-39.

Chapter 4

1. Sir Henry Clinton to William Eden, Sept. 1, 1780, in William B. Willcox, ed., *The American Rebellion: Sir Henry Clinton's Narrative of His Campaigns, 1775-1782* (New Haven, 1954), p. 456.

2. John C. Fitzpatrick, ed., *The Writings of George Washington. . . ,* 39 vols. (Washington, D.C., 1931-44), 10:194.

3. Accounts of the army logistical organization and its development in the Revolutionary period are given in James A. Huston, *The Sinews of War* (Washington, D.C., 1966), pp. 3-74; Erna Risch, *Quartermaster Support of the Army: A History of the Corps, 1775-1939* (Washington, D.C., 1962), pp. 1-73; Louis Clinton Hatch, *The Administration of the American Revolutionary Army* (New York, 1904), pp. 86-123; Victor Leroy Johnson, *The Administration of the American Commissariat During the Revolutionary War* (Philadelphia, 1941).

4. The expense involved in transporting supplies from New England to the middle states by land led one commissary to suggest, half-seriously, that the army would be better off resorting to coastal transport since even if only one boat in three got through, the cost would still be less.

5. The first commissary general was Jonathan Trumbull. In June 1777 the department was divided into two: Trumbull was continued as commissary general of purchases and Charles Stewart appointed commissary general of issues. Trumbull resigned in Aug. 1777 and was succeeded by William Buchanan, who in turn resigned in Mar. 1778, to be succeeded by Jeremiah Wadsworth. The last person to hold the office during the war was Ephraim Blaine, appointed Dec. 2, 1779.

The first quartermaster was Thomas Mifflin, who held the post (except for a few months in the summer of 1776 when it was filled by Stephen Moylan) until Oct. 1778, when he resigned. The office remained effectively vacant until Feb. 25, 1778, when Nathanael Greene accepted it. Greene served until Aug. 1780 and was succeeded by Timothy Pickering.

6. Huston, *Sinews of War,* p. 6; John Adams was the first president of the board. Richard Peters, the secretary, was the closest the board came to having a permanent member in its early years. The first members of the board who had no congressional duties were appointed in Oct. 1777. They were Thomas Mifflin, Timothy Pickering, and Robert H. Harrison.

7. Henry Laurens to John Laurens, May 16, 1778, quoted in Jennings B. Sanders, *The Evolution of the Executive Departments of the Continental Congress, 1774-1789* (Chapel Hill, 1935), p. 13n.

8. Risch, *Quartermaster Support of the Army,* pp. 27-29.

9. Pickering to Trumbull, June 28, 1777, in Douglas S. Freeman, *George Washington,* 7 vols. (New York, 1948-57), 4:441n.

10. Risch, *Quartermaster Support of the Army,* p.7.

11. Risch, *Quartermaster Support of the Army,* pp. 29, 42; Huston, *Sinews of War,* p. 21; Hatch, *Administration of the Army,* p. 98; Johnson, *Administration of the American Commissariat,* pp. 102-03.

12. Risch, *Quartermaster Support of the Army,* p. 62.

13. Huston, *Sinews of War,* pp. 22, 33-34.

14. Risch, *Quartermaster Support of the Army,* pp. 45-46.

15. Edmund C. Burnett, ed., *Letters of Members of the Continental Congress,* 8 vols. (Washington, D.C., 1921-36), 2:393-94; Fitzpatrick, *Writings of Washington,* 9:134; Johnson, *Administration of the American Commissariat,* pp. 70-76.

By early winter with the army supply system in disarray, Congress realized its error and on Nov. 27 elected Joseph Trumbull to the Board of War. To his credit, since he had been accused by some members of Congress of being unpatriotic, Trumbull accepted the appointment. He was, unfortunately, in ill health and died on July 23, 1778. Johnson, *Administration of the American Commissariat,* pp. 86-87.

16. Risch, *Quartermaster Support of the Army,* pp. 31-33.

17. Freeman, *Washington,* 4:559, 573.

18. He was replaced by James Thompson, appointed December 22, 1777.

19. Johnson, *Administration of the American Commissariat,* p. 95; Fitzpatrick, *Writings of Washington,* 10:192.

20. Risch, *Quartermaster Support of the Army,* pp. 33-37; Huston, *Sinews of War,* pp. 58-62; Don Higginbotham, *The War of American Independence* (New York, 1971), pp. 304-05; Johnson, *Administration of the American Commissariat,* pp. 96-97.

21. Fitzpatrick, *Writings of Washington,* 10: 192-93.

22. The price of flour was advanced from 26s. to 33s. per hundredweight (it had been 12s. 6d. at the beginning of the war). Beef, which had been £3 4s. a hundredweight, was advanced to £4 7s. Johnson, *Administration of the American Commissariat,* p. 102.

23. Risch, *Quartermaster Support of the Army,* p. 46; Johnson, *Administration of the American Commissariat,* pp. 136-37.

24. Charles H. Lesser, ed., *The Sinews of Independence: Monthly Strength Reports of the Continental Army* (Chicago, 1976), p. xxxi. It also helped that the winter was mild and that the tactical situation allowed Washington to disperse his forces considerably, thus easing the transportation problem. Huston, *Sinews of War,* pp. 62-63. Washington gave most of the credit for the army's vast

improved logistical services to the new commissary and quartermaster generals, Wadsworth and Greene. Fitzpatrick, *Writings of Washington,* 12:277.

25. In early 1781 the Council of Pennsylvania quoted Continental currency at 175:1 against specie. Huston, *Sinews of War,* p. 66. What Johnson calls a "speculation mania" was also at work. News that a French fleet and army would arrive drove prices almost out of sight in Philadelphia in 1778. Flour reached 70s. a hundredweight (hard money) that Aug. Johnson, *Administration of the American Commissariat,* pp. 142-43.

26. Fredrich Kapp, *The Life of John Kalb* (New York, 1884), p. 183, quoted in Risch, *Quartermaster Support of the Army,* p. 56; Huston, *Sinews of War,* pp. 63-66.

27. Sanders, *Executive Departments,* pp. 15-16; Risch, *Quartermaster Support of the Army,* pp. 57-58.

28. For instance, the Delaware Assembly adjourned in Nov. 1780 without providing the supplies required in the requisitions of that year.

29. Risch, *Quartermaster Support of the Army,* pp. 64-65; Huston, *Sinews of War,* pp. 68-69; Hatch, *Administration of the Army,* pp. 104, 107.

30. Fitzpatrick, *Writings of Washington,* 18:413, 427-28.

31. M. F. Treacy, *Prelude to Yorktown* (Chaptel Hill, 1963), pp. 54-60.

32. Lesser, ed., *Sinews of Independence,* p. xxxi. The army declined from 18,334 in Jan. 1780 to 9,498 by June.

33. Fitzpatrick, *Writings of Washington,* 20:470.

34. A good account of the logistical side of the struggle to mount the Yorktown campaign is in Huston, *Sinews of War,* pp. 75-85.

35. Higginbotham, *War of American Independence,* p. 390.

36. Ibid. These figures are, of course, for Continental regulars. Washington often commanded a much larger force but the difference was made up by state levies and militia. There were wild fluctuations in the size of his force. It went from 9,498 in June 1780 to 21,043 in Sept. and was back down to 6,723 in Dec. Lesser, ed., *Sinews of Independence,* pp. xxxi, 172-93.

37. See Ira D. Gruber, *The Howe Brothers and the American Revolution* (New York, 1972); William B. Willcox, *Portrait of a General: Sir Henry Clinton in the War of Independence* (New York, 1964); and Franklin B. Wickwire and Mary Wickwire, *Cornwallis: The American Adventure* (Boston, 1970).

38. See Piers Mackesy, *The War for America, 1775-1783* (Cambridge, Mass., 1964).

39. For a more detailed account of the army logistical organization see R. Arthur Bowler, *Logistics and the Failure of the British Army in America, 1775-1783* (Princeton, 1975), pp. 12-40. British government contracting procedures are dealt with in Norman Baker, *Government and Contractors* (London, 1971).

40. British Public Record Office, London, Treasury 64/101, 72 (hereafter cited as T).

41. T 64/106, 20-6; T 64/108, 18-19, 38-39.

42. See David Syrett, *Shipping and the American War, 1775-1783* (London, 1970), for the organization of the communications link between Britain and the army in America.

43. Bowler, *Logistics,* p. 63.

44. T 64/118, 18-9.

45. T 64/119, 4-5; 64/114, 20-2.

46. Bowler, *Logistics,* chap. 3.

47. T 1/518; Howe to Treasury, Dec. 1, 1775, "Notes of S[ir] Henry Clinton Relative to the Campaign of 1778"; British Museum, Add. Mss. 34, 416, 153-59; T 64/114, 117-20.

48. A graph of the army's provisions reserves throughout the war is in Bowler, *Logistics,* app. 1.

49. Bowler, *Logistics,* pp. 247-52; Baker, *Government and Contractors,* p. 9.

50. T 27/33, 236-37.

51. T 64/106, 29-44.

52. Bowler, *Logistics,* pp. 64-65.

53. Fitzpatrick, *Writings of Washington,* 7:95.

54. Eric Robson, *The American Revolution in its Political and Military Aspects, 1763-1783* (New York, 1954), pp. 161-62; T Colonial Office, 5/95, 86; Bernard A. Uhlendorf, ed., *Revolution in America* (New Brunswick, N.J., 1957), pp. 155-56, 509.

55. "Journal of Captain John Peebles of the 42d or Royal Highland Regiment during the War of Independence," Scottish Record Office, GD21/492; H. M. Lydenberg, ed., *James Robertson, Lieutenant-General Royal Engineers, His Diaries and Sketches in America, 1762-1780* (New York, 1930).

56. E. Stuart Wortley, ed., *A Prime Minister and His Son* (London, 1925), p. 20, Mar. 29, 1777.

57. Eric Robson, ed., *Letters from America, 1773-1780* (Manchester, England, 1951), pp. 38-39, 101-02.

58. R. W. Pettengill, trans. and ed., *Letters from America* (Port Washington, N.Y., 1964), p. 164.

59. Congress directed that accounts of such incidents be collected. A number were published in the *Pennsylvania Evening Post,* Apr. 24, May 10, 26, 1777. They are now in W. A. Whitehead et al., ed., *Archives of the State of New Jersey, 1631-1800,* 2d ser. (Trenton, 1901), 1:347-53, 362-67. See also Varnum Lansing Collins, ed., *A Brief Narrative of the Ravages of the British and Hessians at Princeton in 1776-77* (Princeton, 1906).

60. "Journal of Col. Stephen Kemble," *The Kemble Papers,* Collections of the New-York Historical Society, 2 vols. (New York, 1884), 1:91, 96. Leonard Lundin, in *Cockpit of the Revolution: The War for Independence in New Jersey* (Princeton, 1940), pp. 171-87, asserts that the British victories in the late fall of 1776 brought about the virtual collapse of the Revolution in New Jersey but that the depredations of the British troops revived it. Willcox, *Portrait of a General,* p. 350, and Wickwire and Wickwire, *Cornwallis,* pp. 25-28, suggest that the same results followed British operations in Virginia and the Carolinas. See also John Shy, "The American Revolution: The Military Conflict Considered as a Revolutionary War," in *Essays on the American Revolution,* ed. Stephen J. Kurtz and James H. Hutson (Chapel Hill, 1973), pp. 133-43.

61. Bowler, *Logistics,* chap. 5.

Chapter 5

1. Peter Paret, "The History of War," *Daedalus* 100 (1971):376-96, discusses the way in which military history has been cut off from the study of history in general. My own book, John Shy, *A People Numerous and Armed* (New York, 1976), tries to reintegrate the two for the Revolutionary period, and the present essay is a continuation of that effort.

2. Benjamin Rush, Nov. 13, 1775, in *Lee Papers,* Collections of the New York Historical Society, 4 vols. (New York, 1871-74), 1:216.

3. The adjutant general of Hessian troops described Rawdon's Volunteers of Ireland as one of the finest regiments in the army. Bernard A. Uhlendorf, ed., *Revolution in America* (New Brunswick, N.J., 1957), p. 264. Rawdon's original letter to Major Rugeley, Camden, July 1, 1780, and his subsequent explanation to Cornwallis, Dec. 5, 1780, British Public Record Office, London, Colonial Office 5/101, 283-84, 413. Robert L. Meriwether, *The Expansion of South Carolina, 1729-1765* (Kingsport, Tenn., 1940), pp. 136-46, describes the character of the Waxhaws settlement, while more information on the origins of some of the settlers is in Robert W. Ramsey, *Carolina Cradle* (Chapel Hill, 1964).

4. The best overall account of colonial American society in the eighteenth century is James Henretta, *The Evolution of American Society, 1700-1815* (Lexington, Mass., 1973).

5. The classic account of the phenomenon is Benjamin Franklin, "Observa-

tions Concerning the Increase of Mankind" (1751), in *The Papers of Benjamin Franklin,* ed. Leonard W. Labaree and William B. Willcox, 15 vols. to date (New Haven, 1959—), 4:255 ff. A modern analysis is J. Potter, "The Growth of Population in America, 1700-1860," in *Population in History,* ed. D. V. Glass and D. E. C. Eversley (London, 1965).

    6. James G. Leyburn, *The Scotch-Irish: A Social History* (Chapel Hill), p. 172.

    7. Potter, "Growth of Population."

    8. See Leyburn, *The Scotch-Irish,* on the Scotch-Irish. A recent estimate for German immigration is in Howard B. Furer, *The Germans in America, 1607-1970* (Dobbs Ferry, N.Y., 1973), p. 4. James T. Lemon, *The Best Poor Man's Country* (Baltimore, 1972), discusses both Scotch-Irish and Germans in eighteenth-century Pennsylvania, where most of the impact of immigration was felt. Philip D. Curtin, *The Atlantic Slave Trade: A Census* (Madison, Wis., 1969), p. 140, is the best estimate of black immigration; and Winthrop D. Jordan, *White Over Black* (Chapel Hill, 1968), pp. 116 ff., discusses the general fear of slave insurrection after about 1740.

    9. The best picture of this elite is still Leonard W. Labaree, *Conservatism in Early America* (New York, 1948); but see also James K. Martin, *Men in Rebellion* (New Brunswick, N. J., 1973). The operation of "deference" is discussed in J. R. Pole, "Historians and the Problem of Early American Democracy," *American Historical Review* 67(1961):626-46.

    10. The major instances of violent outbreaks included the Green Mountain Boys, waging civil war over land grants between the Connecticut and Champlain valleys well before the Revolution; land riots in New Jersey and New York; something like open warfare between Pennsylvania authorities and Connecticut settlers in the upper Susquehanna Valley; the so-called Paxton Boys in the middle Susquehanna, massacring Indians and threatening Philadelphia itself; Regulators in both North and South Carolina, using vigilante violence, with a pitched battle needed to stamp them out in the former colony; and, while the seaboard debated the Boston crisis in 1774-75, fighting between Pennsylvania and Virginians for control of the Pittsburgh area.

    11. Bernhard Knollenberg, *George Washington: The Virginia Period, 1732-1775* (Durham, N.C., 1964), pp. 44-50.

    12. For two New England towns and their early response to the war, see Howard K. Sanderson, *Lynn in the Revolution,* 2 vols. (Boston, 1909), and Jonathan Smith, *Peterborough, New Hampshire, in the American Revolution* (Peterborough, N.H., 1913).

    13. *Historical Statistics of the United States, Colonial Times to 1957* (Washington, D.C., 1960), p. 756; Allen French, *The First Year of the American Revolution* (Boston, 1934), p. 52; and Charles H. Lesser, ed., *The Sinews of*

Independence: Monthly Strength Reports of the Continental Army (Chicago, 1976), pp. 2-3, for July.

14. Russell F. Weigley discusses Washington's "orthodoxy" in *The American Way of War* (New York, 1973), pp. 13-17, and his views on citizen soldiers in *Towards an American Army* (New York, 1962), pp. 1-9. Paul David Nelson of Berea College is currently engaged in a study of American military leaders' attitudes toward the militia during the Revolutionary period.

15. Quoted in Allen French, "General Haldimand in Boston," *Massachusetts Historical Society Proceedings* 66(1942):91.

16. Richard H. Kohn, *Eagle and Sword* (New York, 1975), explores the connection between Federalism and the army after the war.

17. Charles A. Lofgren, "Compulsory Military Service Under the Constitution: The Original Understanding," *William and Mary Quarterly*, 3d ser. 33(1976):76-79, is an informed sketch of actual practice during the war.

18. The point is illustrated and developed in my essay, "Hearts and Minds in the American Revolution: The Case of 'Long Bill' Scott and Peterborough, New Hampshire," in Shy, *A People Numerous and Armed,* and originally published under a different title in *The American Revolution,* ed. J. Parker and C. Urness (Minneapolis, 1975).

19. The best account of wartime finance is E. James Ferguson, *The Power of the Purse* (Chapel Hill, 1961), and the most thorough treatment of military supply and its problems is a manuscript by Erna Risch, to be published by the Center of Military History, Department of the Army, Washington, D.C. The basic prosperity of America failed to sustain the war effort because that prosperity had three components: surplus production, marketing mechanisms, and a distribution system. The war simply overtaxed the distribution system and, eventually, the marketing mechanisms. The distribution system had developed in the colonial period as a pattern of fairly short, low-volume overland hauls to navigable water, which was by far the most efficient means of transportation. The war effectively closed the routes of water transportation, and required long-distance, high-volume overland shipments, frequently *across* the river valleys; i.e., in "unnatural" directions for which there was little or no colonial precedent. The marketing mechanisms had developed in the colonial period on the basis of paper money and credit, both dependent on mutual confidence; runaway wartime inflation naturally broke down these marketing mechanisms. Surplus production no doubt diminished during the war, but did not disappear; the problem lay in marketing and distributing the surplus. J. A. Edwards of University College Swansea (Wales) helped me to clarify my thinking on this point, and I am indebted to him.

20. This analysis of British strategy and its problems derives from my essay "The American Revolution: The Military Struggle Considered as a Revolution-

ary War," in *Essays on the American Revolution,* ed. Stephen J. Kurtz and James H. Hutson (Chapel Hill, 1973), and republished in Shy, *A People Numerous and Armed.* My understanding of the subject depends heavily on the work of Piers Mackesy, William B. Willcox, Paul H. Smith, and Ira D. Gruber.

21. The view of the loyalists as essentially "minority" groups belongs to William H. Nelson, *The American Tory* (Boston, 1961), pp. 85-92. Robert McCluer Calhoon, *The Loyalists in Revolutionary America, 1760-1781* (New York, 1973), is the fullest, most recent survey; on p. 562 Calhoon indicates that Nelson's concept has stood up well to the test of further research.

22. Not often do contemporary records or local historians describe the line between Whigs and Tories in ethnic or religious terms; there were good reasons not to do so during the war, and there have been well-known inhibitions against doing so ever since. But close study of the areas committed to one side or the other supports the view that ethnic and religious differences were important determinants of Revolutionary behavior. For example, German settlements in the Carolina back-country appear to have provided much of the manpower for loyalist militia units in that region, although the Scottish role is better known; while other Tories in arms were often described as "regulators," referring to the prewar vigilante insurrections. But on German loyalism, see Edward McCrady, *The History of South Carolina in the Revolution 1775-1780* (New York, 1901), pp. 33 ff., and Robert O. Demond, *The Loyalists in North Carolina during the Revolution* (Durham, N.C., 1940), pp. 54-55. And for an Anglican view of the Waxhaws settlement before the war, there is the Reverend Charles Woodmason (Jan. 25, 1767): "a finer body of land is no where to be seen—But it is occupied by a sett of the most lowest vilest crew breathing—Scotch Irish Presbyterians from the North of Ireland" (Richard J. Hooker, ed., *The Carolina Backcountry on the Eve of the Revolution* [Chapel Hill, 1953], p. 14).

23. This transition in political attitudes between 1776 and 1787 is fully and beautifully described by Gordon Wood, *The Creation of the American Republic, 1776-1787* (Chapel Hill, 1969), but Wood does not relate the transition specifically to the experience of war; I do.

Chapter 6

1. There are several versions of this oration. See, for one, Caleb Stark, *Memoirs and Official Correspondence of General John Stark . . .* (orig. pub. 1860; reprint ed., Boston, 1972), p. 60.

2. Francis V. Greene, *The Revolutionary War and the Military Policy of the United States* (New York, 1911), p. 112.

3. C. H. Van Tyne, *The War of Independence* . . . (Boston, 1929), p. 115.

4. Nathanael Greene to Jacob Greene (?), Sept. 28, 1776, in Richard K. Showman, ed., *The Papers of General Nathanael Greene,* 1 vol. to date (Chapel Hill, 1976—), 1:303. The same opinion appears in George Weedon to Washington, Dec. 4, 1777, Washington Papers, Library of Congress.

5. Memoirs and Correspondence of John Lacey, New-York Historical Society.

6. Washington to James Clinton, Oct. 28, 1780, in John C. Fitzpatrick, ed., *The Writings of George Washington.* . . , 39 vols. (Washington, D.C., 1931-44), 22:260.

7. William B. Reed, *The Life and Correspondence of Joseph Reed,* 2 vols. (Philadelphia 1847), 2:355.

8. Jackson to Henry Knox, Aug. 27, 1777, Henry Knox Papers, Massachusetts Historical Society.

9. Hugh Hastings, ed., *The Public Papers of George Clinton,* 10 vols. (New York and Albany, 1898-1914), 2:169; Daniel Morgan to Horatio Gates, June 24, 1780, Horatio Gates Papers, New-York Historical Society.

10. Louis Morton, "The Historian and the Study of War," *Mississippi Valley Historical Review* 48(1962):600; Don Higginbotham, "American Historians and the Military History of the American Revolution," *American Historical Review* 70(1964):27-28. The same reasons likely explain the neglect of militia in the colonial period. The only pre-World War II doctoral study is Morrison Sharp, "The New England Trainbands in the Seventeenth Century" (Ph.D. diss., Harvard University, 1938). Further speculation on this neglect appears in Richard H. Marcus, "The Militia of Colonial Connecticut, 1639-1775: An Institutional Study" (Ph.D. diss., University of Colorado, 1965), p. 2.

11. John Shy, *A People Numerous and Armed: Military Aspects of the American Revolution* (New York, 1976), pp. 165-67. Edward C. Papenfuse and Gregory A. Stiverson, "General Smallwood's Recruits: The Peacetime Career of the Revolutionary War Private," *William and Mary Quarterly,* 3d ser. 30(1973):117-32; Mark E. Lender, "The Enlisted Line: The Continental Soldiers of New Jersey" (Ph.D. diss., Rutgers University, 1975); John Sellers, "The Origins and Careers of the New England Soldier: Non-commissioned Officers and Privates in the Massachusetts Continental Line" (paper delivered at a meeting of the American Historical Association, December 1972); idem, "The Common Soldier in the Revolution," in *Military History of the American Revolution: Proceedings of the 6th Military History Symposium, USAF Academy,* ed. Stanley J. Underal (Washington, D.C., 1976), pp. 151-61.

12. In short, if the monetary inducements were so attractive, and if so many

Americans were experiencing decreasing economic opportunities and hard times, then the securing of adequate enlistments should not have been such a severe problem for the Continental army. The historians who have found growing indices of stratification in society include James T. Lemon, Gary B. Nash, James A. Henretta, Jackson T. Main, and Kenneth Lockridge.

13. A. S. Sally, ed., *Documents Relating to the History of South Carolina during the Revolutionary War* (Columbia, S.C., 1907), pp. 51-55, 61-67; Walter Clark, ed., *The State Records of North Carolina,* 16 vols. (Winston, Raleigh, and Goldsboro, N.C., 1895-1906 [vols. numbered consecutive to William L. Saunders, ed., *The Colonial Records of North Carolina*]), 24:15. This is not to say, however, that the pay-bounty factor was not important for many men—how many is anybody's guess. But it could work to influence militiamen as well as Continentals. Militiamen could usually avoid service in the field by securing substitutes; that is, men who were called out—usually only a part of each company—could hire less well-to-do neighbors or transients. In two Pennsylvania counties 38.2% and 54.3% respectively of all those drafted employed substitutes. Arthur J. Alexander, "Service by Substitute in the Militia of Lancaster and Northampton Counties (Pennsylvania) during the War of the Revolution," *Military Affairs* 9(1945):278-82. It has been suggested that the war produced a new kind of soldier in the militia, the perpetual substitute, serving in the place of one man, then another, and so on; that in some units he constituted the actual infrastructure of the organization. James B. Bartholomees, "Fight or Flee: The Combat Performance of the North Carolina Militia at the Battle of Cowpens" (M.A. thesis, Duke University, 1976).

14. Ronald Hoffman, "The 'Disaffected' in the Revolutionary South," in *The American Revolution: Explorations in the History of American Radicalism,* ed. Alfred F. Young (DeKalb, Ill., 1976), pp. 273-318; Steven J. Rosswurm, "Lower Class Culture and Activity in Philadelphia: The Crowds and Militia" (Ph.D. diss. in progress, Northern Illinois University). I am grateful to Mr. Rosswurm for sharing some of his findings with me.

15. David C. Skaggs, *Roots of Maryland Democracy* (Westport, Conn., 1973), p. 162. For the removal of loyalist militia officers in one town, see Ronald L. Boucher, "The Colonial Militia as a Social Institution: Salem, Massachusetts, 1764-1775," *Military Affairs* 37(1973):125-29.

16. Alfred F. Young to the author, May 18, 1976. Young is well known for his work on artisans and other non-elites in early America. He and two of his graduate students have been examining the role and place of artisans and farmers in Whig military organizations. Besides the study by Steven J. Rosswurm cited in n. 14, see Walter Wallace, " 'Oh Liberty! Oh Virtue! Oh My Country!': An Exploration of the Minds of New England Soldiers during the American Revolution" (M.A. thesis, Northern Illinois University, 1974).

17. *Journals of the Provincial Congress . . . of New York,* 2 vols. (Albany, 1842).

18. John P. Beeker, *The Sexagenary: or, Reminiscences of the American Revolution* (Albany, 1866), pp. 21-22.

19. Ronald Hoffman, *A Spirit of Dissension: Economics, Politics, and the Revolution in Maryland* (Baltimore, 1973), p. 196. See also Adrian C. Leiby, *The Revolutionary War in the Hackensack Valley* (New Brunswick, N.J., 1962), p. 29.

20. In any case, in the 1790s the militia commander's "chance of political preferment" was excellent; "the step from general to governor or senator was not uncommon" (John K. Mahon, *The American Militia: Decade of Decision, 1789-1800* [Gainesville, Fla., 1960], pp. 34-35). See also Marcus Cunliffe, *Soldiers and Civilians* (New York, 1968).

21. Griffith J. McRee, *The Life and Correspondence of James Iredell,* 2 vols. (New York, 1857-58), 1:272.

22. Julian P. Boyd, ed., *The Papers of Thomas Jefferson,* 19 vols. to date (Princeton, 1950—), 4:260, 6:78-79n; Emory G. Evans, *Thomas Nelson of Yorktown* (Williamsburg, Va., 1975), pp. 102-03.

23. I owe this point about Clinton to Alan C. Aimone of the U.S. Military Academy Library, who is examining the New York militia in the Revolution. But also see Alfred F. Young, *The Democratic Republicans of New York* (Chapel Hill, 1967), pp. 38-39. General William Livingston, head of the New Jersey militia, was elected governor of the state in 1777. His successor as ranking militia officer, General Philemon Dickinson, unsuccessfully opposed Livingston in the gubernatorial elections of 1778, 1779, and 1780. David Bernstein, "New Jersey in the American Revolution: The Establishment of Government Amid Civil and Military Disorder, 1770-1781" (Ph.D. diss., Rutgers University, 1969), p. 238.

24. Shy, *A People Numerous and Armed,* p. 168.

25. Greene to Nicholas Cooke, June 18, 1775, and Greene to Samuel Ward, Sr., Jan. 4, 1776, in Showman, *Papers of Greene,* 1:87, 176. For attitudes of other New Englanders toward militia, see Frank C. Mevers, ed., *The Papers of Josiah Bartlett* (forthcoming).

26. Fitzpatrick, *Writings of Washington,* 5:239.

27. Ibid., 7:272-73. For an extended discussion of Washington's advocacy of concentration, see Russell F. Weigley, *The American Way of War* (New York, 1973), chap. 1.

28. Boyd, *Papers of Jefferson,* 4:110, 142, 151.

29. Hastings, *Papers of Clinton,* 4:289.

30. Generally, the primary thrust of militia reform was toward bringing state troops more quickly into service when needed. To accomplish this, it was necessary to eliminate or modify the practice of "classing," making only select

portions of the militia eligible for active duty at specified times. Governors also required more authority to act decisively when their legislatures were not in session. Legislators whose sections were not threatened by the enemy—from West Jersey in 1780, for example—often slowed or blocked militia reform. Bernstein, "New Jersey in the American Revolution," pp. 311-12, 317-19, 331, 348-51; Richard B. Morris, ed., *John Jay, The Making of a Revolutionary: Unpublished Papers, 1745-1780,* 1 vol. to date (New York, 1975—), 1:375-76n; Arthur J. Alexander, "Pennsylvania's Revolutionary Militia," *Pennsylvania Magazine of History and Biography* 69(1945):15-25.

31. Evans, *Nelson,* pp. 62, 103-04.

32. Hastings, *Papers of Clinton,* 5:602; Fitzpatrick, *Writings of Washington,* 18:389.

33. Lawrence H. Gipson, *The British Empire before the American Revolution,* 15 vols. (Caldwell, Idaho, and New York, 1936-69), 7:viii and passim. See also R. Arthur Bowler, *Logistics and the Failure of the British Army in America, 1775-1783* (Princeton, 1975); Norman Baker, *Government and Contractors* (London, 1971); David Syrett, *Shipping and the American War, 1775-1783* (London, 1970).

34. Walter Millis, *Arms and Men* (New York, 1956), pp. 34-35.

35. Quoted in Hoffman, *Spirit of Dissension,* p. 149.

36. Quoted in Hugh F. Rankin, *Francis Marion: The Swamp Fox* (New York, 1973), p. 2.

37. Leiby, *Hackensack Valley,* p. 139.

38. Richard A. Shrader, "William Lenoir: A Biography" (Ph.D. diss. in progress, University of North Carolina at Chapel Hill), chap. 2.

39. Hastings, *Papers of Clinton,* 4:158, 159.

40. Washington's heavy dependence on Dickinson's militia before Monmouth is reflected in the Virginian's letters to the New Jersey officer. Fitzpatrick, *Writings of Washington,* 12:19, 28, 66, 86, 95, 96, 100, 103, 107, 110, 111, 113, 118, 125. The Monmouth campaign has been described as the most notable success of the state's militia in the war. Bernstein, "New Jersey in the American Revolution," pp. 331-32.

41. E. Stuart Wortley, *A Prime Minister and His Son . . .* (London, 1925), pp. 101-02.

42. "Diary of John Ewald," an edited manuscript in the possession of Joseph Tustin, who kindly permitted me to use it.

43. Charles Ross, ed., *Correspondence of Charles, First Marquis Cornwallis,* 3 vols. (London, 1859), 1:81. See also Banastre Tarleton, *A History of the Campaigns of 1780 and 1781 in the Southern Provinces of North America* (London, 1787), p. 496.

44. Other militia contributions to the regular army included moving supplies,

garrisoning forts and towns, and guarding prisoners of war. To illustrate: Maryland militia escorted captured British soldiers through the state and in 1780 served as guards at a prisoner-of-war camp in Frederick County. Lucy Bowie, "German Prisoners in the American Revolution," *Maryland History Magazine* 40(1945):190.

45. For the contributions of southern militia, see Robert C. Pugh, "The Revolutionay Militia in the Southern Campaigns, 1780-1781," *William and Mary Quarterly*, 3d ser. 14(1957):154-75; and two forthcoming essays by Clyde R. Ferguson: "Carolina and Georgia Patriot and Loyalist Militia in Action, 1778-1783," and "Carolina Partisan-Militia in Action, 1779-1782: Traditional Function in a Revolutionary Situation."

46. Such leaders were superb social psychologists; they recognized the values and preconceptions of their men, factors that historians must master as well if we are to understand how and why men fought in the War of Independence. We need to begin with studies at the company level. Did whole companies come out, or were companies, like regiments, often composites as a result of the classing system? Did men come from the same very immediate area—within a few miles of each other? What sort of family, religious, and economic connections existed between them before their military service? Muster rolls and local town and county records afford us a way of getting at answers to these and other questions. For a promising start in this direction, see Bartholomees, "Fight or Flee," which stresses the value of social cohesion.

47. Shy, *A People Numerous and Armed*, p. 190.

48. Don Higginbotham, *The War of American Independence* (New York, 1971), pp. 94, 375, 412-14, 432; and idem, "Military Leadership in the American Revolution," in *Leadership in the American Revolution*, Library of Congress, (Washington, D.C., 1974), pp. 103-07. So too up to a point did British commanders, or so one gathers from their correspondence. But there nevertheless was an ambivalence on their part as to how to wage war on a daily basis, especially concerning how closely to limit the severity of loyalist tactics. Shy, *A People Numerous and Armed*, pp. 175-84; Robert M. Calhoon, "Civil, Revolutionary, or Partisan: The Loyalists and the Nature of the War for Independence," in *Military History of the American Revolution*, ed. Underal, pp. 93-109.

49. There are numerous cases of the militia's participation in politics. I use the terms "politics" here to denote efforts to shape or influence local or state level matters such as elections, economic issues, and, in the case of Pennsylvania, even constitution-making in 1776. In Philadelphia the militia was highly involved in trying to help chart the course of Whig domestic affairs from the outset of the war. These urban militiamen—unlike those described in previously mentioned studies of other areas—were primarily laborers and poorer artisans. See Charles S. Olton, *Artisans for Independence* (New York, 1975); Eric Foner, "Tom Paine's

Republic: Radical Ideology and Social Change," in *The American Revolution,* ed. Young, pp. 195-96, 215-17; Foner, *Tom Paine and Revolutionary America* (New York, 1976), chaps. 4-5; John K. Alexander, "The Fort Wilson Incident of 1779; A Case Study of the Revolutionary Crowd," *William and Mary Quarterly* 31(1974):589-612. Rosswurm, "Lower Class Culture and Activity in Philadelphia," sees the "excesses" of the militia as a logical result of their social situation; they were "pre-political people," prior to the Revolution, who had become "politicized and organized," and the militia was the "vehicle" by which this was brought about. Rosswurm to the author, Mar. 16, 1777. In some ways the militia (later the National Guard) has continued to be heavily involved in politics. See Martha Derthick, *The National Guard in Politics* (Cambridge, Mass., 1965).

50. Dennis P. Rogers, *New Jersey in the American Revoluiton* (Trenton, 1975), pp. 73, 74; Leiby, *Hackensack Valley,* p. 227; Fitzpatrick, *Writings of Washington,* 12:57n. There were in New Jersey complaints of militia officers billeting their men in private homes and seizing private property. Bernstein, "New Jersey in the American Revolution," p. 327.

51. Joseph Hart to Lacey, Jan. 20, 1778, and Lacey to Hart, Feb. 11, 1778, Lacey Papers, New-York Historical Society.

52. William Moultrie, *Memoirs of the American Revolution. . . ,* 2 vols. (New York, 1802), 1:203.

53. Leiby, *Hackensack Valley,* pp. 225-26.

54. Greene finally persuaded Governor John Rutledge of South Carolina in Sept. 1781 to issue a full pardon to all loyalists who had fought with the British on condition that they serve in the patriot militia. See Hoffman, "The 'Disaffected' in the Revolutionary South," pp. 297, 310-11.

55. Howard H. Peckham, *The Toll of Independence* (Chicago, 1975).

56. Reed, *Joseph Reed,* 2:335.

Chapter 7

1. Memorandum of John Day, Aug. 22, 1775, Edward Hand Papers, Peter Force Transcripts, Library of Congress. Evidently such "psychological warfare" as the Day memorandum was common, since Charles Lee received virtually the

same document from General Burgoyne. See Hand to Jasper Yeates, Aug. 29, 1775, ibid.

2. For American admiration of the British constitution, see Gordon Wood, *The Creation of the American Republic, 1776-1787* (Chapel Hill, 1969), pp. 11, 44-45, 200-03, 262-63, 575-76.

3. Don Higginbotham, *The War of American Independence* (New York, 1971), p. 83; Elbridge Gerry to the Massachusetts delegates in Congress, June 4, 1775, Elbridge Gerry Papers, Library of Congress. For the traditional fear of standing armies, see Richard H. Kohn, *Eagle and Sword* (New York, 1975), pp. 1-6.

4. Adams to Gates, June 18, 1776, in Edmund C. Burnett, ed., *Letters of Members of the Continental Congress,* 8 vols. (Washington, D.C., 1921-36), 1:497.

5. For debates and concern about military power, see Burnett, *Letters of Members of the Continental Congress*, 2:198, 202, 262-63, 269, 300-01; 3:34, 162, 176-78, 255-56; Higginbotham, *War of American Independence,* pp. 205-08; George W. Greene, *The Life of Nathanael Greene. . .* , 3 vols. (New York, 1867-71), 3:255-56.

6. L. H. Butterfield, ed., *The Adams Papers: Diary and Autobiography of John Adams,* 4 vols. (Cambridge, Mass., 1961), diary, Oct. 1776, 2:447.

7. See Roger J. Champagne, *Alexander McDougall and the American Revolution in New York* (Schenectedy, N.Y., 1975), p. 103.

8. Trumbull to Moylan, Jan. 17, 1780, Jonathan Trumbull Papers, Peter Force Transcripts, Library of Congress.

9. Washington to Moylan, Feb. 3, 1780, in John C. Fitzpatrick, ed., *The Writings of George Washington. . .* , 39 vols. (Washington, 1931-44), 17:482. Moylan's responses to Trumbull are dated Jan. 20, 1780, Jan. 26, 1780, and Feb. 7, 1780 [last misdated 1778], Trumbull Papers. For a survey of relations between the army and state governments, see Margaret B. Macmillan, *The War Governors in the American Revolution* (New York, 1943), pp. 116-17, 134-63, 185-86, 195-218.

10. For a complete list of general officers appointed by Congress, see Henry A. Muhlenberg, *The Life of Major General Peter Muhlenberg of the Revolutionary Army* (Philadelphia, 1849), pp. 453-56, or Jonathan Gregory Rossie, *The Politics of Command in the American Revolution* (Syracuse, 1975), pp. 219-21. Two other lists, dated Jan. 9, 1778 and Dec. 4, 1778, are in the Peter Force Papers Miscellany, Library of Congress. The list in Francis B. Heitman, *Historical Register of Officers of the Continental Army . . .* (orig. pub. 1914; reprint ed., Baltimore, 1967), pp. 9-10, omits several names. Because this paper concentrates on 1780, I have emphasized for research those generals then in service. One

list is dated Jan. 1, 1780, in the Henry Knox Papers, Massachusetts Historical Society, 5:113. For an official roster of the thirty-seven generals in service in 1780, see Edward Hand to Jasper Yeates, Mar. 29, 1780, Edward Hand Papers, New York Public Library. Hand was then adjutant general.

11. Greene to John Adams, June 2, 1776, in G. W. Greene, *Nathanael Greene,* 2:423-24.

12. John Shy, "Charles Lee: The Soldier as Radical," in *George Washington's Generals,* ed. George A. Billias (New York, 1964), pp. 28-31; John R. Alden, *Charles Lee, Traitor or Patriot?* (Baton Rouge, 1951), p. 114; George M. Curtis III, "The Goodrich Family and the Revolution in Virginia, 1774-1776," *Virginia Magazine of History and Biography* 84(1976):68-71.

13. Examples of Washington's orders are Washington to Benedict Arnold, Sept. 14, 1775, and Washington, Circular to the States, Aug. 27, 1780, in Fitzpatrick, *Writings of Washington,* 3:491; 19:449-50; for instances of conflict and admissions of violence, see Champagne, *Alexander McDougall,* p. 106; Greene to John Jay, Feb. 20, 1779, Nathanael Greene Papers, William L. Clements Library, University of Michigan; Frank Landon Humphreys, *Life and Times of David Humphreys. . . ,* 2 vols. (New York, 1917), 1:121; G. W. Greene, *Nathanael Greene,* 3:219; William Heath to John Sullivan, July 29, 1778, in Otis G. Hammond, ed., *Letters and Papers of Major-General John Sullivan. . . ,* Collections of the New Hampshire Historical Society, 3 vols. (Concord, N.H., 1930-39), 2:146; Joseph Reed to Congress, 1777, in William B. Reed, *The Life and Correspondence of Joseph Reed,* 2 vols. (Philadelphia, 1847), 1:240. John Paterson justified the use of force and Greene threatened to use it when circumstances dictated. See Paterson to William Heath, May 7, 1780, in Thomas Egleston, *The Life of John Paterson . . .* (New York, 1898), p. 217; Greene to Col. Hathaway, Jan. 1780, Greene Papers, Clements Library; Enoch Poor to Trumbull, Feb. 11, 1780, Trumbull Papers.

14. Greene to Reed, Jan. 9, 1781, in Reed, *Joseph Reed,* 2:344; Washington to Gouverneur Morris, Dec. 10, 1780, in Fitzpatrick, *Writings of Washington,* 20:458. See also Horatio Gates to Jefferson, July 19, 1780, in Julian P. Boyd, ed., *The Papers of Thomas Jefferson,* 19 vols. to date (Princeton, 1950—), 3:496.

15. Mark E. Lender, "The Enlisted Line: The Continental Soldiers of New Jersey" (Ph.D. diss., Rutgers University, 1975), pp. 175-82, 219-28.

16. See Hammond, *Papers of Sullivan,* 1:534-37, 565-66; 3:273; Theodore Thayer, *Nathanael Greene* (New York, 1960), pp. 271-73, 276-77; Louis C. Hatch, *The Administration of the American Revolutionary Army* (orig. pub. 1904; reprint ed., New York, 1971), pp. 103-04, 107-11. For the political aspects of the generals, see, for example, Thayer, *Nathanael Greene,* pp. 212-20; Higginbotham, *War of American Independence,* chap. 9; Rossie, *Politics of*

Command, passim; H. James Henderson, *Party Politics in the Continental Congress* (New York, 1974), pp. 104, 113-20.

17. Greene to Alexander McDougall, Jan. 25, 1778, Alexander McDougall Papers, New-York Historical Society.

18. For indications of the nature of the debate, see Burnett, *Letters of Congress,* 3:32, 34, 162, 170, 174, 176-78, 255-56; Henderson, *Continental Congress,* pp. 120-24.

19. John Adams autobiography, Aug. 1776, in Butterfield, *Diary and Autobiography of Adams,* 3:409-10.

20. Quoted in Lender, "Enlisted Line," p. 125. This study provides the best description of the makeup of the Continental army, especially pp. iv, 111-34, 175-82, 190-92. See also Edward C. Papenfuse and Gregory A. Stiverson, "General Smallwood's Recruits: The Peacetime Career of the Revolutionary War Private," *William and Mary Quarterly,* 3d ser. 30(1973):117-32; John R. Sellers, "The Common Soldier in the Revolution," in *Military History of the American Revolution: Proceedings of the 6th Military History Symposium, USAF Academy,* ed. Stanley J. Underal (Washington, D.C., 1976), pp. 151-61; John C. Miller, *Triumph of Freedom, 1775-1783* (Boston, 1948), pp. 500-01, 506-07. For contemporary British views of the Continental army, see Piers Mackesy, *The War for America, 1775-1783* (Cambridge, Mass., 1964), pp. 31-32.

21. Greene to Henry Laurens, Jan. 12, 1778, Greene Papers, Clements Library. For officers complaints in 1777 and 1778, see also Hatch, *Administration of the Army,* pp. 94-95.

22. See, for example, Lender, "Enlisted Line," pp. 219-28; Maryland officers to Governor Thomas Johnson, 1779, Otho H. Williams Papers, Maryland Historical Society; Arthur St. Clair to Joseph Reed, Mar. 6, 1779, in William H. Smith, ed., *The St. Clair Papers,* 2 vols. (Cincinnati, 1882), 1:462-67.

23. Robert Honeyman journal, Dec. 3, 1778, Library of Congress.

24. Samuel Shaw to ———, Mar. 22, 1779, in Josiah Quincy, *The Journals of Major Samuel Shaw* . . . (Boston, 1847), p. 54.

25. Huntington to Andrew Huntington, Jan. 8, 1780, *Huntington Papers: Correspondence of the Brothers Joshua and Jedidiah Huntington,* Collections of the Connecticut Historical Society, vol. 20 (Hartford, 1923), pp. 437-38. See also Shaw to ———, Mar. 22, 1779, in Quincy, *Samuel Shaw,* pp. 54-55; Robert Honeyman journal, Mar. 16, 1780. For examples of officer grievances over pay at this time, see Joseph Ward to Samuel Huntington, Nov. 26, 1779, Joseph Ward Papers, Chicago Historical Society; New York officers to Washington, Feb. 1, 1780, in Hugh Hastings, ed., *The Public Papers of George Clinton,* 10 vols. (Albany, 1898-1914), 5:478-80.

26. "Unless speedy measures are taken to pay off the army, the consequences must be dangerous to the States," John Stark wrote John Sullivan. "A hint to the wise is sufficient. The army apprehend less danger from the sword of the enemy, than from the ingratitude of their government" (Stark to Sullivan, Dec. 10, 1780, in Caleb Stark, *Memoirs and Official Correspondence of General John Stark . . .* [orig. pub. 1860; reprint ed., Boston, 1972], p. 232). See also St. Clair to Reed, Sept. 5, 1780, in W. H. Smith, *St. Clair Papers,* 1:523-24; McDougall to Greene, Aug. 8, 1780, McDougall Papers.

27. Jackson to Knox, Feb. 28, 1782, quoted in Hatch, *Administration of the Army,* pp. 116-17. See also Greene to O. H. Williams, June 6, 1782, in Reed, *Joseph Reed,* 2:470.

28. See especially James McHenry to Alexander Hamilton, Aug. 11, 1782, in Harold G. Syrett, ed., *The Papers of Alexander Hamilton,* 24 vols. to date (New York, 1961—), 3:129.

29. For a sense of the officers' feelings at war's end, see Greene to O. H. Williams, June 6, 1782, in Reed, *Joseph Reed,* 2:470; [John Armstrong, Jr.], Address to the Officers of the American Army, Mar. 11, 1783, in Worthington C. Ford, ed., *Journals of the Continental Congress, 1774-1789,* 34 vols. (Washington, D.C., 1904-37), 24:295-97; "A Letter to a Member of Congress," 1783, in Arthur St. Clair Papers, Peter Force Transcripts, Library of Congress. The Continental army officer corps deserves a book-length study. The best description of the feelings in the corps and its activities is Sidney Kaplan, "Pay, Pension and Power: Economic Grievances of the Massachusetts Officers of the Revolution," *Boston Public Library Bulletin* 3(1951):15-34, 127-42.

30. Francis Dana to Hamilton, July 25, 1779, in H.G. Syrett, *Papers of Hamilton,* 2:108. Dana was relating a story he heard from the Reverend William Gordon, who had it from another man. Hamilton, of course, vehemently denied it, and there is no proof for the story. See John Brooks to Hamilton, July 9, 1779; Hamilton to Dana, July 11, 1779; Brooks to Hamilton, Aug. 8, 1779; Gordon to Hamilton, Aug. 25, 1779; Hamilton to Gordon, Sept. 5, 1779; in Syrett, *Papers of Hamilton* 2:91, 99, 108-09, 125-26, 141-43.

31. Greene to Lewis Morris, Sept. 14, 1780, Greene Papers, Clements Library. For the warnings, see St. Clair to Reed, in W. H. Smith, *St. Clair Papers,* 1:523-24; Stark to Sullivan, Dec. 10, 1780, in Stark, *John Stark,* p. 232; McDougall to Greene, Aug. 8, 1780, McDougall Papers.

32. Reed to [Greene?], Sept. 1780, in G. W. Greene, *Nathanael Greene,* 3:344.

33. Memorandum of Lewis Nicola, enclosed in Nicola to Washington, May 22, 1782, Washington Papers, Library of Congress.

34. Yeates to Edward Hand, July 4, 1783, Hand Papers, Force Transcripts;

Greene to Reed, Apr. 23, 1783, and Greene to O. H. Williams, Apr. 11, 1783, in Reed, *Joseph Reed,* 2:395-96, 474-75.

35. Smith to Elias Boudinot, Apr. 1783, "Letters from William Peartree Smith to Elias Boudinot . . . ,'' *Proceedings of the New Jersey Historical Society,* 1st ser. 4(1849):122.

36. Jefferson to Washington, Apr. 16, 1784, in Boyd, *Papers of Jefferson,* 7:106-07.

37. William Floyd to George Clinton, Dec. 21, 1779, in Hastings, *Papers of Clinton,* 5:426. For the crisis of 1780 and its background, see Henderson, *Continental Congress,* chaps. 7-9; Miller, *Triumph of Freedom,* chaps. 18, 22-23; E. James Ferguson, *The Power of the Purse* (Chapel Hill, 1961), pp. 44-47, 59-69, 92-112.

38. Shaw to ———, June 20, 1780, in Quincy, *Samuel Shaw,* p. 75; Reed to Washington, June 5, 20, 1780, in Reed, *Joseph Reed,* 2:209, 215; Rufus Rockwell Wilson, ed., *Heath's Memoirs of the American War Reprinted from the Original Edition of 1798* (New York, 1904), pp. 255-56.

39. Timothy Pickering to John Pickering, June 13, 1780, Timothy Pickering Papers, Massachusetts Historical Society; Reed, *Joseph Reed,* 2:209, 214; Samuel Paterson to Caesar Rodney, June 22, 1780, William B. Sprague Collection of Caesar and Thomas Rodney, Peter Force Papers, Library of Congress; minutes of the New England Convention, Nov. 1780, in Charles J. Hoadley and Leonard Labaree, eds., *The Public Records of the State of Connecticut,* 45 vols. (Hartford and New Haven, 1894-1943), 3:571; William Moultrie, *Memoirs of the American Revolution. . . ,* 2 vols. (New York, 1802), 2:220.

40. Luzerne to Vergennes, Apr. 16, 1780, in Fitzpatrick, *Writings of Washington,* 18:211n. I have used the translation in G. W. Greene, *Nathanael Greene,* 3:256. For talk of dictators, see William Livingston to John Witherspoon, Dec. 28, 1780, William Livingston Papers, Massachusetts Historical Society; Greene to Lewis Morris, Sept. 14, 1780, Greene Papers, Clements Library.

41. Henry Knox to Lucy Knox, 1777, Knox Papers, 4:87; Don R. Gerlach, *Philip Schuyler and the American Revolution in New York, 1733-1777* (Lincoln, Neb., 1964), pp. 301-02.

42. Jedidiah Huntington to Jabez Huntington, Nov. 11, 1777, *Huntington Papers,* 20:379; Greene to William Smallwood, Mar. 16, 1778, Miscellaneous Manuscripts, New-York Historical Society; John Adams to Sullivan, June 3, 1777, in Hammond, *Papers of Sullivan,* 1:368; Allan Nevins, *The American States During and After the Revolution, 1775-1789* (New York, 1924), p. 492.

43. Wayne to Richard Peters, Apr. 12, 1778, Anthony Wayne Papers, Historical Society of Pennsylvania. See also George Weedon to Greene, Sept.

20, 1779, in Mrs. Catesby Willis Stewart, *The Life of Brigadier General William Woodford of the American Revolution,* 2 vols. (Richmond, 1973), 2:1086-88.

44. Washington to George Mason, Mar. 27, 1779, in Fitzpatrick, *Writings of Washington,* 14:301.

45. McDougall to [Elisha Boudinot], Nov. 1, 1778, Miscellaneous Manuscripts Collection, Library of Congress.

46. Boudinot to McDougall, Jan. 22, 1779, McDougall Papers. McDougall's feelings at this time are described excellently in Champagne, *Alexander McDougall,* chaps. 9-11. For statements not cited above by generals in 1789 and 1779, on similar and related subjects, see Wayne to Gouverneur Morris, May 16, 1778, Wayne Papers; Gates to Henry Laurens, June 3, 1778, Horatio Gates Papers, New-York Historical Society; Greene to Charles Pettit, Jan. 2, 1779, William B. Sprague Collection of Nathanael Greene Papers, Peter Force Transcripts, Library of Congress; George Weedon to Greene, Mar. 10, 1779, Greene Papers, Clements Library; Lachlan McIntosh to Benjamin Lincoln, Aug. 4, 1779, Miscellaneous Collection, William L. Clements Library.

47. Sullivan to McDougall, Jan. 27, 1781, in Hammond, *Papers of Sullivan,* 3:273. See also Thomas Burke to Sullivan, Oct. 12, 1777, and Sullivan to Burke, Oct. 27, 1777, in Hammond, *Papers of Sullivan*, 1:534-37, 565-66.

48. General officers to Congress, Dec. 31, 1777, in Hammond, *Papers of Sullivan* 1:606-08; Champagne, *Alexander McDougall*, p. 135; Hatch, *Administration of the Army,* pp. 55-57; Greene to [Knox?], Feb. 26, 1778, Miscellaneous Manuscripts, New-York Historical Society; Mordecai Gist to John Amory, Nov. 19, 1777, Mordecai Gist Papers, Peter Force Transcripts, Library of Congress; Jedidiah Huntington to Jabez Huntington, Dec. 29, 1777, *Huntington Papers,* 20:390-91; John Clark to Greene, Jan. 10, 1778, Greene Papers, Clements Library.

49. Varnum to Sullivan, May 27, 1778, in Hammond, *Papers of Sullivan,* 2:60.

50. Parsons to Root, Aug. 29, 1779, in Charles S. Hall, *Life and Letters of Samuel Holden Parsons* (Binghamton, N.Y., 1905), p. 267. For the finances of the generals, see, for example, Sullivan to Washington, Feb. 1778, and Mar. 2, 1778, in Hammond, *Papers of Sullivan,* 2:17-19; Gates to Robert Morris, May 12, 1779, Gates Papers; Peter Muhlenberg to the Board of War, Dec. 20, 1780, in Muhlenberg, *Peter Muhlenberg,* pp. 213-15; John Stark to the president of Congress, Sept. 1, 1781, in Stark, *John Stark,* p. 232.

51. Willard M. Wallace, "Benedict Arnold: Traitorous Patriot," in *George Washington's Generals,* ed. Billias, pp. 163-92; Rossie, *Politics of Command,* p. 210; George A. Billias, *General John Glover and His Marblehead Mariners* (New York, 1960), pp. 177-91. Five major generals and two brigadiers resigned in 1778 and 1779.

52. See, for example, Hand to Richard Peters, Dec. 24, 1777, Hand Papers, Force Transcripts.

53. Washington to the president of Congress, Aug. 20, 1780, in Fitzpatrick, *Writings of Washington,* 19:408. For other examples of calls for a regular army, see Washington, "Remarks on Plan of Field Officers for Remodeling the Army," Nov. 1777, ibid., 10:125-26; field officers' plan for reorganizing the army, [1777], Gist Papers, Force Transcripts; Greene to Smallwood, Mar. 16, 1778, Miscellaneous Manuscripts, New-York Historical Society; William Heath to Washington, Mar. 21, 1778, in *The Heath Papers,* Collections of the Massachusetts Historical Society (Boston, 1898-1905), 7th ser. 4:221-22; William Irvine to Reed, and Greene to Reed, Mar. 18, 1781, in Reed, *Joseph Reed,* 2:117-18, 349; Steuben to Trumbull, Apr. 20, 1779, Trumbull Papers, Force Transcripts; Greene to Knox, May 20, 1782, Knox Papers.

54. Greene to Samuel Blachley Webb, Dec. 21, 1779, in Worthington C. Ford, ed., *Correspondence and Journals of Samuel Blachley Webb,* 3 vols. (New York, 1894), 2:231. For the quartermaster troubles, see Hatch, *Administration of the Army,* pp. 97-98, 103, 107-08.

55. Greene to Sullivan, Dec. 3, 1779, in Hammond, *Papers of Sullivan,* 2:171.

56. Greene to Charles Pettit, Jan. 2, 1780, Greene Papers, Clements Library.

57. Greene to James Duane, Apr. 16, 1779, ibid.

58. Greene to Clement Biddle, June 29, 1780, in Reed, *Joseph Reed,* 2:468-69. See also Greene to Catherine Greene, Aug. 14, 1780, Nathanael Greene Papers, William A. Read Collection, William L. Clements Library; Greene to William Greene, Sept. 3, 1780, and Greene to Nathaniel Peabody, Sept. 6, 1780, Greene Papers, Clements Library.

59. Huntington to Andrew Huntington, July 17, 1780, *Huntington Papers,* 20:441; Paterson to Heath, May 7, 1780, *Heath Papers,* 7th ser. 5:62.

60. Paterson to Heath, Mar. 31, 1780, *Heath Papers,* 7th ser. 5:44.

61. See Heath to the Massachusetts General Assembly, Apr. 7, 1780, and Heath to Robert Howe, Apr. 26, 1780, in *Heath Papers*, 7th ser. 5:51-55, 59; Heath to Clinton, Nov. 5, 1780, in Hastings, *Papers of Clinton,* 6:382-85.

62. Knox to Joseph Ward, July 28, 1780, Ward Papers. See also Knox to Heath, Mar. 17, 1780, *Heath Papers,* 7th ser. 5:41; St. Clair to Reed, Sept. 5, 1780, in W. H. Smith, *St. Clair Papers,* 1:524; Hand to Jaspar Yeates, Sept. 10, 1780, Hand Papers, New York Public Library.

63. Wayne to Washington, Mar. 19, 1781, Washington Papers. See also Wayne to Col. Johnston, Mar. 25, 1780, and Wayne to Robert Harrison, May 20, 1780, Wayne Papers.

64. McDougall to Egbert Benson, Feb. 9, 1778, McDougall Papers.

65. Greene to McDougall, Feb. 11, [1779], ibid.

66. McDougall to Greene, Mar. 24, 1779, Nathanael Greene Papers, American Philosophical Society Library. See also McDougall to Reed, Mar. 25, 1779, in Reed, *Joseph Reed,* 2:59.

67. McDougall to Greene, May 29, 1780, Greene Papers, Clements Library.

68. McDougall to Greene, Aug. 8, 1780, McDougall Papers. The petition, signed by sixteen American generals and Lafayette, dated July 11, 1780, is in the Greene Papers. It is printed, along with a petition from the New England generals to their state governments, dated Oct. 7, 1780, in Stark, *John Stark,* pp. 221-29. See also Robert Howe to Greene, July 14, 1780, and Ezekiel Cornell to Greene, Aug. 15, 1780, Greene Papers, Clements Library; Stark to Sullivan, Nov. 20, 1780, John Stark Papers, Peter Force Transcripts, Library of Congress; Sullivan to Stark, Nov. 28, 1780, in Hammond, *Papers of Sullivan,* 3:224-25. The mission is covered excellently in Champagne, *Alexander McDougall,* chap. 11.

69. Knox claimed that "the system is so abominably defective that it ought to be chang'd instantly" (Knox to McDougall, Mar. 4, 1781, McDougall Papers).

70. Armstrong to Gates, Feb. 16, 1780, Gates Papers.

71. See Lachlan McIntosh to Benjamin Lincoln, Aug. 4, 1779, Miscellaneous Collection, Clements Library; Schulyer to Greene, Mar. 22, 1780, in Burnett, *Letters of Congress,* 5:90-91; Wayne to Robert Harrison, May 20, 1780, and Wayne to Reed, Sept. 17, 1780, Wayne Papers; Hamilton to James Duane, Sept. 3, 1780, in H. G. Syrett, *Hamilton Papers,* 2:400-18; Hand to Jasper Yeates, Sept. 10, 1780, Hand Papers, New York Public Library; Greene to Lewis Morris, Sept. 14, 1780, Greene Papers, Clements Library; Henry Lee to Thomas Sim Lee, Sept. 18, 1780, Emmet Collection, New York Public Library; Mordecai Gist to Robert Munford, Oct. 24, 1780, Mordecai Gist Papers, Maryland Historical Society; Greene to McDougall, Oct. 30, 1780, and Knox to McDougall, Mar. 4, 1781, McDougall Papers; Washington to James Duane, Dec. 26, 1780, in Fitzpatrick, *Writings of Washington,* 21:14. For the nature of the link between nationalists and generals, I benefited from conversation with Joseph L. Davis, whose study, tentatively titled "Sectionalism and the Politics of Revolutionary America," is in press at the University of Wisconsin Press.

72. Schuyler to Washington, Jan. 21, 1781, in Jared Sparks, ed., *Correspondence of the American Revolution . . . Letters . . . to George Washington,* 4 vols. (Boston, 1853), 3:213.

73. Arnold to Samuel Holden Parsons, Sept. 8, 1780, Benedict Arnold Papers, Peter Force Transcripts, Library of Congress.

74. Arnold to Parsons, Sept. 12, 1780, ibid.

75. Quoted in Higginbotham, *War of American Independence,* p. 85.

76. F. Michaelis to George Beckwith, Oct. 4, 1783, Bancroft Transcripts, New York Public Library. For veneration of Washington by 1780, see Marcus

Cunliffe, *George Washington: Man and Monument* (London, 1959), pp. 13, 14, 18, 21, 106-07, 158-62.

77. Sullivan to Washington, Dec. 1, 1779, in Hammond, *Papers of Sullivan,* 3:169. See also Greene to Sullivan, July 23, 1778, in Hammond, *Papers of Sullivan* 2:103-04.

78. Greene to Reed, May 10, 1780, in Reed, *Joseph Reed,* 2:191.

79. For the rank competition, see Champagne, *Alexander McDougall,* p. 107; Howard P. Moore, *A Life of General John Stark of New Hampshire* (Boston, 1949), pp. 236-38; Muhlenberg, *Peter Muhlenberg,* pp. 126-40; Parsons to McDougall, Oct. 17, 1780, McDougall Papers; Robert Howe to [Congress?], June 8, 1777, Force Papers, Miscellany; Weedon to Greene, Oct. 5, 1778, Greene Papers, Clements Library; Weedon to Greene, Sept. 20, 1779, in Stewart, *William Woodford,* 2:1086-88; Mordecai Gist to Washington, Nov. 30, 1777, and Gist to Thomas Johnson, Sept. 19, 1777, Gist Papers, Force Transcripts; Moses Hazen to Sullivan, Apr. 30, 1781, in Hammond, *Papers of Sullivan,* 3:308-12.

80. Edward Hand diary, Aug. 5, 1779, Emmet Collection, New York Public Library. See also James Wilkinson to St. Clair, Sept. 21, 1777, Oct. 7, 1777, in W. H. Smith, *St. Clair Papers,* 1:443, 444.

81. Quoted in Don Higginbotham, ''Military Leadership in the American Revolution,'' in *Leadership in the American Revolution,* Library of Congress, (Washington, D.C., 1974), p. 101. See also Benjamin Rush to Wayne, Sept. 26, 1776, in Burnett, *Letters of Congress,* 2:108; William Irvine to Wayne, Nov. 19, 1778, Wayne Papers; Rossie, *Politics of Command,* passim.

82. See Hatch, *Administration of the Army,* p. 7; Kenneth R. Rossman, *Thomas Mifflin and the Politics of the American Revolution* (Chapel Hill, 1952), p. 57. I am greatly indebted to Mary Wright for researching in the secondary sources the social, economic, and political backgrounds of over sixty American generals of the Revolution. The backgrounds and career patterns of the generals were compared with James K. Martin's conclusions in *Men in Rebellion* (New Brunswick, N.J., 1973).

83. John Adams autobiography, Oct. 1776, in Butterfield, *Diary and Autobiography of Adams,* 3:446.

84. Elias Dayton to Abraham Clark, Nov. 1777, Emmet Collection, New York Public Library.

85. See James Clinton to George Clinton, Sept. 8, 1780, in Hastings, *Papers of Clinton,* 6:185.

86. McDougall to Washington, Oct. 30, 1780, in Sparks, *Letters to Washington,* 3:136. See also ''Aristides'' [Greene] to McDougall, Oct. 30, 1780, McDougall Papers; Champagne, *Alexander McDougall,* chap. 12.

87. See, for example, Greene to Reed, Aug. 6, 1781, in Reed, *Joseph Reed,*

2:363-64; Greene to Weedon, Oct. 1, 1782, George Weedon Papers, American Philosophical Society Library; Wayne to Benjamin Rush, Sept. 20, 1779, May 10, 1782, Miscellaneous Manuscripts Collection, Library of Congress.

88. Adams, address to the cadets at West Point, Aug. 1821, in Charles Francis Adams, ed., *The Works of John Adams,* 10 vols. (Boston, 1850-56), 10:419. See also Douglass Adair, "Fame and the Founding Fathers," in *Fame and the Founding Fathers,* ed. Edmund P. Willis (Bethlehem, Pa., 1967), pp. 27-52.

89. Sullivan to Washington, Jan. 29, 1781, in Hammond, *Papers of Sullivan,* 3:276-77.

90. Hand to Jasper Yeates, July 17, 1781, Hand Papers, Force Transcripts.

91. McDougall to Greene, May 29, 1780, Greene Papers, Clements Library.

92. McDougall to Greene, Mar. 21, 1780, ibid. See also Gates to Heath, Apr. 30, 1779, in *Heath Papers,* 7th ser. 4:299-300; Wayne to Col. Johnston, Mar. 25, 1780, Wayne Papers; Greene to Washington, Oct. 31, 1780, in Sparks, *Letters to Washington,* 3:139; Knox to William Knox, July 20, 1781, in Francis S. Drake, *Life and Correspondence of Henry Knox* . . . (Boston, 1873) p. 66.

93. Greene to Lewis Morris, Sept. 14, 1780, Greene Papers, Clements Library. See also Greene to Washington, Oct. 31, 1780, in Sparks, *Letter to Washington,* 3:139.

94. For examples, see Israel Putnam to Trumbull, Jan. 1779; Jedidiah Huntington to Trumbull, Apr. 2, 1780; Robert Howe to Trumbull, Apr. 27, 1780; Parsons to Trumbull, Jan. 14, 30, 1781, and Feb. 5, 1781, Trumbull Papers, Force Transcripts. Also, Wayne and Irvine to the Pennsylvania officers, Aug. 12, 1780; Wayne and Irvine to Washington, Aug. 11, 1780; and Wayne to Reed, Sept. 3, 1780, Wayne Papers. Gates to Heath, Apr. 30, 1779, and Heath to Jeremiah Powell, Sept. 2, 1779, in *Heath Papers,* 7th ser. 4:299-300, 316; Parsons to Jesse Root, Aug. 29, 1779, in Hall, *Samuel Holden Parsons,* pp. 266-69; St. Clair to Reed, Mar. 6, 1779, in W. H. Smith, *St. Clair Papers,* 1:462-67; Carl Van Doren, *Mutiny in January* . . . (New York, 1943).

95. For the outcome of the generals' petition to Congress, see Ford, *Journals of Congress,* 17:689, 725-27, 770-73, 777-78; 18:958-59, 1099-1100; Champagne, *Alexander McDougall,* p. 163.

96. See n. 71 above.

97. Lincoln to Knox, Jan. 23, 1781, Knox Papers.

98. John Paterson et al. to Heath, Feb. 5, 1782; to Knox, Feb. 5, 1782; and to the Massachusetts delegates, Feb. 5, 1782, in Egleston, *John Paterson,* pp. 254, 255-56, 257-59. Also Heath to Knox, June 24, 1782; Knox to Lincoln, Aug. 19, 1782; and Lincoln to Knox, Aug. 26, 1782, Knox Papers.

99. Williams to Greene, Dec. 22, 1782, Nathanael Greene Papers, Library of Congress.

100. For McDougall's role and the conspiracy, see Kohn, *Eagle and Sword,* chap. 2.

101. Morris to Knox, Feb. 7, 1783, in Burnett, *Letters of Congress,* 7:34n; Morris to Greene, Feb. 15, 1783, in Jared Sparks, *The Life of Gouverneur Morris,* 2 vols. (Boston, 1832), 1:250-51.

102. Knox to McDougall, Feb. 21, 1783, Knox Papers. See also Knox to Gouverneur Morris, Feb. 21, 1783, ibid.

103. Greene to Morris, Apr. 3, 1783, in Sparks, *Gouverneur Morris,* 1:251-52.

104. For Gates's role, see Paul David Nelson, "Horatio Gates at Newburgh, 1783: A Misunderstood Role," with rebuttal, and C. Edward Skeen, "The Newburgh Conspiracy Reconsidered," with rebuttal, *William and Mary Quarterly,* 3d ser. 29(1972):143-58, 31(1974):273-98. I am indebted to Nelson for allowing me to read in advance portions of his newly published *General Horatio Gates* (Baton Rouge, 1976).

105. Armstrong to Christopher Van Deventer, Jan. 29, 1816, Christopher Van Deventer Collection, William L. Clements Library.

106. See Washington, speech to the officers, Mar. 15, 1783, in Fitzpatrick, *Writings of Washington,* 26:227. The positions of Knox, Greene, and McDougall have been discussed in the text. For the opinions of other generals, see Hand to Yeates, Mar. 17, 1783, Apr. 3, 1783, Hand Papers, Force Transcripts: Jedidiah Huntington to Andrew Huntington, Mar. 18, 1783, *Huntington Papers,* 20:460; draft of a speech [Putnam?], Mar. 1783, Knox Papers, 12:22; Hand to Irvine, Apr. 19, 1783, Bancroft Transcripts; Kohn, *Eagle and Sword,* pp. 314, 315, 316.

107. Gordon to Gates, Feb. 26, 1783, in "Letters of the Reverend William Gordon. . . ," *Proceedings of the Massachusetts Historical Society* 63(1931):488.

108. Morris to Greene, May 18, 1783, Greene Papers, Library of Congress.

109. It was *"then,"* remembered Benjamin Lincoln in 1798, that "he trembled for his country" (E. S. Thomas, *Reminiscences of the Last Sixty-Five Years. . . ,* 2 vols. [Hartford, 1840], 1:125).

110. Humphreys to Greene, May 30, 1780, in Humphreys, *David Humphreys,* 1:150. At the time, Humphreys was Greene's aide, having served already as brigade major to Parsons and aide to Putnam. Less than a month after writing to Greene, Humphreys became aide to Washington.

111. "Institution of the Society of the Cincinnati," May 13, 1783, Society of Cincinnati Papers, Peter Force Transcripts, Library of Congress. Generals set up the society, wrote the charter, and virtually to a man joined it. See journal of the meeting, May 10-13, 1783; journal of the Society, June 19, 1783; Gates to

Steuben, Aug. 20, 1783; St. Clair to Steuben, Sept. 3, 1783; "List of officer
Names, who have signed the Cincinnati Society," in William Smallwood to
Washington, Nov. 29, 1783, Cincinnati Papers.

Chapter 8

I am grateful to the Connecticut Historical Association for permission to quote
from manuscripts in its possession. I also wish to acknowledge my appreciation to
the National Endowment for the Humanities and the American Council of
Learned Societies for grants relating to this project.

1. Ira D. Gruber, *The Howe Brothers and the American Revolution* (New
York, 1972), p. vii; the same question was the premise around which William B.
Willcox's "Too Many Cooks: British Planning Before Saratoga," *Journal of
British Studies* 2(1962):56-90, and "Rhode Island in British Strategy, 1780-
1781," *Journal of Modern History* 17(1945):304-31 were written. See also
Frederick Wyatt and William B. Willcox, "Sir Henry Clinton: A Psychological
Exploration in History," *William and Mary Quarterly,* 3d ser. 16(1959):3-26.

2. Cf. Don Higginbotham, "Military Leadership in the American Revolution," in *Leadership in the American Revolution,* Library of Congress
(Washington, D.C., 1974), pp. 103-04; John Shy, "The American Revolution:
The Military Conflict Considered as a Revolutionary War," in *Essays on the
American Revolution,* ed. Stephen G. Kurtz and James H. Hutson (Chapel Hill,
1973), pp. 121-56; Russell F. Weigley, *The American Way of War* (New York,
1973), chaps. 1-2.

3. Piers Mackesy, *The War for America, 1775-1783* (Cambridge, Mass.,
1964), p. 55; also idem, "British Strategy in the War of American Independence," *Yale Review* 52(1963):547-48; Paul H. Smith, *Loyalists and Redcoats*
(Chapel Hill, 1964), passim.

4. See Edwin G. Burrows and Michael Wallace, "The American Revolution: The Ideology and Psychology of National Liberation," *Perspectives in
American History* 6(1972): 295-99.

5. Weigley, *The American Way of War,* chap. 2; and idem, *The Partisan
War: The South Carolina Campaign of 1780-1782* (Columbia, S.C., 1970).

6. Mackesy, "British Strategy," p. 548; Eric Robson, *The American
Revolution in Its Political and Military Aspects, 1763-1783* (London, 1955), pp.

108-111; Paul H. Smith, "The American Loyalists: Notes on Their Organizations and Numerical Strength," *William and Mary Quarterly*, 3d ser. 25(1968): 259-77, gives the most judicious estimate available as to the extent of British reliance on American manpower.

7. R. Arthur Bowler, *Logistics and the Failure of the British Army in America, 1775-1783* (Princeton, 1975), passim; Mackesy, *War for America*, pp. 65 ff.; idem, "British Strategy," p. 543.

8. See Peter Force, ed., *American Archives . . .* (Washington, D.C., 1837-53), 4th ser. 1:653n; Charles Lee, *Strictures on a Pamphlet, entitled, A Friendly Address to All Reasonable Americans . . .* (Philadelphia, 1774), p. 7.

9. Daniel Dulany, *Considerations on the propriety of imposing taxes in the British Colonies . . .* (New York, 1765), pp. 21 ff.; John Dickinson, "The Farmer's Letters to the Inhabitants of the British Colonies," in *Political Writings of John Dickinson, Esquire . . .* (Wilmington, Del., 1801), 1:222-23; also Force, *American Archives*, 4th ser. 1:1168.

10. Force, *American Archives*, 4th ser. 1:415, 947; also 6:169, 299; John Adams's notes on debates Sept. 26, 27, 28, 1774, in Edmund C. Burnett, ed., *Letters of Members of the Continental Congress*, 8 vols. (Washington, D.C., 1921-36), 1:49, 53; Lee, *Strictures*, 5n.

11. Such was the expectation of "Americanus" in *Connecticut Gazette*, Dec. 30, 1774.

12. Thomas Paine, "Common Sense," in Philip S. Foner, ed., *The Complete Writings of Thomas Paine*, 2 vols. (New York, 1945), 1:32, 36, 41.

13. Washington to the president of Congress, Sept. 8, 1776, in John C. Fitzpatrick, ed., *The Writings of George Washington. . . ,* 39 vols. (Washington, D.C., 1931-44), 6:27 29; Force, *American Archives*, 5th ser. 3:589-90; Jedidiah Huntington to Jonathan Trumbull, Nov. 7, 1776, Jonathan Trumbull Papers, Connecticut State Library, 5:249 (hereafter cited as JT:CSL).

14. Mackesy, *War for America*, pp. 495, 512-13; idem, "British Strategy," p. 557.

15. John Dalrymple, *The Address of the People of Great Britain to the Inhabitants of America* (London, 1775), reprinted in Force, *American Archives*, 4th ser. 1:1413.

16. Force, *American Archives*, 4th ser. 1:654n; Lee, *Strictures*, pp. 6-8.

17. E. James Ferguson, *The Power of the Purse* (Chapel Hill, 1961), chap. 1; Joseph A. Ernst, *Money and Politics in America: 1755-1775* (Chapel Hill, 1973), passim; also Marc Egnal and Joseph Ernst, "An Economic Interpretation of the American Revolution," *William and Mary Quarterly*, 3d ser. 29(1972): 18-19.

18. Ferguson, *Power of the Purse*, p. 32. Depreciation rates varied with local circumstances. In July 1777 Continental money was 4:1 in Boston whereas in

Philadelphia it was 3:1; cf. T. Boutineau to J. Wadsworth, July 30, 1777, Jeremiah Wadsworth Papers, Connecticut Historical Society, Box 125 (hereafter cited as JW:CHS).

19. Worthington C. Ford, ed., *Journals of the Continental Congress, 1774-1789,* 34 vols. (Washington, D.C., 1904-37), 5:845 (hereafter cited as JCC). The subscription of state currency would have been subject to the discretion of the commissioners of the treasury or the Continental treasurer.

20. These figures are extrapolated from data supplied by R. V. Harlow, "Aspects of Revolutionary Finance," *American Historical Review* 35(1929): 50-51 (insert), using a conversion rate of $3.33 to £1. Also J. E. D. Binney, *British Public Finance and Administration 1774-92* (Oxford, 1958), particularly appendix 1.

21. Ferguson, *Power of the Purse,* p. 31; also William Williams to Jonathan Trumbull, Sept. 30, 1777, in Burnett, *Letters of Congress,* 2:505.

22. *JCC,* 5:541, 600, 604, 608, 609, 611, 612, 615, 616, 621, 624, 628, 635, 636, 639, 674, 677; 6:1098 ff.; Josiah Bertlett to William Whipple, Sept. 10, 1776, in Burnett, *Letters of Congress,* 2:83.

23. Samuel Chase to Philip Schuyler, Aug. 9, 1776; William Williams to Oliver Wolcott, Aug. 12, 1776; and Edward Rutledge to Robert R. Livingston, Aug. 19, 1776, in Burnett, *Letters of Congress,* 2:44, 48, 56; also William Williams to Joseph Trumbull, Oct. 7, 1776, Joseph Trumbull Papers, Connecticut Historical Society.

24. Henry Laurens to John Rutledge, Sept. 10, 1777, in Burnett, *Letters of Congress,* 2:491; *JCC,* 9:956; interesting comments on the beginning of the depreciation are also contained in Nicholas Street, *The American State acting over the part of the children of Israel in the Wilderness . . .* (New Haven, 1777), pp. 24, 26.

25. *JCC,* 5:762 ff.

26. Examples of such legislation by the states are to be found in Charles J. Hoadley and Leonard Labaree, eds., *The Public Records of the State of Connecticut,* 45 vols. (Hartford and New Haven, 1894-1943), 1:5-6, 62-65.

27. Congress recommended this expedient on Nov. 22, 1777; see *JCC,* 9:971.

28. See for instance Connecticut's attempt to "draft" men into the three-year army in the spring of 1777; Hoadley and Labaree, *Public Records,* 1:207-09, 240-42. Virginia's experience was similar; see W. W. Hening, ed., *The Statutes at Large Being a Collection of All the Laws of Virginia* (Richmond, 1809-23), 9:338-43.

29. The policy of the states' retiring their currency issues was first proposed by the convention of the New England states together with New York that met in Springfield, Massachusetts, at the end of July and beginning of Aug. 1777.

Hoadley and Labaree, *Public Records,* 1:603, 606. Congress endorsed the proposal on Nov. 22, 1777. *JCC,* 9:955-56. For Connecticut's compliance, see Hoadley and Labaree, *Public Records,* 1:531.

30. Franklin, Deane, and A. Lee to Committee of Secret Correspondence, Jan. 17, 1777, in Frances Wharton, ed., *The Revolutionary Diplomatic Correspondence of the United States,* 6 vols. (Washington, D.C., 1889), 2:250.

31. *JCC,* 7:158.

32. William Carmichael to Committee of Secret Correspondence, Nov. 2, 1776, in Wharton, *Revolutionary Diplomatic Correspondence,* 2:187; cf. also Henry Laurens to John Rutledge, Sept. 10, 1777, in Burnett, *Letters of Congress,* 2:489.

33. *JCC* 8:724-25.

34. *JCC,* 9:785, 788, 793, 797, 801, 834, 925, 932, 934; see also 981, 985.

35. Ibid., 9:955.

36. Ferguson, *Power of the Purse,* p. 37.

37. J. Tracy to J. Wadsworth, May 7, 1778 in JW:CHS, Box 126.

38. Congress downgraded the importance of the alliance in its address to the people of May 8, 1778; *JCC,* 11:477-78 (p. 477 quoted).

39. *JCC,* 10:327-28, 345, 361; Wadsworth's undated memo to S. Huntington, [Mar. 1778], JW:CHS, Box 126; cf. also F. Dyer to W. Williams, Feb. 17, 1778, and to J. Wadsworth, Mar. 10, 1778, in Burnett, *Letters of Congress,* 3:88, 121.

40. *JCC,* 11:569; Hoadley and Labaree, *Public Records,* 2:12-13.

41. Peter Colt to R. Flint, Nov. 3, 1778; John Chester to Wadsworth, Nov. 24, 1778; J. Lloyd to Wadsworth, Dec. 1, 1778; and J. Watson to Wadsworth, Jan. 4, 1779, JW: CHS, Box 127.

42. The inspiration for Connecticut's price-fixing law came from a convention that met in New Haven in Jan. 1778. Cf. Hoadley and Labaree, *Public Records,* 1:613-18, 524-28; for the sources of popular support behind the Regulating Act, see *Connecticut Courant,* June 7, 1778.

43. P. Colt to Wadsworth, June 3, 1779, JW:CHS, Box 128.

44. There were ten separate emissions dated May 20, 1777, totaling $16 million and ending only on Apr. 18, 1778. There were five emissions dated Apr. 11, 1778, ending Sept. 5, 1778, and totaling $25 million.

45. *JCC,* 13:20-22.

46. Chaloner and White to Wadsworth, May 24, 1779, JW:CHS, Box 128; also Henry Laurens, Notes on Proceedings, May 19, 1779; William Whipple to Josiah Bartlett, May 21, 1779; Daniel St. Thomas Jenifer to Thomas Johnson, Jr., May 24, 1779, in Burnett, *Letters of Congress,* 4:219, 223, 232-33; Anne Bezanson, "Inflation and Controls, Pennsylvania, 1774-1779," *Journal of*

Economic History 8(1948):15-17 supplement. John K. Alexander, "The Fort Wilson Incident of 1779: A Case Study of the Revolutionary Crowd," *William and Mary Quarterly,* 3d ser. 31(1974): 589-612.

47. *JCC,* 14:626.

48. R. Flint to Wadsworth, July 20, 1779, JW:CHS, Box 128.

49. Hoardley and Labaree, *Public Records,* 2:286-87. Virginia was less scrupulous in complying with Congress's requisition (Hening, *Statutes,* 10:148, 168), and its authorizing the issue of £1 million notes in the spring session of 1779 undercut Congress's plan (ibid., 10:31; R. H. Lee to G. Mason, in Burnett, *Letters of Congress,* 4:256).

50. The factors accounting for the grain crisis were best summarized by the Committee of Congress appointed to meet with the minister of France in Feb. 1779 about procuring grain for the French fleet. Minutes of their meeting in *JCC,* 13:327.

51. David Klingaman, "Food Surpluses and Deficits in the American Colonies, 1768-1772," *Journal of Economic History* 31 (1971): 558 (table), 563-65.

52. Hoadley and Labaree, *Public Records,* 2:121, 125-26; P. Colt to R. Flint, Nov. 1, 1778, JW:CHS, Box 127.

53. P. Colt to Wadsworth, Sept. 15, 1778; J. Cuyler to Wadsworth, Sept. 20, 1778; and J. Bayley to Cuyler, Sept. 22, 1778, JW:CHS, Box 126; Colt to Flint, Oct. 3, 5, 17, 24, 1778; Cuyler to Flint, Oct. 8, 1778; and Wadsworth to Board of Treasury, Oct. 8, 1778, JW:CHS, Box 127.

54. Colt to J. Reed, Oct. 25, 1778, and to Flint, Nov. 8, 1778, JW:CHS, Box 127.

55. *JCC,* 12:876-7 8, 901-02; also Wadsworth to E. Blaine, Oct. 15, 1778, and Colt to Flint, Oct. 24, 1778, JW:CHS, Box 127.

56. Blaine to Wadsworth, Mar. 17, 1779; Chaloner and White to Wadsworth, Mar. 18, 1779; and Wadsworth to Committee of Congress, Mar. 27, 1779, JW:CHS, Box 127; Board of War to Wadsworth, May 18, 1779, and Chaloner and White to Wadsworth, May 20, 22, 24, 1779, JW:CHS, Box 128.

57. Cuyler to Wadsworth, June 8, 1779, JW:CHS, Box 128.

58. J. Watson to Wadsworth, May 1, 1779, and Wadsworth to Morris and Whipple, May 5, 1779, JW:CHS, Box 128.

59. The assumption is that available manpower was the principle limitation on production.

60. J. Lloyd to Wadsworth, July 4, 1779, JW:CHS, Box 128; J. K. Alexander, "Fort Wilson Incident," p. 595.

61. Bezanson, "Inflation and Controls," pp. 9-14, dates the chronic shortage in West India produce from Sept. 1776. The phenomenon appears to have affected New England as well. Colt to Wadsworth, Nov. 3, 1778, JW:FHS, Box 127; J. Tracy to Wadsworth, Apr. 15, 1779, JW:CHS, Box 128.

62. Jonathan Trumbull to Wadsworth, Mar. 27, 1779, and Wadsworth to Committee of Congress, [Mar. 28?, 1779], JW:CHS, Box 127.

63. Colt to Wadsworth, June 6, July 2, 1779, JW:CHS, Box 128.

64. J. Jeffrey to Wadsworth, and Colt to Wadsworth, Aug. 28, 1779, JW:CHS, Box 129; Jonathan Trumbull to Baron Johan Diruk Vander Copellen, Aug. 31, 1779, Jonathan Trumbull, Sr. Papers, Connecticut Historical Society.

65. Commissary agents initially attributed the high prices in the Boston market to the scarcity caused by the Convention army and the French fleet the preceding autumn. Colt to Flint, Feb. 13, 1779, JW:CHS, Box 127. By May they were aware that other factors were at work. Wadsworth to Gates, May 3, 1779, and to Morris and Whipple, May 5, 1779, JW:CHS, Box 128. A similar situation developed less ambiguously in Philadelphia. Blaine to Wadsworth, Mar. 17, 1779, JW:CHS, Box 127; Chaloner and White to Wadsworth, Apr. 18, May 22, and 24, 1779, JW:CHS, Box 128.

66. Colt to Wadsworth, Feb. 17, 1779, JW:CHS, Box 127.

67. The Board of War advised this course be taken in its letter to Wadsworth, May 18, 1779, JW:CHS, Box 128.

68. Cuyler to Wadsworth, July 14, 1779, JW:CHS, Box 128. The prizes brought into Boston in the summer helped replenish the salt supply. Colt to Wadsworth, July 27, 1779, JW:CHS, Box 128, and Aug. 18, 1779, JW:CHS, Box 129; but by autumn salt was again in short supply. Wadsworth to Jonathan Trumbull, Sept. 16, 1779, and Colt to Wadsworth, Oct. 14, 1779, JW:CHS, Box 129.

69. Hoadley and Labaree, *Public Records,* 2:224-27; J. Watson to Wadsworth, May 7, 1779, JW:CHS, Box 128. The same thing happened in New York. Watson to Colt, and Colt to Wadsworth, July 1, 1779, ibid.

70. Colt to Wadsworth, Oct. 14, 1779, and Flint to Wadsworth, Nov. 7, 1779, JW:CHS, Box 129.

71. H. Wyckoff to Wadsworth, Sept. 15, Oct. 24, 1779, and David Van Ness to R. Flint, Sept. 29, 1779, JW:CHS, Box 129.

72. Cuyler to Wadsworth, Apr. 12, 1779, JW:CHS, Box 128; Colt to Wadsworth, Oct. 14, 1779, JW:CHS, Box 129.

73. Flint to Wadsworth, July 20, 1779, JW:CHS, Box 128.

74. Colt to Wadsworth, June 16, 1779, JW:CHS, Box 128; Governor Trumbull to Wadsworth, Sept. 16, 1779, JW:CHS, Box 129.

75. Flint to Wadsworth, July 6, 1779, and J. Lloyd to Wadsworth, July 13, 1779, JW:CHS, Box 128; A. Keyes to Wadsworth, Aug. 3, 1779, and Jonathan Trumbull, Jr., to Wadsworth, Aug. 3, 1779, JW:CHS, Box 129; also Charles Carroll of Carrollton to William Carmichael, May 31, 1779, in Burnett, *Letters of Congress,* 4:240.

76. Chaloner and White to Wadsworth, Aug. 13, 1779, JW:CHS, Box 129; Bezanson, "Inflation and Controls," p. 16.

77. J. Reed to Wadsworth, Oct. 25, 1779; Flint to Wadsworth, Nov. 7, 1779; and Colt to Wadsworth, Nov. 30, 1779, JW:CHS, Box 129; H. Champion to Wadsworth, Dec. 3, 1779, JW:CHS, Box 130.

78. Cuyler to Wadsworth, Oct. 14, 1779; copy of R. L. Hooper to Blaine, Nov. 10, 1779; R. L. Hooper to Wadsworth, Nov. 12, 1779; and J. Child to Wadsworth, Nov. 2, 1779, JW:CHS, Box 129; I. Tichner to Cuyler, Nov. 22, 1779, and G. Coffman to Flint, Dec. 23, 1779, JW:CHS, Box 130.

79. Colt to Wadsworth, Nov. 30, 1779, JW:CHS, Box 129, gives a good account of the currency's collapse. For speculation see Barnabas Deane to Wadsworth, Dec. 8, 1779, JW:CHS, Box 130.

80. Hening, *Statutes,* 10:50-55, 148. The controversial nature of Virginia's action is reflected in John Armstrong to Washington, Jan. 12, 1780; Ezekiel Cornell to William Greene, June 18, 1780; and William Grayson to General Smallwood, June 26, 1780, in Burnett, *Letters of Congress,* 5:9, 225, 245n.

81. *JCC,* 16:262-67.

82. Weigley, *The American Way of War,* chap. 2; M. F. Treacy, *Prelude to Yorktown* (Chapel Hill, 1963), chap. 5; Louis Gottschalk, *Lafayette and the Close of the American Revolution* (Chicago, 1942), chaps. 9-11.

83. Washington to the Secretary at War, Nov. 6, 1782, and to Trumbull, Nov. 13, 1782, in Fitzpatrick, *Writings of Washington,* 25:322, 335.

84. Washington to John Sullivan, Feb. 4, 1781, ibid., 21:183, and Washington to William Livingston, Jan. 12 [13], 1782, ibid., 23:444; Congress had recommended that the states pass such a law on Nov. 14, 1780. *JCC,* 18:1053.

85. Washington to Governor Trumbull, Apr. 12, 1777, in *Collections of the Massachusetts Historical Society* 5th ser. 10(1888):55; Wadsworth to Trumbull, Apr. 6, 1779, ibid., 7th ser. 2(1902):385; J. Shipman to Trumbull, Jan. 13, 1778, and Thaddeus Betts to Trumbull, Jan. 21, 1778, JT:CSL, 8:43, 51.

86. O. Wolcott to Trumbull, Nov. 30, 1779; Enock Poor to Trumbull, Feb. 11, 1780; D. Waterbury to Trumbull, June 16, Aug. 24, 1781; William Ledyard to Trumbull, Sept. 3, 1781, and J. Mead to Trumbull, Jan. 14, 1782, JT:CSL, 10:252; 11:60; 14:290, 90; 16:15.

87. Civil Authority and Selectmen of Greenwich to Trumbull, Jan. 15, 1781, JT:CSL, 14:36.

88. D. Weir to J. Robinson, Feb. 14, 1779, and Robinson to Weir, Apr. 13, 1781, British Public Record Office, London, Treasury 64/114, 119 (hereafter cited as T).

89. Weir to Robinson, Dec. 21, 1778, in 64/114.

90. J. Madison to E. Pendleton, Jan. 23, 1781, in Burnett, *Letters of Congress,* 5:543.

91. Elizabeth B. Schumpeter, *English Overseas Trade Statistics, 1697-1808* (Oxford, 1960), pp. 64, 67. Schumpeter's tables give figures for only one out of every five years. Caesar Moreau, *State of the Trade of Great Britain with all Parts of the World* (London, 1824), gives figures for yearly aggregate exports to specific regions without distinguishing between the items exported. Moreau's figures show exports hovering between 1.5% and 2.2% of the 1774 aggregate in the years 1776-78, then rising to 14% in 1779, 31% in 1780, and 32% in 1781. In 1782 exports fell back to 10% of the 1774 figure, reflecting a loss of confidence by British traders in the American trade.

92. Ternay to Trumbull, Oct. 23, 1780, and Destouches to Trumbull, Jan. 1, 1781, JT:CSL, 13:99; 14:3; Washington to Trumbull, Nov. 13, 1782, in *Collections of the Massachusetts Historical Society,* 5th ser. 10(1888):276.

93. Trumbull to Washington, Aug. 31, 1780, *Collections of the Massachusetts Historical Society,* 5th ser. 10(1888):203; Washington to John Sullivan, Feb. 4, 1781, in Fitzpatrick, *Writings of Washington,* 21:182.

94. Ferguson, *Power of the Purse,* chap. 8.

95. The western frontier was subject to the most pressure. J. Mead to Trumbull, Oct. 24, 1777; G. S. Silliman to Trumbull, Apr. 30 and May 1, June 20, July 13, 1778; J. Mead to Trumbull, June 17, 1779; Wolcott to Trumbull, Nov. 30, 1779; Abraham Tyler to Trumbull, Feb. 14, 1780; E. Mygatt to Trumbull, Apr. 19, 1780; J. Mead to Trumbull, May 9, 1780; Silliman to Trumbull, June 4, 1780; E. Lockwood to Silliman, June 13, 1780; B. Beebe to Trumbull, June 25, 1780; Silliman to Trumbull, July 3, 1780; L. Wells to Trumbull, Aug. 11, 1780; J. Mead to Silliman, Sept. 1 and 8, 1780; J. Mead to Trumbull, Jan. 15, 1781, JT:CSL, 6:150; 8:123; 125, 127, 145; 9:244; 10:252, 11:61, 145, 177, 239; 12:9, 46, 70, 202, 266, 280; 14:37. But the entire coast shared the problems of the western frontier in lesser degree. J. Shipman to Trumbull, Jan. 12, 1778; W. Ledyard to Trumbull, Feb. 28, 1781; Saybrook Committee to Trumbull, April 26, 1782, JT:CSL, 8:43; 14:37; 16:103.

96. W. Ledyard to Trumbull, Jan. 30, 1781, JT:CSL, 14:67; Hoadley and Labaree, *Public Records* 3:448.

97. Trumbull to Clinton, July 20, 1781, *Collections of the Massachusetts Historical Society,* 7th ser. 3:248-49. Connecticut had not acted without careful investigation, and the government had accumulated considerable evidence about subversive networks of illicit traders. S. H. Parsons to Washington, March 3, 14, 1781, in Charles S. Hall, *Life and Letters of Samuel Holden Parsons* (Binghamton, N.Y., 1905), pp. 341-43, 346-48; depositions dated Mar. 12, 1781, and Parsons to Trumbull, Mar. 13, 1781, JT:CSL, 14:125, 128. Clinton's and Arbuthnot's proclamation was issued on Dec. 29, 1780, not 1781 as recorded in Roger P. Bristol, *Supplement to Charles Evans' American Bibliography* (Charlottesville, Va., 1970).

98. B. Brown to Trumbull, Aug. 18, 1780, and John Mackay to Trumbull, Aug. 21, 1780, JT:CSL, 12:235, 242.

99. Henry Scudder to Trumbull, Nov. 29, 1780, JT:CSL, 12:174; documents relating to the case of Colonel William Worthington of Saybrook in Connecticut State Archives: Revolutionary War, 1st ser., 21:219-62, Connecticut State Library; also the allegations against General Parsons in Hall, *Samuel Holden Parsons,* pp. 419 ff.

100. W. Ledyard to Trumbull, July 12, 1780; B. Talmadge to Trumbull, Jan. 4, 1783; Authority and Selection of Guilford, Jan. 8, 1783, JT:CSL, 12:88; 18:2, 8.

101. W. Williams to Trumbull, Mar. 29, 1780, JT:CSL, 11:122; Hoadley and Labaree, *Public Records,* 3:6, 331; 4:132; 5:110; Trumbull's address to the Connecticut legislature of Jan. 29, 1782, and the report of the committee appointed to investigate the charges against him in *Connecticut Courant,* Mar. 26, 1782.

102. Hoadley and Labaree, *Public Records,* 4:337-39; 5:29, 37.

103. A copy of the petition framed by the committee appointed by the Hartford town meeting on Jan. 29, 1783, is in the Papers of the Connecticut General Assembly, Connecticut Historical Society. It was followed by a counterpetition, signed by twenty-two prominent citizens, against the people presuming to interfere in such matters.

104. Thomas Mumford, Daniel Rodman, Joshua Huntington, and Giles Mumford, "To the Public," (March 25, 1783), *Connecticut Gazette,* Mar. 28, 1783; see also S. McClellan to Trumbull, Mar. 27, 1783, JT:CSL, 18:76.

105. The definition of shoreline being used in this computation includes islands and rivers to a point where tidal water narrows to 100 feet.

106. Washington to Trumbull, Oct. 18, 1780, *Collections of the Massachusetts Historical Society,* 5th ser. 10(1888):210; Trumbull to Clinton, July 20, 1781, ibid., 7th ser. 3:251; Circular of the president of Congress to the States, Jan. 15, June 1, 1781, JT:CSL, 14:34, 266.

Chapter 9

1. Don Higginbotham, *The War of American Independence.* (New York, 1971), p. 103. See also ibid., p. 57.

2. Piers Mackesy, *The War for America, 1775-1783* (Cambridge, Mass., 1964), p. 4.

3. Some Prussian examples: In 1776 the rank and file were evenly divided between natives and foreigners (most of whom were non-Prussian Germans)— 78,767 to 78,280—a relationship that remained unchanged to the end of Frederick's reign. In 1787 new regulations called for a slight preponderance of natives in all branches except the hussars, where natives and foreigners were to be equal in number. At the outbreak of the Wars of the French Revolution natives outnumbered foreigners by some 20,500 men in the infantry and by some 4,000 men in the cavalry. In the officer corps the percentage of natives was still higher, although as late as 1805, as many as one-third of all infantry officers holding the rank of lieutenant colonel or higher were foreigners. For additional statistics, and remarks on the politically significant appeal that Prussian service had for foreigners, see Peter Paret, *Clausewitz and the State* (New York, 1976), p. 59. Austrian manpower policies of the period aree analyzed in Jürg Zimmerman, *Militärverwaltung und Heeresaufbringung in Osterreich bis 1806,* vol. 3, *Handbuch zur deutschen Militärgeschichte* (Frankfurt, 1965).

4. Mackesy, *War for America,* p. 31.

5. On this aspect of the war, see John Shy, ''The American Revolution: The Military Conflict Considered as a Revolutionary War,'' in *Essays on the American Revolution,* ed. Stephen J. Kurtz and James H. Hutson (Chapel Hill, 1973), pp. 121-56.

6. I have discussed the revolutionary elements on both sides of the conflict in the Vendée in Peter Paret, *Internal War and Pacification: The Vendée, 1789-1796,* Center of International Studies, Research Monograph no. 12 (Princeton, 1961).

7. For analyses of English and Continental conditions, see R. Arthur Bowler, *Logistics and the Failure of the British Army in America, 1775-1783* (Princeton, 1975), and *Heeresverpflegung,* vol. 6, *Studien zur Kriegsgeschichte und Taktik,* ed. Military History Section I of the Great General Staff (Berlin, 1913), pp. 2-73.

8. The following discussion is based on Peter Paret, ''Colonial Experience and European Military Reform at the End of the Eighteenth Century,'' *Bulletin of the Institute of Historical Research* (1964): 47-59.

9. It is nevertheless notable that such a balanced, critical interpreter of Prussian history as Hajo Holborn defines the aim of the Austro-French alliance as ''the total destruction of Prussia'' *(A History of Modern Germany* [New York, 1964], pp. ii, 235).

10. Since the military aspects of this conflict have been largely ignored in the literature, it may be useful to mention the two best brief accounts: Curt Jany, *Geschichte der Preussischen Armee,* rev. ed. (Osnabrück, 1967), pp. iii, 107-

29; and far superior analytically, Colmar von der Goltz, *Von Rossbac bis Jena* (Berlin, 1906), pp. 408-17. The chapter dealing with the war in Paul B. Bernard, *Joseph II and Bavaria* (The Hague, 1965), is better on the diplomatic maneuvers than on the course of operations.

Afterword

1. Eric Robson, *The American Revolution in its Political and Military Aspects* (New York, 1954).

2. Ernest Kipping, ed., *The Hessian View of America* (Monmouth Beach, N.J., 1971), p. 34.

3. David Griffiths, "Nikita Panin, Russian Diplomacy and the American Revolution," *Slavic Review* 28(1969):12.

4. Paul Smith, *Loyalists and Redcoats* (Chapel Hill, 1964), p. 173.

5. Russell F. Weigley, *The American Way of War* (New York, 1973), p. 12.

6. Piers Mackesy, "Professionals and Amateurs: A Commentary," U.S. Military Academy Symposium on the American Revolution, West Point, N.Y., April 22, 1976.

7. Pauline Maier, "The Beginnings of American Republicanism, 1765-1776," in *The Development of a Revolutionary Mentality,* Library of Congress (Washington, D.C., 1972), pp. 99-118.

8. Mackesy, "A Commentary."

9. Piers Mackesy, *The War for America, 1775-1783* (Cambridge, Mass., 1964), p. xiv.

INDEX

Adams, John, fears armies, 104, 105, 107, 115, 119, 175n
Age of Limited Warfare, 159. *See also* Military doctrine; Strategy
American Campaigns (Steele), 34
American Revolution (Robson), 47, 158
American Revolution, as an anti-colonial movement, 3-13. *See also* War of Independence
American Revolution Bicentennial, 72
American society: its effect on the war, 72-82 passim; and expanding population, 75, 77, 80; and land, 75, 77; and immigration, 75, 77; and social elite, 76, 77; institutional weaknesses of, 76, 77, 79, 80, 81; and provincialism, 76-77, 80, 81
Amherst, Gen. Jeffery, 15-16, 17
Anglican church, 76
Anne Arundel County, Md., 96
Annual Register, 96, 97
Appeal to Arms (Wallace), 43
Arms and Men (Millis), 35, 36, 95, 96
Armstrong, John, 115, 122
Arnold, Gen. Benedict, 30, 38, 45, 61, 93, 112, 116
Articles of Confederation, 111, 120, 130, 132

Barras, de Saint-Laurent, Comte de, 43
Bennington, battle of, 83, 99
Bergen County, N. J., 97, 98
Bever, Samuel. *See Cadet, The*
Biddle, Clement, 58
Bigelow, John. *See Principles of Strategy*
Billias, George A., 45
Board of Ordnance, British, 62
Board of War, American, 56, 57, 58
Boston, 23, 24, 38, 49, 73
Boudinot, Elias, 111
Bowler, R. Arthur, 125, 128, 160, 161, 164
Boyd, Adam, 101
Brandywine, Battle of, 26
British Museum, 72, 82
Buchanan, William, 58
Buell, Richard, 161, 163, 164
Bunker Hill, Battle of, 23
Burgoyne, Gen. John, 18, 25, 26, 27, 30, 83, 161; service in Portugal, 16; plan for invading New York, 25; impact of his surrender, 27
Burke, Thomas, 112

Cadet, The (Bever), 18
Caesar, Julius. *See Commentaries*

Caldwell, James, 100
Camden, Battle of, 73, 110, 125
Canada, 3, 16, 24, 25, 27, 37, 38, 48, 49, 51
Carleton, Gen. Guy, 16, 18
Caswell, Richard, at Moore's Creek Bridge, 89, 90
Catherine the Great, 7
Chamier, Daniel, 64
Charleston, S. C., 29, 110, 125, 127
China, 12
Chinese Revolution, 4, 5
Civil-military conflict, American, 104-123. See also Continental Army; Continental Congress; Washington, George
Clark, George Rogers, 100
Clausewitz, Karl von, 32, 38, 46
Clinton, George, 85, 90, 94, 119
Clinton, Gen. Henry, 24, 26, 31, 55, 65, 66, 67, 141; pre-Revolutionary service of, 16, 17, 18; appointed commander in chief, 27; early plans of, 28-29; complains of provisions, 54, 65, 66
Clinton, James, 119
Commentaries (Caesar), 19, 20, 21, 22, 159
Commissary Department: American, 57, 58, 59, 133, 135, 136, 137, 139, 140, 175n; British, 54, 63, 64, 65, 67, 69
Concord, Battle of, 23
Congregational church, 76
Connecticut, 24, 29, 135, 137; flooded with Continental currency, 133, 134, 163; illicit trade in, 140, 141, 142, 143
Constitution, federal, military provisions of, 102
Continental Army, 14, 24, 25, 26, 31,

40, 41, 49, 57, 58, 61, 65, 73, 78, 84, 85, 87, 101, 105, 113, 148, 152. See also Militia; Strategy; Tactics; Washington, George
Continental Association, 93
Continental Congress, 37, 38, 55, 56, 57, 58, 59, 60, 62, 83, 90, 91, 94, 95, 104, 105, 106, 107, 108, 109, 117, 118, 119, 129, 130, 133, 134, 138, 139; economic policy of, 128; loan office certificates, 129, 132, 134; taxation by, 131; French financial support of, 132; requisitions of, 132, 137, 138. See also Civil-military conflict; Currency, Continental; Washington, George
Conway, Thomas, 107, 117
"Conway Cabal," 37, 118
Cornell, Ezekiel, 89
Cornwallis, Gen. Charles, Earl, 16, 18, 29, 45, 51, 61, 66, 74, 93, 99, 127, 161
Corsica, 6
Coudray, Phillip Du, 112
Crafts, Thomas, 85
Cunliffe, Marcus. See Washington, George
Currency, Continental, 60, 128, 129, 131, 134, 138, 163

Dalrymple, Campbell. See Military Essay
Dartmouth, earl of (William Legge), 15
Davidson, William L., 89
Davis, Robert, 96
Day, John, 104
Destouches, Adm. Chevalier, 43
Dick Act, 102
Dickinson, Gen. Philemon, 98

Duncan, William, 19

Earle, Richard T., 88
Economy, colonial, 126, 129, 181n
Estaing, Adm. Charles Hector, Comte
    d', 135, 136
Ewald, John, proposal for defeating
    patriot irregulars, 99

Ferguson, Patrick, 98
Feuquières, Marquis of. *See Memoirs*
Flexner, James T., 45
Florida, 28, 29
Floyd, William, 110
Forage, British problem, 58, 67, 68
Fort Schuyler, 95
Fort Washington, 127
France, 6, 10, 11, 132, 133
Frederick the Great, 153
Freeman, Douglas S.: *George
    Washington*, 44; assessment of
    Washington, 44, 45, 48, 49
French Alliance, 41, 48, 55, 61, 81,
    82; aid to patriots, 9, 132; French
    role at Yorktown, 9, 41; signed, 26,
    27, 127; French purchases in
    America, 135, 141
French Revolution, 6, 8
Frothingham, Thomas G. *See
    Washington: Commander in Chief*
Fuller, J. F. C. *See Military History of
    the Western World*

Gage, Gen. Thomas, 16, 17, 23, 63
Gansevoort, Peter, 89
Gates, Gen. Horatio, 78, 83, 85, 100,
    104, 110, 117; at Newburgh, 122
Genoa, 6
George III, 3, 12, 15, 22, 23
Georgia, 29, 73
Germain, Lord George: pre-war

career, 15, 18; on the conduct of the
    war, 25, 26, 28
German mercenaries, 69, 83
German settlers, 75, 81
Germantown, battle of, 41
Giap, Vo Nguyen, 39
Gipson, Lawrence H., 95
Glover, Gen. John, 112
Gordon, William, 122
Grain crisis in America, 135, 136, 137
Greene, Christopher, 92
Greene, Francis V., 43
Greene, Gen. Nathanael, 34, 38, 40,
    48, 58, 61, 84, 89, 92, 100, 101; in
    the South, 39; as a strategist, 44, 45,
    115, 117, 118, 119, 121, 122;
    civil-military relations, 106, 107,
    108; as quartermaster general, 113
Greene, Nathanael (Thayer), 45, 46
Green Mountain Boys, 180n
Greenwich, Conn., 140
Gruber, Ira D. *See Howe Brothers*

Hackensack Valley, 97, 101
Halleck, Henry H., 32, 33
Hamilton, Alexander, 108
Hand, Gen. Edward, 118, 120
Hart, B. H. Liddell. *See Strategy*
Hartford, Conn., 142
Hay, A. Hawkes, 98
Hazen, Col. Moses, 118
Heard, Gen. Nathaniel, 98
Heath, Gen. William, 68, 114
Henry, Patrick, 94
Herkimer, Gen. Nicholas, 85
Higginbotham, Don, 4, 8, 43, 44, 48,
    144, 145
History of Warfare (Montgomery),
    34, 35
Howe, Gen. Robert, 118
Howe, Gen. William, 23, 27, 49, 50,

64, 66, 67, 91, 101, 127; pre-war
    career of, 16, 17, 18; views on
    beating rebels, 24, 25, 26, 31
Howe Brothers (Ira D. Gruber), 47,
    159, 161
Huntington, Gen. Jedidiah, 114, 119

India, 11
Indians, 87, 91, 98, 135
Inflation. *See* Currency, Continental

Jackson, Colonel, 85
Jackson, Henry, 108
Jacobite Rebellion, 15
Jameson, J. F., 95
Jay, John, 105
Jefferson, Thomas, 90, 93, 109
Jomini, Antoine Henri, Baron de, 32,
    33

Kalb, Baron Johann de, 61
Kemble, Stephen, 69, 70
Kentish Guards, 92
Kettle Creek, Battle of, 97
King's Mountain, Battle of, 97, 98
Knox, Dudley W. *See Naval Genius of
    George Washington*
Knox, Gen. Henry, 85, 111
Kohn, Richard H., 163

Lacey, Gen. John, 84, 98, 100
Lafayette, Marie Joseph, Marquis de,
    6, 139
Laurens, Henry, 56
Lexington, Battle of, 23
Lee, Charles, 106, 117; on coastal
    defense, 42; on American soldiers,
    73, 78, 82
Lee, Richard Henry, 94
Lenoir, William, 98
Leslie, Gen. Alexander, 93

Ligonier, Field Marshal John, 15, 16,
    17
Lillington, Alexander, 90
Lincoln, Gen. Benjamin, 100
Livingston, William, 119
Logistics: American, 54-62; British,
    62-71, 125; European, 151, 160
Long Island, Battle of, 49
Loyalists, 23, 26, 95, 96, 97, 98, 106,
    125; military units, 14; in the South,
    27; ministry's view of, 30, 160;
    vindictive behavior of, 81, 161; as
    minority groups, 81, 182n;
    American efforts to win over, 101
Loyal Nine, 85
Luzerne, César Anne, Chevalier de la,
    110

Mackesy, Piers. *See War for
    America, The*
McDougall, Gen. Alexander, on
    officers' grievances, 105, 111, 113,
    114, 115, 118, 119, 120
Madison, James, 140
Mahan, Alfred T., 34
Mahan, Dennis H., 33
Maier, Pauline, 163
Mao Tse-tung, 39
Marion, Gen. Francis, 89, 96
Marlborough, John Churchill, Duke
    of, 22
Massachusetts Provincial Congress,
    104
Mathew, Gen. Edward, 93
Mella, Bernardo Vieira de, 5, 8
Memoirs (Marquis of Feuquières), 19,
    20, 21, 22, 24
Mifflin, Gen. Thomas, 58, 104, 117
Military doctrine: British, 14, 17, 18,
    21, 30; French, 18, 19, 20, 21;
    classical, 18, 19, 20, 21, 22;

American, 32, 33, 34; Napoleonic, 151. *See also* Military history, writings on
Military Essay (Dalrymple), 18, 19
Military history, writings on: impact of Napoleonic warfare, 32, 33; of World War I, 37; studies on by American military men, 39-47 passim; of World War II, 43, 44, 45; of Vietnam, 44, 158
Military History of the Western World (J. F. C. Fuller), 34, 46
Military Institutions (Vegetius), 19, 20, 21, 22, 159
Militia, 47, 76, 113, 163; drafts, 79; institutional structure, 83, 84, 89, 91, 92, 162; Greene's view of, 84; Washington's view of, 84, 90, 91, 92; militia-continental friction, 85; motives for service, 86, 87, 184n; officers, 87, 88, 89, 90; opposes loyalists, 95, 96, 97, 98; efforts to reform, 94, 102, 103, 185-186n
Millis, Walter. *See Arms and Men*
Minden, Battle of, 15
Montgomery, Field Marshal Viscount. *See History of Warfare*
Montgomery, Gen. Richard, 38, 78
Moore's Creek Bridge, Battle of, 90, 97
Morgan, Gen. Daniel, 85, 100
Morris, Gouverneur, 121, 122
Morris, Robert, 116, 120, 141
Moultrie, Gen. William, 101
Moylan, Stephen, 105
Muhlenberg, Gen. Peter, 94
Mumford, Thomas, 142, 143

Napoleon, 32, 33, 52, 149, 165
Naval Genius of George Washington (Knox), 37, 38, 41, 42, 43, 51

Navy Board, British, 62, 64, 67
Nelson, Thomas, 90, 94
Newburgh conspiracy, 117, 121, 122, 123, 163
New Jersey, 26, 97, 98, 101
New Kent County, Va., 94
Newport, 26
New York, 26, 94, 140, 143
New York City, 23, 24, 26, 29, 37, 140
Nicola, Lewis, 109
North, Frederick, 15
North Carolina, 23, 29, 73, 90, 97

Orrery, earl of. *See Treatise of the Art of War*

Palmer, Dave R. *See Way of the Fox*
Panin, Nikita, 159
Paoli, Pasquale, 6, 9
Paret, Peter, 36, 159, 164, 165
Parsons, Gen. Samuel H., 112, 116, 118, 119
Partisan warfare. *See* Militia; Tactics
Paterson, Gen. John, 114
Peebles, John, 68
Penobscott expedition, 136, 137
Peter III, 7
Philadelphia, 25, 26, 29, 30, 50, 64, 138
Phillips, Gen. William, 93
Pickens, Gen. Andrew, 96, 100
Polish insurrection of 1794, 149
Portsmouth, Va., 106
Portugal, 5, 16
Potter, James, 98
Preston, Richard A. (co-author of *Men in Arms*), 34
Prince Edward Island, 3, 5
Princeton, battle of, 25, 37, 41, 50, 64, 127

Principles of Strategy (Bigelow), 33, 34
Pugachev, Emilian, 6, 7, 8, 9

Quartermaster Department: American, 57, 58, 59, 113, 175n; British, 70

Ramsour's Mill, Battle of, 97
Rawdon, Lord Francis, 73, 74, 81, 82
Recife, Brazil, 5
Reed, Joseph, 84, 103, 109, 118, 119
Reveries (Saxe), 19, 20, 21, 22, 24, 159
Rhode Island, 24, 30, 135, 142
Rifle companies, 87
Robertson, James, 68
Robinson, John, 67
Robson, Eric. *See American Revolution*
Root, Jesse, 112
Ropp, Theodore. *See War in the Modern World*
Royal Volunteers of Ireland, 73, 74, 79
Russia, 6, 10
Russian Revolution, 4, 5, 8

St. Lucia, 28, 29
St. Petersburg, 7, 9
Sandwich, John Montagu, earl of, 15
Saratoga, N. Y., 27, 83, 84
Saxe, Maurice, Comte de. *See Reveries*
Schuyler, Gen. Philip, 90, 100, 111, 112, 116, 117
Scotch Irish, 73, 74, 75, 81
Sears, Isaac, 105
Seven Years' War, 16, 62, 63, 95, 154, 156
Seymour, Moses, 142

Shy, John, 90, 100, 160, 161, 162
Simpson, James, 162
Slaves, role in War of Independence, 81, 82, 86, 91
Smallwood, Gen. William, 118
Smith, Paul, 160
Smith, Richard, 142
Smith, William P., 109
South Carolina, 28, 29, 73, 74, 81, 125
Soviet Union, 12
Spain, 127
Springfield, Battle of, 51
Stark, John, 83, 84, 89, 99
Stark, Molly, 83
States, American, economic policies: taxation, 131, 135, 160; price regulation, 138
Steele, Matthew F. *See American Campaigns*
Steuben, Friedrich Wilhelm von, 152
Stirling, Lord (William Alexander), 118, 119
Stony Point, Battle of, 50
Strategy, 17, 22, 23, 46; conventional, 14, 28, 29; British, 23, 24, 25, 26, 27, 28, 29, 30, 31, 46, 47; origins of the concept, 32, 33, 38, 159; American, 38, 39, 42, 43, 44, 45, 46, 47, 48, 49, 50, 51, 52, 53. *See also* Military doctrine
Strategy (Hart), 34
Stuart, Charles, 99
Sullivan, Gen. John, 112, 117, 118, 120, 135
Sumner, Gen. Jethro, 94
Sumter, Gen. Thomas, 87, 89, 96

Tactics, 22, 36, 44; light infantry, 15, 150; definition of, 38; irregular, 39, 40, 69, 91, 150; linear, 150, 152

Thayer, Theodore. *See Greene, Nathanael*
Thornsbury, Joseph, 59
Toulon, 149
Treasury, British: responsibilities for provisions, 63, 64, 65, 66
Treatise of the Art of War (Orrery), 18, 19, 21, 22
Trenton, Battle of, 25, 37, 41, 50, 64, 127
Trumbull, Jonathan, 105, 119, 141, 142, 143
Trumbull, Joseph, 58

Uniform Militia Act, 102
United Empire Loyalists, 3
Upton, Emory, 35, 85
Ural River, 7

Valley Forge, Pa., 55, 58, 64, 107
Van Schaick, Goose, 85
Van Tyne, C. H., 84
Varnum, Gen. James M., 92, 112
Vegetius, Flavius. *See Military Institutions*
Vendée, 149
Vietnam War, 39, 44; compared to War of Independence, 11-12, 124, 158
Virginia, 6, 94, 135, 138, 139

Wadsworth, Jeremiah, 133
Wagon department, American, 58, 59
Wallace, Willard M. *See Appeal to Arms, An*
War for America, The (Mackesy), 47, 145, 162, 164
War in the Modern World (Ropp), 34, 35
War of attrition. *See* Military doctrine; Military history
War of Austrian Succession, 11, 15

War of Bavarian Succession, 154, 155
War of Independence: compared to European conflicts of the seventeenth and eighteenth centuries, 144-157; limited impact on early professional literature, 152, 164
War Office: American, 56, 57; British, 62
Washington: Commander in Chief (Frothingham), 37, 38, 39, 40, 41, 43, 46, 161
Washington, George, 6, 8, 25, 26, 27, 30, 32, 55, 61, 62, 64, 73, 74, 77, 100, 102, 105, 106, 107, 110, 115, 162; other studies of, 37, 44, 47; on preserving his army, 40, 41, 91, 127, 165; on sea power, 41, 42, 43; Freeman's view of, 44, 45, 48; Palmer's view of, 47, 48, 49, 51, 52; Weigley's view of, 50, 51, 52; on a traditional military response, 78, 86; on civilian control, 117, 123
Washington, George (Cunliffe), 45, 48
Waxhaws district, 73, 74, 81
Wayne, Gen. Anthony, 101, 111
Way of the Fox (Palmer), 47, 48, 49, 50, 161
Weedon, Gen. George, 94, 118
Weigley, Russell F., 159, 161, 164
West Point, N. Y., 30, 119
Whitemarsh, Battle of, 27
Wilkinson, James, 107
Willcox, William B., 46, 47
Wise, Sydney F. (co-author of *Men in Arms*), 34

Yates, Joseph, 109
Yorktown, 30, 41, 48, 51, 127
Young, Alfred F., 88, 184n

ABOUT THE EDITOR

Don Higginbotham, a specialist in early American history, has taught at the College of William and Mary, Longwood College, and Louisiana State University, and is currently Professor of History at the University of North Carolina, Chapel Hill. He has previously published *Daniel Morgan: Revolutionary Rifleman, The War of American Independence, Atlas of the American Revolution*, and *The Papers of James Iredell*. He is currently working on a biography of George Washington.

DATE DUE

NOV 1 1979		
MAR 1 8 1982		
JAN 0 5 1988		
DEC 1 7 1993		
APR 2 0 2001		